Sport in the Global Society

General Editor: J.A. Mangan

FRANCE AND THE 1998 WORLD CUP

FRANCE AND THE 1998 WORLD CUP

The National Impact of a World Sporting Event

Editors

HUGH DAUNCEY
GEOFF HARE

University of Newcastle upon Tyne

FRANK CASS

LONDON • PORTLAND, OR

First published in 1999 in Great Britain by
FRANK CASS PUBLISHERS
Newbury House, 900 Eastern Avenue
London, IG2 7HH

and in the United States of America by
FRANK CASS PUBLISHERS
c/o ISBS, 5804 N.E. Hassalo Street
Portland, Oregon 97213-3644

Website: http://www.frankcass.com

British Library Cataloguing in Publication Data

France and the 1998 World Cup : the national impact of a
world sporting event. – (Sport in the global society ; no. 7)
1. World Cup (Football championship : 2. Nationalism and
sports
I. Dauncey, Hugh II. Hare, Geoffrey
796.3'34668

ISBN 0-7146-4887-6 (cloth)
ISBN 0-7146-4438-2 (paper)
ISSN 1368-9789

Library of Congress Cataloging-in-Publication Data

France and the 1998 World Cup: the national impact of a world
sporting event / edited by Hugh Dauncey and Geoff Hare.
p. cm. – (Sports in the global society, ISSN 1379-9789: vol. 7)
Includes bibliographical references and index.
ISBN 0-7146-4887-6 (cloth). – ISBN 0-7146-4438-2
1. World Cup. 2. Soccer – Social aspects – France. 3. Soccer –
– Economic aspects – France. 4. Nationalism and sports – France.
5. Sports and state – France. I. Dauncey, Hugh, 1961– .
II. Hare, Geoff, 1945– . III. Series: Cass series – sport in the
global society : 7.
GV943.5.F73   1999   98-47286
796.334'0944—dc21   CIP

This group of studies first appeared as a special issue of *Culture, Sport, Society* (ISSN 1461-
0981), Vol.1, No.2, December 1998, published by Frank Cass

Printed in Great Britain by Antony Rowe Ltd., Chippenham, Wilts

Contents

List of Illustrations

Foreword

GÉRARD HOULLIER

It is almost stating the obvious to say that the 1998 World Cup has completely transformed the way football is seen in France. However, what now seems self-evident was almost unthinkable only a few months ago.

Riding contentedly on the crest of the wave, or should I say the tidal-wave, created by the success of Aimé Jacquet and his players, French football is nevertheless keeping the basics strongly in mind. The success of *les Bleus* in eventually acquiring the World Cup crown that had eluded them ever since the invention of the competition by our fellow countryman Jules Rimet was due in part to the high standards of technical training available in France. French training and coaching methods are admired internationally, as is amply demonstrated by the interest shown in young French players by big foreign clubs. Coaching policy in France is under the control of the *Direction Technique Nationale* (DTN) of the French Football Federation, and the DTN has always made coaching its principal objective. Ever concerned to improve its activities, in the early 1990s the DTN even introduced a far-reaching scheme of Youth Development ('pré-formation' or 'pre-training') for very young players, who can learn advanced skills in seven football centres across France. The current élite of young players of the French First Division have all developed their skills in one of these centres, and the policy of Youth Development has turned out to be a total success, promising a rosy future for French football in the coming years.

Entertainment and thrills were above all what the French general public – long-term fans and last-minute supporters alike – was keen to see, as the saga of *les Bleus* developed during France 98. In the space of a few weeks, under the influence of the Tricolour victory, the 1998 World Cup was transformed from an international sporting event of the first order into a new social phenomenon, as the lives of French people, men and women alike (women having suddenly taken a passionate interest in our sport) were put on hold for a whole month in the summer. In helping reveal a lost or at the least half-hidden national identity, football generated an unbelievable feeling of identification with France's Blue-White-and-Red national flag.

Never since the Liberation of Paris from German occupation in 1944 had the French people come together in such great numbers; and in addition to the inspiring procession on the Champs-Elysées the day after the Final, perhaps one of the most striking and enduring images of this harmonious unity was the presence of President Chirac and Prime Minister Jospin, despite their differing political ideals, side-by-side (almost hand-in-hand) in the official stand at the France v. Brazil final.

Four months have passed since the crowning glory of *les Bleus*, but the popular enthusiasm they sparked has not diminished. This new interest in football is demonstrated in many ways: by a noticeable increase in the numbers of registered amateur players (boys and girls alike); by the persisting enthusiasm of women for the game (in mid-October, France's first match in the Stade de France since the World Cup showed that women fans were retaining their interest in the team beyond the emotionally charged but fleeting imagery of last summer); by record match attendances in the professional divisions; by the renewed boom in club merchandising. Examples abound of how French football is enjoying its World Cup. It is without doubt the start of a new era.

GÉRARD HOULLIER
Liverpool FC
November 1998

Foreword

OLIVIER POIVRE D'ARVOR

> Some people think football is a matter of life and death. I don't like that
> attitude. I can assure them it is much more serious than that.
> Bill Shankly, remark on BBC television, 1981

It was about time. There was a huge sigh of relief that evening of 12 July.
In Saint-Denis and in the four corners of France and Navarre. I was there
and rather well placed to see the three French goals, with a ticket that hadn't
been stolen, but obtained honestly. Afterwards it was a long night, and while
it is true I was not born at the time of the Liberation of France in 1944, nor
very aware of politics in May 1968, my memory of the Champs-Elysées
will stay with me for a long time.

But straightaway something else became evident. While victory was
won on the Stade de France pitch, what was at stake in this magnificent
game of football had to be measured elsewhere. And if I say it was about
time, really about time, it is of course because by beating Brazil, and by
having qualified for the Final, France had above all exorcised its own
demons: the spectre of racism, the headlong rush back towards intolerance,
the catastrophic image of a country hemmed in by fear, hatred and
introspection.

Born as I was in Rheims when the town had a great team, I love football.
But like millions of my compatriots, I was taken by surprise by the
extraordinary effect on public opinion that the competition produced. I can
well remember the editors of this volume passionately telling me about their
topic: the impact on France of the World Cup. This was a full year before
joyful hostilities were declared on the pitch. At the time the idea had seemed
curious, not to say bizarre: how could a game transform society?

Living in London, I had, in the weeks preceding the opening of the
competition, suffered under the often unjustified and irrational criticism of
the organisation of the competition appearing in the most imbecile and
demagogic columns of the tabloid press. Oh, the famous affair of the official
World Cup knives which would be used to stab English supporters! Oh, the
accusations of cheating and fraud in the distribution of tickets! Old Franco-
British rivalries. I was however very saddened to see Scotland eliminated

from the tournament so early. And England too, even if a France–England final would have made my life as a French diplomat in London ... difficult.

By the quarter-finals something had crystallised. Articles in the press about the multicoloured team, young women in the street in love with Zidane, Karembeu, Desailly and other 'blacks et *beurs*' (Black and North African players) ... the semi-final set the seal on it: through its football team, France wanted to be reconciled with itself. Millions of us were in the streets, expectant and happy.

Living abroad for ten years, trying to give my host cultures an open and enlightened image of my country, always hanging on to old certainties ('the country of the Rights of Man', the Enlightenment, 'French culture is made up of borrowings from abroad'), I had felt ashamed. Ashamed at every national, regional and local election. Ashamed that this image of a racist country was being popularised beyond our frontiers. The night of 12 July, for the first time in a long while, I could breathe more easily. No, it's not true, that is not the France we love. Le Pen is just a very bad dream.

The summer has come and gone. The phenomenon is still with us. Something lasting, I think I can safely say. But at the same time, a doubt crosses my mind. What if France had not qualified for the quarter- and semi-finals? What if Desailly had scored an own goal? What if Zidane had got injured? That is a lot of 'ifs'. Alas, only one thing is certain: France has won a World Cup, but Le Pen has not been eliminated.

OLIVIER POIVRE D'ARVOR
Cultural Counsellor, French Embassy
Director of the Institut français in the United Kingdom
November 1998

Series Editor's Preface

Was the 1998 World Cup really about sport at all? The editors of this volume assert that soccer was almost the last thing on the mind of the bidders: 'the 1998 World Cup was staged for external consumption. It was to celebrate France's position as one of the major economic and political powers (a country definitively "dans la cour des grands")' (p.1). Only then was it to serve as a shop window for French culture, society and sport. Almost as an afterthought, they add that certainly one purpose was to promote French football more widely! Nevertheless, the essential aim was national self-promotion. Of course, this was nothing new. Political projection through sport is a long-established French tradition going back to the Olympic Games of 1924 – but this time it was a far more populist strategy than hitherto, embracing a French President decked out *à la* Mandela in a national football shirt; the People's President celebrating the People's Game no less – most appropriate, perhaps, if somewhat delayed, for the nation of 1789. Logically, however, global 'Grandeur' was to depend on organisational brilliance not soccer success. Given French lack of confidence on the football field this was not surprising. Serendipitous victory came as an unexpected bonus. At long last, the somewhat arrogant observation of Mathew Arnold that 'France, famed in all great arts, in none supreme' was proved wrong.

With the result that a notable consequence of the 1998 World Cup was the promotion of a new national self-confidence:

> French confidence was boosted by the World Cup victory ... Jean-François Kahn identified a new and surprised realisation by the French ... that France can be proud of its achievements in general and that the rest of the world does have things to admire about France rather than just seeing the country as a nation of *râleurs* ('whingers'). (p.212)

Any and all *râleurs*, hostile to the event, were drowned, as Hare and Dauncey observe, 'by the tide of euphoria swelling round by round' (p.214).

John Gay once remarked that the nation allows people to function in the impersonal settings of modern societies by offering the possibility of communication in a common language in which meaning is not dependent on local contexts and usages. In France in the summer of 1998 football was the language of euphoric communal communication: 'The passionate World Cup celebrations on the Champs-Elysées after the Final victory, when over a million people came together to express their elation – scenes repeated in

French towns and cities across the country – showed a sense of fraternity after a history of "guerre franco-française". Many expressed their joy by waving the national flag' (p.216).

Hippolyte Taine, the French nineteenth-century historian and critic, asserted in his *Histoire de la littérature anglaise* that national culture is determined by race, milieu and *moment* (emphasis added). A fresh sense of 'inclusiveness' was the further inestimable emotional gift of success in the international competition. It reached from the top to the bottom of French society.

> Chirac had also been given a number 23 shirt with his name emblazoned on the back. It was this shirt which appeared around the President's shoulders as everyone celebrated victory in the Stade de France on 12 July. The symbolism of such a gift from the players was strong, given the prevalent emphasis on the racial and social inclusiveness of the team and of the importance of its performances for encouraging harmony in French society: the symbolic inclusion of the head of state as an extra member of the national squad marked the solidarity of the French nation from highest office to poorest immigrant children in Marseilles worshipping Zidane. (p.2)

Success gathered in the politician, philosopher and plebeian in a triumphalist rationalisation of the moral value of the victory. It was observed that 'the French victory had caused millions of French people to give collective expression to a sense of belonging to the national community, not through nationalism and exclusiveness, but rather through solidarity, diversity and positive, progressive, human values – in the image of the French team' (p.207).

Thus it appears, as Hare and Dauncey optimistically assert, France discovered the reality of 'une France multiraciale' and decided that it possessed 'une France tricolore et multicolore'. The successful multiracial team epitomised a successful multicultural society. But much more than this, larger problems may have been partially eased if not wholly solved, by victory in the *Mondial*:

> France has been undergoing a crisis of identity to do with the racial and cultural mix of its poor city suburbs that have become ghettos. It has been complicated by growing globalisation of the economy (for which, in France, read Americanisation), the inability to come to terms in the collective memory with Vichy and France's role in the Holocaust, or with resentments left over from the Algerian War. Has the World Cup victory been a defining moment in France's realisation that it is unalterably, and for better or worse (and probably for the

better in the image of their football team) a mixed-race society? Has the victory crystallised a feeling that France is also undeniably in the big league and accepted as such by the rest of the world? There may be a feeling that the World Cup is lifting a long depression, and showing the way forward in terms of national identity. (p.217)

Nations need heroes. This is a truism. The World Cup 1998 also provided France with heroes – in small *and* large measure. Both Chirac and Jospin basked in reflected glory – momentarily heroic rather than villainous – redeemed for the moment by association. But the Carlylean heroic figure of the new multiracial France 'revealed' by France 98 was Zinedine Zidane, soccer international and son of a warehouseman from Algeria. By means, in no small part, of this offspring of a North African immigrant worker, the French people had come together, claimed *Le Journal du Dimanche* (as Hare and Dauncey agree), around the tricolour and national anthem. Patriotism was won back from the National Front.

And if Zinedine Zidane was the personification of inclusiveness, then Aimé Jacquet the French coach was the epitome of France of the post millennium:

> Having been mocked for his provincial accent and his inarticulacy, his refusal to play the communication game, and for generally being unfashionable, he now stood for the virtues of hard work, modesty, humility, respect, honesty, simplicity, authenticity, competence, professionalism. His approach to football had worked: methodical, protecting his players, building teamwork, generosity, valuing character, willingness to work meaning more than natural talent, getting a result rather than being flashy ... (p.219)

So was the 1998 World Cup really about sport? In the summer of 1998 France acquired self-confidence, won admiration for its modernity, found a new racial harmony, discovered new role models – and all because of a game! However, as Hare and Dauncey rightly ask, how permanent are these new found virtues and values, and as a corollary, how permanent is the power of a game to transform national identity and image? Interesting and absorbing questions!

On the world, as distinct from the national, stage the 1998 World Cup poses serious questions associated with the concept of 'autonomy'. While the contributors to this volume provide 'a framework for the understanding and the further study (much to be welcomed) of the impact of the 1998 World Cup on France and French Football' (p.11), issues of global significance are raised in this book – the democratic availability of sport, the freedom of founder sports organisations *vis-à-vis* media, commerce and supranational bodies, public access to play and watch. The former prized and protected independence of sports organisations, for example, is increasingly a thing of the past. The timing and availability of sporting events is more and more a consequence of media demands and control, of commercial strategies allied to the profit motive. The autonomy that only recently set sport apart from other social domains *is*, as Hare and Dauncey claim, in great danger of 'being eroded by the hegemony that commerce, via the tool of television, is beginning to exert on football and other sports' (p.9). In addition, growing subscription to a belief in the entrepreneurial essence of all spectator sport summed up in the brutal but not inappropriate aphorism 'make them pay – one way or another' equally erodes democratic access to, of all things, 'the people's game'. In the post-euphoria of the 1998 World Cup, in France and elsewhere these trends should not be overlooked, ignored or unchallenged. Appreciation of the importance of the State in recognising, emphasising and ensuring that sport serves all the community and not just the profiteers and privileged is more necessary now than ever before.

Finally, Bourdieu, Elias and Dunning are singled out for praise by Hare and Dauncey for using sport as a standpoint from which to observe change in society and culture. To end on a sanguine note, after a congratulatory nod of appreciation to the editors and contributors of this attractive volume, the trio is in good company. This Series, which provided the editors of this highly readable and topical volume with the opportunity to follow in the trio's footsteps, was founded, among other things, to do *just* that – hence the appearance in Sport in the Global Society of *France and the 1998 World Cup*. And it is good to report that there will be a steady flow of other contributors to the Series in due course, committed to this important, stimulating and challenging task.

J.A. MANGAN
International Research Centre for
Sport, Socialisation and Society
University of Strathclyde
November 1998

Acknowledgements

Thanks to: Frank Cass, Jonathan Manley, and Tony Mangan for believing in the project; the contributors for getting the work in (relatively) on time; John (Max) Roach for translations and comments; the French Embassy (London) for help with travel costs (H. Dauncey and G. Hare); CNRS conference 'Football et cultures', Paris, May 1998 (Jean-Michel Faure, Charles Suaud, Rémi Lenoir and Patrick Mignon) for invitation to participate and contacts; Newcastle University Small Research Grants for help with travel cost (G. Hare); *Financial Times* Paris Office, INSEP, Institut Français de Presse, International Herald Tribune for documentation, library facilities and other help; The Institut National de l'Audiovisuel; James Bannister, Peter Berlin, Jacques Bonnet, Jacques-Marie Bourget, Jean-François Danis, Jacques Dauvin, Les Davison, Jo de Linde, James Eastham, Guy-Laurent Epstein, Marie-Claude Gédor, Catherine Hare, James Hickey, Chrystel Hug, Bruno Martini, Ann McKeever, Stuart Nimmo, Véronique Pabois, Philippe Peybernes and Victor Sinet, for other help; and Aimé Jacquet and *les Bleus* for making it all come together at the end.

The Editors and Publisher would like to thank the French Embassy for its generous sponsorship of this book.

Ambassade de France à Londres

Acronyms

AS	Association sportive
CFI	Comité français interfédéral
CFA	Championnat de France amateur (equivalent of D4)
CFO	Comité français d'organisation de la Coupe du monde
CIM	Centre international des médias
CIRTV	Centre international de radio et télévision
CNOSF	Comité national olympique et sportif français
CNRS	Centre national de la recherche scientifique
COBOF	Comité pour l'organisation du boycott de la Coupe du monde de football en France
CPP	Centre principal de presse
CRS	Compagnies républicaines de sécurité
D1	Division 1
D2	Division 2
DATAR	Délégation à l'aménagement du territoire et à l'action régionale
DICOM	Délégation interministérielle à la Coupe du monde
DOM	Départements d'outre-mer
DNCG	Direction nationale de contrôle de gestion
FA	Football Association
FAS	Fédération des associations de supporters
FFF	Fédération française de football
FFFA	Fédération française de football association
FGSPF	Fédération gymnastique et sportive des patronages de France
FIFA	Fédération internationale de football assocation
FLN	Front de libération nationale
FNDS	Fonds national pour le développement du sport
GIA	Groupe islamique armé
HLM	Habitation à loyer modéré
INSEE	Institut national de la statistique et des études économiques
INSEP	Institut national du sport et de l'éducation physique
IOC	International Olympic Committee
ISL	International Sport Leisure
LFA	Ligue de Football Association
LNF	Ligue nationale de football
OM	Olympique de Marseille
PC	Parti communiste

PS	Parti socialiste
PSG	Paris Saint-Germain
RAID	Recherche-assistance-intervention-dissuasion
RER	Réseau express régional
RPR	Rassemblement pour la République
SA	Société anonyme
SAOS	Société anonyme à objet sportif
SAEMS	Société anonyme d'économie mixte sportive
SdF	Stade de France
SEM	Société d'économie mixte
SIPECS	Société immobilière parisienne d'études et de constructions sportives
SME	Small and medium sized enterprise
STO	Service de travail obligatoire
SWC	Sony World Cup
TGV	Train à grande vitesse
TOM	Territoires d'outre-mer
UDF	Union pour la démocratie française
UEFA	Union européenne de football association
USFSA	Union des sociétés françaises de sports athlétiques
UNFP	Union nationale des footballeurs professionnels

Introduction: France and France 98

HUGH DAUNCEY and GEOFF HARE

France 98: French Culture, Sport and Society

Why did France want to host the World Cup in 1998? As in 1989, when the Bicentenary of the Revolution celebrated the French contribution to democracy and universal notions of human rights, looking back to a glorious past and highlighting France's legacy to the world, the 1998 World Cup was staged for external consumption. It was to celebrate France's position as one of the major economic and political powers (a country definitively 'dans la cour des grands'), and to serve as shop-window for French culture, sport and society. France 98 was intended to showcase French industry and high technology (construction, TGV, telecommunications, television, luxury goods), to stimulate internal investment (including in the regions), tourism (in the long term). Internally, hosting such an international sporting competition was an opportunity to develop infrastructures (stadiums, transport), to associate national and local politicians with a major world event, and to promote French football to a wider audience.

Whatever the complexities of preparing for France 98, and whatever the pitfalls to be avoided in organising the competition itself or the future problems of running infrastructures such as the Stade de France 'after the circus has left town', France's success in obtaining the World Cup was an important reward for its strategy of national self-promotion.[1] FIFA's choice of France was partly influenced by favourable impressions of French transport and telecommunications (TGV high-speed train and France Telecom), as well as by the French State's recent tradition of *grands travaux*, which suggested that building a new national stadium to comply with FIFA requirements would be unproblematic.

The French have traditionally used both sporting events and architecture to create Grandeur, as recent controversies over the latest Mitterrandian version of 'la politique des grands travaux' have emphasised, and as is also suggested by France's hosting of the 1924 Olympics, the 1938 World Cup, the 1968 Winter Games at Chamonix, the 1984 European Soccer Championships and the 1992 Winter Olympics at Albertville. France has arguably been keener to host these events than comparator European nations, and believes in their efficacy as national self-promotion. The furore of popular, media and academic interest in Euro 96 showed in Britain that hosting a large-scale international sporting contest of this kind is a significant event economically, politically and culturally. Analysts of the European Championships have placed 1996 alongside 1966 in British popular culture and sport in defining the way we were/are, and the 1998 World Cup in France has similarly marked the French collective psyche, as much as it has affected infrastructures and finance.

International football and the French nation have had a special relationship throughout the years: a Frenchman, Jules Rimet, as President of the French Football Federation and of FIFA, was the most influential of administrators in creating the World Cup; a Frenchman scored the first ever goal in a World Cup competition in 1930 in Uruguay – Laurent; a Frenchman, Just Fontaine, holds the record for the number of goals scored in a World Cup Finals competition, 13. The first time the President of the Republic attended the French Cup Final was in 1927 when Rimet invited President Doumergue to present the Cup to winners Olympique de Marseille, but apart from this annual event, until the 1960s sport rarely intruded into public life of the nation and the national political world. When President Auriol received boxer Marcel Cerdan at the Elysée Palace after his world-title winning fight with Tony Zale in 1948, this seemed an exceptional event, but now the use of sport in politics is commonplace, as politicians see the advantages of being associated with sports men and women. Jacques Chirac received all the French medallists after the Atlanta Olympics in 1996, just as he received the French World Cup winning squad at the 14 July garden party in 1998.

Nowadays the nation and its leaders identify readily with the national football team. After the semi-final with Croatia, President Chirac and Prime Minister Jospin talked with the French players in the dressing rooms, each emerging with a player's shirt as a memento. Earlier, Chirac had also been given a number 23 shirt with his name emblazoned on the back. It was this shirt which appeared around the President's shoulders as everyone celebrated victory in the Stade de France on 12 July. The symbolism of such a gift from the players was strong, given the prevalent emphasis on the racial and social inclusiveness of the team and of the importance of its performances for encouraging harmony in French society: the symbolic inclusion of the head of state as an extra member of the national squad marked the solidarity of the French nation from highest office to poorest immigrant children in Marseille worshipping Zidane. There were of course some dissenting voices from the extreme Right amidst the general enthusiasm for the multi-coloured national squad, but Jospin also stressed the multiracial composition of the team in an interview before the Final: 'Quel meilleur exemple de notre unité et de notre diversité que cette magnifique équipe?'[2]

Indeed, although a general political consensus was evident over the staging of the competition, some parties of both the extreme Left and the extreme Right were sceptical about France's motivations. The neo-Trotskyist *Lutte ouvrière* (LO) pilloried the government for allowing an explosion of capitalist greed at all levels from ticket touts to the construction consortia building the Stade de France. For the extreme-Right weekly *Rivarol*, any support in France for the Tunisian, Moroccan, Cameroon or other African teams proved the status of what it called the 'néo-Français', who even if they support the French team do so more because it is the 'bande à Zidane' than because it is the 'Onze tricolore'.[3] Other elements of French society were also opposed to the World Cup, such as the Comité pour l'organisation du boycott de la Coupe du monde de football en France (COBOF). Other less political organisations, like the association 'La coupe est pleine', were created as acts of resistance against the wave of World Cup hysteria felt by some to be over-running the country.

Organising France 98

The structures set up to manage France 98, in terms of the local organising committee and the co-ordinating committees linking it to the State, reflect the French model of promoting sport. As Pierre Bourdieu and others have remarked, sport in France has a particular relation to society (and to the State) involving issues of moral values, public service and anti-commercialism, all of which create tensions in the modern game. In France for example, official recognition (*agrément*) by the Ministry for Youth and Sport allows, for instance, the imposition on sports governing bodies of model statutes ensuring democratic functioning and accountability, and in return for this State tutelage and recognition of the sport's public service mission as being of 'public utility', a sporting body or affiliated club becomes eligible for official grant aid.[4] Thus the Ministry for Youth and Sport delegates to the FFF the monopoly of organisation, regulation and representation of football in France. The tutelage exercised by the State is real and allows supervision of the legality and fairness of the Federation's activities because the FFF's authority has simply been delegated by the State on the behalf of French citizens.

The local organising committee (Comité français d'organisation de la Coupe du monde – CFO) was set up by the FFF as an *association loi 1901* in November 1992. Co-presided by Michel Platini and Fernand Sastre (former FFF president) the Committee was responsible for preparing and organising the World Cup in accord with FIFA guidelines and within financial conditions prescribed by the French State. The chief executive of the CFO was high-ranking civil servant (and *énarque*) Jacques Lambert, who has close links to the State (he was formerly *préfet de la Savoie* 1990–93, responsible for safety and security at Albertville 92). Because of the State's disinclination to invest too heavily itself in the World Cup where other funding was possible, the CFO's organisation of the footballing aspects of the event was dependent financially on ticket sales and on its marketing programme launched in early 1994. The successful attraction of sponsors and the huge demand for tickets allowed the CFO's budget to increase gradually reaching 2.4bn francs in September 1997. The overall financial objective of the CFO was to break even, which it achieved with something to spare, since despite escalating costs of personnel, the creation of accreditation and media centres and hospitality villages, the turnover of the France 98 marketing programme was more than twice that of USA '94, but not without controversy – over ticket allocation, notably, and its relation to corporate hospitality.

The Délégation interministérielle à la Coupe du Monde (DICOM) is more directly answerable to the government, and was created in March 1993 to help co-ordinate the interactions between the State, the CFO, cities, and local and regional authorities. *Délégué interministériel* Noël de Saint-Pulgent worked with *ministre de la Jeunesse et des Sports* Marie-George Buffet (PC) and answered to the prime minister's office. DICOM's responsibilities included co-ordinating the activities of the government bodies and public-sector companies involved, implementing investment and infrastructure development programmes for public amenities financed jointly by the State and the public sector, and providing liaison between government, regions, departments and cities involved in hosting games. More generally, DICOM intended to maximise the economic, social and cultural benefits that France would derive from the World Cup. This kind of interdepartmental co-ordinating structure is a commonly used mechanism in a country where the State has a strong tradition of centralism and interventionism in all aspects of society.

Public funding of French sport is the corollary of State oversight of its governing bodies. In 1994, parliamentary debate over funding for the Youth and Sports ministry was marked by dissatisfaction on Left and Right that the 2.78bn francs budget had fallen below 0.2% of the overall State budget, although France was nevertheless still the European country in which State sports funding was most generous. Further criticisms targeted plans to use Youth and Sports funding to help prepare for the World Cup. Conscious that the Fonds national pour le développement du sport (FNDS) financed by taxation of the State lottery – the Française des jeux – is intended to promote grass-roots activities, and not elite sport, deputies and sporting associations protested against projected FNDS contributions of 170m francs annually from 1995 towards the Stade de France and renovation of provincial grounds.[5] In 1996 sporting associations again reacted badly to the news that government funding for Youth and Sport was declining (despite 78m francs required for the SdF in 1996–97), forcing the FNDS increasingly to take on the support of elite sporting activities (including money to depollute the SdF and 78m francs for renovating other World Cup sites).[6]

Planning the World Cup, from government through the multilateral relations linking the many and varied stakeholders listed above, illustrates the way sport in France, both participatory and spectator, has been seen as a public service, 'une mission de service public', at the very least since the Liberation governments, and as a legitimate concern of the public authorities since the Popular Front and Vichy. One of the official statements made by the French State about what the World Cup was to be revealed some of the public service missions of football and France 98. For Mme Buffet, in addition to the politics and the economics of the competition, the summer of 1998 was to foster a 'fraternal coming-together' ('rassemblement fraternel') and a 'festival of youth, citizenship and solidarity' ('une fête de la jeunesse et de la citoyenneté, de la solidarité').[7] The government was anxious to provide alternative attractions for those not solely interested in football, and the Youth and Sports Ministry devoted 15m francs to 'animations sportives et culturelles autour de la Coupe du monde'. Indeed, during the competition, the minister was apparently more at ease with the political part of her job visiting local sports associations and the 'Ecrans du monde' (giant screens in poor areas) than with the protocol requiring her presence at all the matches involving the French team: 'The World Cup is a bit frightening because of all the money and the violence. But it's unbelievable how many projects it has sparked off and how many people have got involved.'[8]

French Football: Style and Coming of Age?

Colin Cameron, in *Football, Fussball, Voetbal* published before the European Championships of 1996, entitled the chapter devoted to France 'A Coming of Age'.[9] For Cameron, the French success in the 1984 European Championships marked France's emergence as a mature adult member of the world football community. The problem with this view is surely that France still had to wait for success in a *world* football competition, rather than a European championship involving eight teams, staged at home. Before 1998 France's record in international football was disappointing. In 1938, France hosted the third World Cup, losing 1–3 in the quarter-finals to eventual winners Italy. In 1958 in Sweden, the national team shone through the brilliance of Just Fontaine, and reached the semi-finals. More recently, in the 1982 World Cup in Spain, France was beaten by Germany in the semi-finals, a result repeated in Mexico four years later; in 1990 and 1994 France failed to qualify for the Finals, and in the 1996 European Championships the French team flattered to deceive, going out on penalties in the semi-final. Only victory at home in Euro 84 gave French football and France itself reasons for pride. Cameron identifies traits in the French approach to sport in general which he feels have contributed to holding back French football in a state of 'immaturity'; he cites a desire to be seen as good hosts, the absence of a win-at-all-costs attitude, the competition of rugby for supporters' attention and a lack of fervour amongst fans, the constantly changing leagues, clubs, mergers and relocations. He concludes that 'French football is a religion without faith, fit only for agnostics.'[10]

When France was asked to organise the World Cup, it could be argued that it was these agnostics and other sceptics at home and abroad who doubted that France's footballing tradition was strong enough to ensure a successful Finals phase, given the small crowds attracted to professional fixtures. Although French domestic football has many strengths, principally in its capacity to nurture talented young players, poor finances and support for teams had weakened the French Championship in the 1990s by a steady drain of players to more profitable careers in Italy and England. Even if these players were still available for the French national squad, traditional pessimism over the strength of French football at international level was compounded by fears that players scattered throughout Europe would play less easily together than if they were all in the French First Division, and that needs of foreign clubs might conflict with those of the French national side. After a series of scandals involving club finances and local politics in the 1980s, the changes to French ways of organising football brought about by the *Bosman* ruling had unsettled the French D1, as players began to realise they could earn more abroad, away from low crowds and the high costs imposed on employers (the football clubs) by French tax and social security systems.

Semi-final defeats in 1982 and 1986 have strengthened the French psychological block over their inability to beat their neighbours and old enemies across the Rhine. Some cultural commentators see France's lack of footballing success against Germany as proof in sport of what Alain Peyrefitte described as 'le mal français'.[11] Everything seems to confirm the definition of football as 'a simple game, with 22 players, a ball and a referee, and the Germans always win'. France's only successes in world football until 1998 came against Latin opponents (Spain and Portugal in 1984 in the European Championships, and Brazil in the 1984 Olympic final). In 1998 there was relief, for different reasons, that neither the English nor the Germans crossed France's path.

Renewed confidence about hosting the world's biggest sporting event and about France's desire to be seen as a fully accepted member amongst the major powers of the world was expressed in the official anthem of France 98, sung by Axelle Red (from Belgium) and Youssou N'Dour (from Senegal), and entitled 'La cour des grands'. Mistranslated by one British journalist as 'The playground for grown-ups', the song is really best interpreted to mean that hosting the World Cup puts France at the top level in sport and in the Premier League of nations with an international role.[12] The desire to accede to such recognition was nevertheless accompanied by a real lack of confidence in the national team.

Before the World Cup, French expectations of 'les Bleus' were relatively low. Confidence in French football at the international level had been seriously undermined by non-qualification for USA 94, caused by defeats against Israel (described by Platini as the worst ever for France) and Bulgaria. After USA 94 and the change in manager brought about by replacement of Gérard Houllier by Aimé Jacquet, difficulties in finding positions for stars like Cantona or Ginola (the latter blamed for the last-minute defeat against Bulgaria in 1994), and a disappointing performance (certainly in terms of style) in Euro 96, further weakened belief in the national team. It was considered talented, but lacking in the toughness and striking ability which would enable it to do justice to French ambitions. In the mini *Tournoi de France* held in June 1997 to test the organisation for the World Cup, France again failed, and in September 1997 Claude Simonet (president of the FFF) reflected the consensus by declaring that with a world ranking of 15th, France had practically no chance of being a seeded country in the qualifying groups for Euro 2000.[13] This conveniently ignored the fact that Jacquet's teams had lost only three games since he had taken over in 1994.

Before the inaugural friendly match in the Stade de France on 28 January 1998, when France beat Spain 2–1 in front of 80,000 spectators, the national manager Jacquet reiterated the philosophy which was to inform his approach to the World Cup: 'I've said it again and again: my aim is not to please. Because we are supposed to win this World Cup, I'm going to give myself the means to do so.'[14] Jacquet was much criticised by the influential sports daily *L'Equipe*, which could not discern a stable style of play that he was imposing on the national team, or if there was one they did not like it. This developed into retaliation by Jacquet that *L'Equipe* was exploiting its position as the *only* daily sports newspaper to dictate to football.[15] As we shall see in the following analyses, some of the impact of the World Cup on French society, sport and culture was revealed in the way it helped to resolve questions of the 'national style of play', the role of *L'Equipe* in media coverage, and other issues.

Analysing Sport: Legitimacy of Study and Autonomy of Practice?

Both in France and in the English-speaking world of sports studies, it long seemed that French sport and French football in particular were neglected objects of study, even though more recently illuminating studies of various aspects of sport and football in France have appeared. In May 1998, two important academic conferences dealing with football were held in Paris, reflecting the ever-growing interest held by intellectuals in France in the interactions between sport and society. The conference hosted by the Centre national de la recherche scientifique (CNRS) was entitled 'Football et cultures' and that organised by the Institut national du sport et de l'éducation physique (INSEP) was devoted to 'Football : jeu et société'. In an interview with *Libération*, ethnologist Christian Bromberger, a participant in both colloquia, expressed the view that there now exists 'une footballisation de la société'.[16] Studies now increasingly see the sport of football and society, politics, economics and culture as interlinked, and football as one way of revealing aspects of social and cultural change.

Much is owed to seminal articles written in the early 1970s, particularly by Eugen Weber, who drew attention to the social and political significance of French sport. Since then interest has grown gradually, perhaps restrained in France by many intellectuals' inherent disinclination to consider manifestations of popular culture as worthy of serious enquiry, despite innovative work on sport and leisure such as J. Dumazedier's *Vers une civilisation du loisir* (1962), which helped demonstrate the centrality of practices previously thought insignificant.[17] In the UK, Richard Holt's *Sport and Society in Modern France* (1981) helped create more interest in analysing the social context of French sport, encouraging the serious study of topics – such as football – which have sometimes come to be seen as not only a growth area in academic enquiry, but as a media obsession and general metaphor for living.[18] In France, despite the 'anti-foot' movement characterised by an intellectual rejection of popular culture and a left-wing belief in football as opium of the people, attitudes towards analysing sport as popular culture have changed gradually. This reflects in part social scientists' desire to better understand practices of everyday life. It also unpacks the social, cultural and political contributions made by sport to France's traditional preoccupation with grandeur.

The publisher Frank Cass was one of the first to recognise Norbert Elias' and Eric Dunning's seminal work on the sociology of modern sport, at a time when sport, and football even less so, were hardly considered subjects for serious research.[19] Cass journals, in particular the *International Journal of the History of Sport*, and the book series Sport in the Global Society, each initiated and founded by J.A. Mangan, have become key points of reference for study of sport in society. Elias and Dunning saw the autonomous nature of modern sport as distinguishing it both from other types of leisure activity and from other types of confrontation: the existence of uniform written codes of rules, the lower level of violence permitted in bodily contact, and the autonomy of sport as a social activity (whether as an activity in itself or as a spectacle). Football today (and the World Cup) are even further removed from medieval folk football than when Elias and Dunning were writing. Traditional forms of football saw confrontations of pre-established social groups – one village against another, married versus single, one profession against another – and the game reproduced distinctions that pre-existed it or existed outside football. Modern sport has on the other hand no ritual or festive significance outside itself: it is meant to cut across or neutralise the differences that organise society, and by its universally accepted rules to create equal opportunities for players, a literal and metaphorical level playing field for participants, whose skill and team work alone matter. Just as universal suffrage is the expression of political democracy and citizenship, so modern sport reflects an equality of opportunity for members of society, a meritocracy. As Roger Chartier remarks, this does not mean that sports events are not also expressions of multiple oppositions (national, racial, social, or religious).[20] Indeed, as the present examination of France 98 shows, the study of French football is a way of exploring these divergences in French society today, and within a wider context. However, the re-entry of social and national distinctions into football was conditional on modern sport having created for itself a space and time that were its own, an initial autonomy that set it outside other social domains. One of the issues that the study of France 98 cannot escape is indeed the extent to which this autonomy is being eroded by the hegemony that commerce, via the tool of television, is beginning to exert on football and other sports.

The autonomy of modern sport is seen in the timing and spaces that are specific to sport as an activity. In terms of space, football can be seen to have a less dominant position within French sport in general simply by looking at the functions of the main stadiums where football is played. Admittedly the biggest British stadiums are also coming to be used occasionally for events other than football – pop concerts for example, but their quasi-exclusive function has until certain recent developments been professional football. In France, however, the oval architecture and even the names of the World Cup venues – Le Stade Vélodrome (Marseille) and Le Stadium municipal (Toulouse) indicate that they are regularly used for other sporting activities. Similar developments in new stadiums in both countries – in particular the provision of hospitality lounges and luxury private boxes with high-class restaurant facilities – show both the growing globalisation of sport and the new pressures on it from areas of social activity to do with conspicuous consumption, public relations and corporate entertainment that hitherto operated in other domains – the Albert Hall or the Paris Opéra in the nineteenth century, Epsom or Chantilly, and more recently Wimbledon or Roland Garros.

If the placing and architecture of modern stadiums have been a function of the management both of population and potential income, the timing of modern football has depended on work rhythms, leisure habits and, increasingly, on the demands of the media. The frequency of the World Cup tournament – every four years – has been constructed specifically, for maximum exposure, to fall in the middle of the Olympic cycle, itself creating an illusion of an unbreakable tradition. The length of the tournament has grown and grown – France 1998 was the longest ever at 33 days, with the matches timed to allow as many televised games as possible, given a cursory nod in the direction of fairness between teams in so far as the final first round matches of each group were played at the same time. This also heightened the drama for the television audience, it should be said, as for example it allowed a late goal by Norway against Brazil to eliminate Morocco, who believed they were coasting to qualification against Scotland.

Another key element of modern sport, as Elias and Dunning showed, was the elaboration of uniform sets of rules. The history of a given sport is in a sense the history of the universal acceptance of a codified set of rules and of their interpretation and indeed a way of playing, as opposed to local or even national variations. The establishment of national FAs, along the model of the English FA, and then the setting up (on French initiative) of the international body, FIFA, in 1904, were important steps in establishing the autonomy of sport above and beyond the social environment. However, in practice, national and of course international competitions were essential to cementing this in reality. What has happened since Elias and Dunning were first thinking about this autonomisation of sport is that the autonomy of sport has become supranational. The global nature of this autonomy is clear in competitions such as the World Cup. Questions of interpretation of rules across continents have emerged in particular at World Cup tournaments, where FIFA has been understandably keen to ensure the 'level playing field' and therefore the autonomy of the game. The attempt by FIFA to make the game more attractive by tightening up on the interpretation of the tackle from behind or how to punish dissent, gave rise to controversy, despite careful training of referees in FIFA seminars before the start of the 1998 tournament. Uniformity of interpretation of the rules by referees and players, especially between South American styles and European styles, has come a long way since the World Cup competition began in 1930.

The process of globalisation of modern football has been furthered by universal television coverage and the mobility of players attracted to rich western European clubs from Latin America, Africa and Eastern Europe. However, the autonomy that the World Cup represents is challenged by the increasing influence of global commerce over football, which is arguably in danger of being subsumed as a part of the marketing and public relations of multinational companies such as Adidas, Nike and Coca-Cola. An area that needs constant vigilance is the relationship between the regulatory bodies of the sport and the sponsoring companies, in so far as the existence of a corps of regulators who legislate and exercise sanctions in the name of the autonomy of the sport, outside (or above) civil law, is at the heart of modern sport's autonomy. The autonomy of sport's governing bodies has of course been under attack not only from commerce, but also from politics and the State, or rather from supranational organisations such as the European parliament, the European Court of Justice and the European Commission (*Bosman* ruling etc.) It may be that sport may have to embrace the demands of one of these masters to protect it from the other. The French approach hitherto has been to rely on the State's recognition of the public service mission of sport to guarantee sporting values. In the English-speaking world football has sought its independence through making clubs specific kinds of business organisation, which are now all the more open to developments in the direction of commercial, profit-making companies.

Following Elias and Dunning, what French sociologists such as Pierre Bourdieu have taken as read is the legitimacy of the study of what he calls the 'champ sportif', and indeed the importance of studying the internal logic of how certain physical practices, sport, take on new meanings and functions within society. Bourdieu has looked at how television is affecting once autonomous fields such as literature and justice and politics, and now sport.[21] Neither Elias and Dunning nor Bourdieu, while establishing the legitimacy of sport as an object of academic investigation, abstract it from economic, social, political and ideological changes. On the contrary, they use sport as a standpoint from which to observe changes in society and culture. May this study, in all due modesty, attempt to follow that tradition.

France, French Football and the 1998 World Cup

The contributions which make up the rest of this study are chosen to provide a framework for the understanding and further exploration of the impact of the 1998 World Cup on France and on French football. The individual contributions give either a presentation and discussion of the academic, sporting, social, political and economic context of France 98, or analyse the running of various aspects of the competition itself. Pierre Bourdieu's introductory study presents a theoretical socio-political perspective on the place of football and sport in French society, suggesting how the traditional autonomy of French sport from free-market economics is being eroded by neo-liberal approaches to government and the economy. Successive analyses look initially at the French domestic footballing context leading up to France 98, and then investigate France 98 and its relationship to French football, politics and society.

Ian Pickup describes the historical development of French football since its introduction from England in the nineteenth century, discussing the move towards professionalisation, the creation of league and cup competitions and the successes and failures of iconic club and national teams, ending his analysis with the triumph of the French team under Platini in Euro 84. John Marks picks up the theme of the national team and of national footballing heroes before and after Platini in an analysis of the links between football and the French nation. He examines issues surrounding the social and ethnic composition of the national side in 1958 (dominated by Kopa) comparing this with the squads of *les Bleus* in the 1990s. James Eastham provides discussion of the contemporary organisation of French football in the 1980s and 1990s in an analysis of financial and political scandals experienced by French clubs and of difficulties caused for French football by the *Bosman* ruling, high French social security costs, player exoduses, and current transformations in French football induced by television-led commercialisation

Patrick Mignon then analyses the sociology of French football supporters by placing the culture of fandom within the context of the slow industrialisation of French society, the pre-eminent role of Paris in the urban hierarchy and social tensions in a multi-ethnic national community undergoing the stress of economic difficulties; he links this study to the French victory in France 98, discussing the meaning of French people's celebratory identification with the national team. Hugh Dauncey considers the infrastructures required by FIFA for France's hosting of the World Cup in an analysis of the economic and political aspects of selecting and renovating regional stadiums and through a study of the siting, designing, constructing and running of the new national stadium, purpose-built for France 98. Geoff Hare similarly concentrates on the World Cup itself in an analysis of the buying and selling of the competition, the dominance of FIFA and consequent constraints on the local organisers, the negotiation of television rights and of contracts for sponsorship and merchandising, corporate hospitality and the scarcity of tickets for 'real' fans.

Claude Journès provides a discussion of the policing and security of the Finals matches, concentrating on the French State's initial concerns over terrorism and hooliganism, considering the success and failure of measures put in place to ensure the safety of fans inside and outside the stadiums. Lucy McKeever discusses the media coverage of the month of competition, placing press, radio, television and new media treatments of the football in the context of recent developments in French media in general, and sports reporting in particular. For ease of reference to the chronological order of events, a 'Diary' (Dauncey and Hare) of the 1998 World Cup then aims to provide a chronological and narrative account of the major sporting, social, political, cultural and economic aspects of the month of football festivities as they were experienced in France. The concluding study (Dauncey and Hare) brings together most of the issues considered by individual contributors in an attempt to mark out some of the general points to be made about the impact of France 98 on French sport, culture and society.

NOTES

1. The 'circus' metaphor comes from the title of a study of USA '94; see J. Sugden and A. Tomlinson, 'What's Left When the Circus Leaves Town? An Evaluation of World Cup USA 1994', *Sociology of Sport Journal* 13 (1996), 238–58.

2. J. Buob, 'La France voit la vie en bleu', *Le Mondial*, 11 July 1998, i. The English version of Jospin's remark is: 'What better example of our unity and diversity than this magnificent team?' In general, all quotations originally in French will be found translated in the main text with as noted reference to the source of the original French. Only where the actual wording of the French is crucial to the point being argued will the original French be retained.

3. C. Lorne, 'M comme Mondial, métissage, meutes ethniques et magouilles', *Rivarol*, 2391, 19 June 1998, 12.

4. C. Miège, *Les Institutions sportives* (Paris, PUF, 1993), 48.

5. J. Fenoglio, 'Jeunesse et sports: le poids de la Coupe du monde de football', *Le Monde*, 27 October 1994, 12.

6. J.-J. Bozonnet, 'Le mouvement sportif regrette le désengagement financier de l'Etat', *Le Monde*, 12 November 1996, 22.

7. Sports Ministry Website, 'Editorial de Marie-George Buffet' (http://www.jeunesse-sports.gouv.fr/francais/mjs1000.htm).

8. B. Hennion, 'La ministre préfère le terrain aux tribunes', *Libération*, 26 June 1998, 33.

9. C. Cameron, *Football, Fussball, Voetbal* (London, BBC Books, 1995), 158–77.

10. Ibid., 163

11. Y. Bigot, *Football* (Paris, Grasset, 1996), 154.

12. J. Lichfield, 'France hopes for a scoring draw', *Independent on Sunday*, 30 November 1997, 16.

13. 'L'équipe de France "n'a pratiquement aucune chance" d'être l'une des têtes de série des neuf groupes éliminatoires de l'Euro 2000', *Le Monde*, 29 September 1997, 21.

14. B. Hopquin, 'Aimé Jacquet entame la deuxième phase de son chantier', *Le Monde*, 28 January 1998, 24.

15. G. Dutheil, 'Après avoir critiqué Aimé Jacquet, *L'Equipe* se refuse au mea culpa', *Le Mondial*, 11 July 1998, iii.

16. C. Losson and O. Villepreux, 'Il y a une footballisation de la société', *Libération*, 12 May 1998, 22.

17. E. Weber, 'Pierre de Coubertin and the Introduction of organised Sport into France', *Journal of Contemporary History*, 5, 2 (1970), 3–26, and 'Gymnastics and Sports in fin-de-siècle France: opium of the classes', *American Historical Review*, 76 (February 1971), 70–98; J.

Dumazedier, *Vers une civilisation du loisir* (Paris, Le Seuil, 1962).
18. R. Holt, *Sport and Society in Modern France* (London, Macmillan, 1981).
19. N. Elias and J. L Scotson, *The Established and the Outsiders. A Sociological Enquiry into Community Problems* (London, Frank Cass, 1965); E. Dunning (ed.), *The Sociology of Sport. A Selection of Readings* with a foreword by Norbert Elias (London, Frank Cass, 1971), republished as part of N. Elias and E. Dunning, *Quest for Excitement. Sport and Leisure in the Civilising Process* (Oxford, Blackwell, 1986).
20. R. Chartier, 'Avant-propos', N. Elias and E. Dunning, *Sport et civilisation. La violence maîtrisée* (Paris, Fayard, 1994), 15.
21. P. Bourdieu, 'Comment peut-on être sportif?', *Questions de sociologie* (Paris, Editions de Minuit, 1980), 173–95.

The State, Economics and Sport

PIERRE BOURDIEU
(Translated by Hugh Dauncey and Geoff Hare)

Talking about sport scientifically is difficult because in one sense it is too easy: everyone has their own ideas on the subject, and feels able to say something intelligent about it. Even Durkheim would already remark that the main difficulty in doing sociology was caused by the fact that everyone feels they have an innate understanding of it. Social objects are hidden behind a screen of preconstructed discourses which present the worst barrier to scientific investigation, and countless sociologists believe they are talking about the object of study when they are merely relaying the discourse which, in sport as elsewhere, the object produces about itself, whether through its officials, supporters or journalists. Consequently the construction of truly scientific objects implies a break with common representations (what Durkheim termed prenotions) which can notably be effected *by taking these prenotions as the object of study*.

It is therefore necessary to break with preconstructions, but without however avoiding the problems (notably political ones) that preconstructed discourses can involve through a slipping into what I shall call the *escapism of Wertfreiheit* (value-free-ness); or in other words, through systematically taking refuge in that kind of political indifferentism which is value-freeness. I myself have indulged in this *escapism*. It has to be said that, in the world of research, there is a lot of social profit to be gained by giving (and by claiming) the appearance of neutrality (which is taken for objectivity). Although I have always undertaken research on burning issues, the more 'controversial' the subject the more I have tended to remain aloof and to invest more (in terms of time especially) in the task of objectivation. But this *escapism* also very often allows one to obtain great benefits very cheaply. For example, one can undertake descriptive microsociology in giving accounts of a peaceful and unproblematic little rural sports club, or of inner city children playing street basketball;[1] or conversely, huge surveys can be produced on objects involving no major theoretical or empirical issues, such as for instance the social make-up of sports crowds, vaguely linking it to the problem of violence through a discussion of the relationship between violence and the spectators' social origins. The same is true of a certain use of history: research intended to glorify people or institutions is more easily accepted than historical sociology, which can be particularly corrosive, or even explosive and difficult to bear, when it studies the tools of thought of researchers or the research community itself.

This brings me to the problem that I should like to raise here, that of the relations between the State, economics and sport. This is a huge problem that the literature critical of collusion between sport, politics and money treats in its own not very scientific way, thereby running the risk of provoking a reaction of *Wertfreiheit escapism* and turning researchers away from the important issues that the same literature identifies, for example drug taking, business approaches in sport, the economic and political impact of commercialising football as a product, etc. These difficult problems must be treated seriously, but in order to be able to resolve them scientifically, the task of constructing the object of study requires great care. I shall therefore try to produce in draft form a programme of research, in other words a coherent system of questions susceptible of a scientific treatment.

Sport and Economics

When one considers the recent development of sport and more particularly that of football, a trend towards commercialisation becomes evident. This trend affects the whole of the space of sporting activities, but differentiates itself in each sport according to each sport's own internal logic and especially, according to the specific logic in each case of the relationship between the sport's practitioners and television, which is the veritable Trojan Horse for the entry of commercial logic into sport. This process is hidden by discussion of little North African or Senegalese children playing football with tin cans or rag balls (underprivileged classes of underdeveloped countries often serve as football nurseries where promoters of commercialised football can find players to make their teams competitive), or, closer to home, by discussion of small amateur clubs whose always fragile survival depends of the unfailing self-sacrifice of unpaid volunteers. The major determining principle of all these changes is that alongside football as *practice*, and alongside sport undertaken by amateurs, particularly in small-town clubs where people can play amateur sport until they are quite old, has arisen football as *spectacle*. This latter is produced in order to be commercialised in the form of *televised spectacle*, a *commercial product* which is especially profitable because football is very widely practised and therefore engenders very extensive interest, and because it requires relatively little interpretative capital: people believe that because they have kicked a ball around they know all they need to understand and discuss a football match, which is not the case for every sport. Some sports make many more demands in terms of interpretation: the uninitiated understand nothing and, most importantly, realise they understand nothing. Clubs are increasingly becoming capitalist businesses, some quoted on the Stock Exchange and producing licit and illicit profits. All this is well known, but what are less well known are all the consequences that derive from it.

Amongst other factors involved in this commercialisation must be mentioned the extension to sport of the rules of neo-liberal economics, as symbolised by the notorious *Bosman* ruling, which will never be discussed in an academic conference although a paper on its social implications ought to be essential. Indeed this measure is very similar to others affecting other practices, such as for example the OECD Multilateral Agreement on Investment, against which French creative artists and performers have protested. The explicit objective of this ruling, according to its supporters, is to extend the workings of the free market and to put an end to what might, by analogy, be called *French (sporting) exceptionalism* by preventing town halls from continuing to subsidise football clubs. This free market logic is encouraged to differing extents by the sports policies of different countries.

But to return to the other important factor, television, I have shown in an article on the Olympic Games that through the intervention of television this ritual celebration of universal values has become a medium for nationalism.[2] Starting from an apparently universal spectacle (although there is a lot of nationalism on show in stadiums themselves: the opening parade by national teams, national flags, national anthems, etc.), each different national television channel makes a selection of what it shows according to its own commercial logic, thereby creating its own national and potentially nationalistic spectacle of the Olympic Games, which no one sees in their totality. This contributes to turning sport into an issue of importance for nation-states, with a host of much studied consequences, such as the appearance of authoritarian training methods and, especially, of performance-enhancing drug taking. I am thinking here, for example, of the book by the American author John Hoberman, *Mortal Engines*, which demonstrates that drug taking does not happen merely incidentally, but is a structural feature of sport as it is today.[3]

Sport visible as spectacle hides the reality of a system of actors competing over commercial stakes. There is an obvious analogy with the artistic field, where the artist is merely the visible agent without whom there would obviously be no work of art, and where the work of art only exists as such by virtue of the activities of critics and of other artists in competition and so on, in other words all that I term the artistic field. Sport as spectacle, in the form that we know it as televised sporting spectacle, presupposes a system of competition in which, alongside sporting actors transformed into objects of spectacle, there are other actors. These are sports industry managers who control television and sponsoring rights, the managers of television channels competing for national broadcasting rights (or rights covering linguistic areas), the bosses of major industrial companies such as Adidas or Coca-Cola competing with each other for exclusive rights to link their products with the sports event, and finally television producers.

This conversion of sport into commercial spectacle and into an advertising medium is also visible within football. The soccer World Cup is also a world cup for the media and for consortia locked in headlong competition. Among the social effects of this 'mediatisation' of football are to be found: the increase in the number of matches (with the growth of European and international competitions); the increase in the number of matches televised; the trend for pay-TV channels to obtain exclusive rights for matches; the fact that the time and date of matches are more and more determined by the needs of television; changes to the structure of competitions; corruption scandals; the birth of globe-trotting cosmopolitan players, often coming from economically dependent countries and changing clubs every two or three years – the effect of which is to transform the relationship between supporters and players.

As an aside, I should mention that, since the media field is not completely heteronomous, the logic of seeking competitive advantage through differentiation (shared by all fields) has brought about (as shown by Françoise Papa) stylistic innovation in television production and commentary – a form of art for art's sake (initiated in particular by Canal Plus)[4] – this is to say things done by TV producers to compete with their rivals, and which may pass unnoticed by the general public.

Sport and the State

This process of 'commercialisation' is resisted to differing degrees in different countries, according to the strength of their statist traditions, as shown by the comparative analysis of England and France (in a conference paper by Dauncey and Hare).[5] In England, this process started very early: clubs very quickly became limited companies quoted on the Stock Exchange and, once engaged with the logic of capitalist profit-making, they broke their solidarity with second, third and fourth division clubs and set up an independent league. They have kept their secondary income, built new stadiums away from working-class districts, developed full commercial sponsorship, and bought foreign players, especially from African countries, which has meant that the cosmopolitanism of the players has conflicted with the local values of the club's fans. The major consequence of all this is a break in the chain of player development in which a player used to be able to begin in a village club and finish in the national team. There was a kind of career path offering the possibility of upward mobility for children of those social classes who had little opportunity of succeeding in the only career path valued today, which is education. Between grass-roots sport and sport as spectacle, between small amateur sports clubs and big professional teams there were links that were very important from the perspective of the very function of sport and of the relations between sport as practice and sport as spectacle. These links were very important also from the perspective of democratic values.

In the eyes of economic neo-liberals, French football professionalism has developed 'late' and in an 'incomplete' way, leaving an important role to unpaid volunteers (for neo-liberalism everything that is not neo-liberal is 'archaic', 'out-dated' and 'old-fashioned' – something like an amalgam of the French National Front and Communist Party). Although in the 1980s the logic of business was getting in thanks to television (bidding up of broadcasting rights etc.), France remained wedded – in the field of sport as elsewhere – to the ideology of the 'public service', and the 'commercialisation' process met with resistance from the amateur structures of sport (despite the economic difficulties they were experiencing because of dwindling crowds and reduced public subsidies and so on). France has a considerable educational infrastructure and links between the school system and sport, since sport has always had an eminently educational function (for example, elite sportsmen and women visit schools to warn against drug taking). The link between clubs and a large-scale volunteer-based sports development infrastructure has not (yet) been broken, explaining why French clubs have become a breeding ground serving other clubs throughout Europe. Unpaid voluntary work and amateurism are continuing both in the running of clubs and in the ranks of players, and football is still fulfilling its function of civic integration, especially for children of immigrants. Unfortunately, the neo-liberal rot has already infected the fruit of 'public service' and many of football's current problems (although this does not just affect football – think of the HIV-infected blood transfusion affair or the Crédit Lyonnais deficit) derive from the fact that many people are playing at running a private enterprise for purposes of speculation, high profits and salaries, while retaining the protection offered by being in the public service.

Scientific Utopia

The more their analysis is scientifically well-founded, the more sociologists have the right (the duty?) to be normative, in contrast to what is encouraged by *Wertfreiheit escapism*. In other words, one may be normative, but only after paying one's scientific dues. The programme of research which is sketched here should allow scientific answers to normative questions such as asking whether French exceptionalism – that is to say the very special relationship between sport and the State which makes sport a public service, public health service or civic education service – is merely an out-of-date · idiosyncrasy doomed to be swept away by the forces of money.

If I feel myself entitled to ask this question without being accused of complacent nostalgia for a national model, it is because a few years ago I wrote a paper entitled 'Two Imperialisms of the Universal', in which I demonstrated that two countries have sought – and are still seeking – to impose their own particular conception of universality on the world, namely France and the United States, and that it is therefore quite natural for these two would-be universal cultural models to be in conflict with each other in almost every domain, and especially in the cultural domain.[6] It is only by rejecting the imperialism of the universal implied in any ambition to universalise a given model that this French vision can be defended – a vision that I can all the more confidently defend as it is nowadays under serious threat and thereby holds little threat itself.

This model, which follows in the tradition of the Enlightenment, attempts to defend a number of choices making up a systematic whole: the choice of 'solidarity' or 'solidarism' over 'individuality' or 'individualism'; the choice of 'social security' against 'individual private insurance'; the choice of the 'collective' over the 'individual'. However, those neo-liberals who attack the French model do so in the name of a very specific view of the State, which they describe as totalitarian, collectivist, destructive of individuality and liberty, the incarnation *par excellence* of this model of the State in their view being the Soviet Union. In opposition to this Marxist vision that paradoxically they take as their own, one should here set out a defence of the Hegelian or Durkheimian vision according to which the State, far from being reducible solely to a class-based State, is also society's self-awareness; it is society which 'thinks itself' and goes beyond its conflicts to find in the universal a compromise between opposing interests, in other words in public service, the general interest, education, disinterested amateurism and large-scale independent non-profit-making educational organisations. One peculiarity of the Hegelian State – of which the State of the French Third Republic was nearly an exact incarnation – is that it feels a responsibility for *bodies* through provision of social security and health policy (especially in terms of protection against drug addiction), through consumer protection and sports policy. From this perspective, it is understandable why drugs represent a key issue and pose specific problems in France: French people find it particularly intolerable that it is through sporting activity – which is supposed to fight against addiction – that a new form of drug abuse has emerged in the form of performance-enhancement.

The economic and symbolic forces which today threaten sport as a disinterested practice – notably the forces of great global ceremonies like the World Cup – can be combated either by caricature (which can ridicule or discredit) or utopia (which can propose alternatives to what exists). But not just any utopia. A scientifically-based and realistic utopia, proposing a coherent and universalist model and with a reasonable chance of being implemented, should advocate for example: emphasis on the educational value of sport; the strengthening of the State's moral and legal support for the ideas and interests of the national sports federations' un-paid officials; stronger measures against corruption; encouragement of coaching centres for young players; more emphasis on the development of young players as opposed to reliance on the transfer market; restoring continuity between grass-roots clubs and elite sportsmen and women; promotion of young people's realistic identification with famous players facilitated by a real model of advancement, and for children of immigrants the promotion of social integration through sport. A body of law specifically applying to sport should be developed, along with a Sports Charter, governing not only sportsmen and women (like the Olympic oath), but also commentators, heads of television channels, etc. The aim of all this would be to restore, in the world of sport, those values which the world of sport proclaims and which are very like the values of art and science (non-commercial, ends in themselves, disinterested, valuing fair play and the 'way the game is played' as opposed to sacrificing everything for results). In this utopia journalists would hold an eminent position, notably sports journalists, who, being dominated within the field of journalism, and consequently sometimes more lucid and more critical than others, could play the role of critical conscience for the sporting world.

NOTES

This is a shortened English version – translated by Hugh Dauncey and Geoff Hare – of the keynote presentation made at the CNRS Conference 'Football et cultures' held in Paris, 13–16 May 1998. A full French version of this paper is to be included in a special forthcoming number of the journal Sociétés et Représentations, which is devoted to the proceedings of the Conference.

1. The French term 'banlieue', which literally means 'suburb', is here translated as 'inner-city' in order to communicate the French connotations of social deprivation and underprivilege, and social and racial tension.
2. P. Bourdieu, 'Les jeux olympiques', Actes de la recherche en sciences sociales, 103, June 1994, 102–3.
3. J. Hoberman, Mortal Engines: The Science of Performance and the Dehumanization of Sport (New York, Maxwell-Macmillan, 1992).
4. F. Papa, 'Logique médiatique et stratégie des chaînes', Sociétés et Représentations (forthcoming).
5. H. Dauncey and G. Hare, 'Télévision et commercialisation du football', Sociétés et Représentations (forthcoming).
6. P. Bourdieu, 'Deux impérialismes de l'universel', in C. Fauré and T. Bishop (eds.), L'Amérique des Français (Paris, Seuil, 1992), 149–55.

French Football from its Origins to Euro 84

IAN PICKUP

The 1998 World Cup in France was not the first to be staged in that country, but since the 1938 Finals the professionalisation and the commercialisation of the game have been such that both on and off the field the global spectacle that was France 98 could scarcely be further removed from its pre-war antecedent. The French sporting identity has emerged gradually over the years, not only in football, but also in rugby and cycling, for example. The heady days of France's home victory in the 1984 European Championships marked the end of a long period of glorious failure during which such national icons as Raymond Kopa and Just Fontaine and their team, Reims (in the 1950s), and also Saint-Etienne (in the 1970s), played in the Gallic fashion (with individual flair and a high level of technical excellence) but did not – like the national team – win a single European competition. Kopa's three European Cup medals were won with the giants of Spanish football, Real Madrid.

Euro 84 was an important step in laying the ghost of perceived inferiority complexes which had seemed to manifest themselves whenever the French national team had to face more successful European rivals. The perennial under-achievers of European and world football had finally assembled a team which could live with Europe's best and provide a spectacle which enhanced the 'French' sporting identity in the eyes of the millions of television viewers at home and abroad, albeit with a charismatic captain bearing an Italian surname (Michel Platini).

It is beyond dispute that the modern game of football (or soccer), and also its close relative, rugby, were born in the public schools of England in the nineteenth century[1] and that a number of Englishmen played a significant role in the early development of the game in France. But football soon spread rapidly in the *Hexagone* amongst the indigenous population and France has been part of all of the major developments of the modern game from the outset.

It is the purpose of this essay to set the staging of France 98 in a historical context which will highlight social and cultural aspects of the development of the 'beautiful game' in France. Our survey begins in the late nineteenth century.

The Early Years: 1872–1900

As shown in the Introduction to this volume, Elias and Dunning[2] distinguish between the social functions of the primitive or embryonic forms of football practised in France from the Middle Ages (games like *la choule, la soule* and *la barette*), 'tough ball games played between villages',[3] and modern codified versions of sports, as developed in Victorian England in the public schools before they were taken up be the working classes of the Midlands and the North. After the formation of the first English clubs in the 1850s and 60s and the creation of England's Football Association in 1863, France soon followed suit with the birth of the first French club, Le Havre Athletic Club, in 1872. It is, then, in the aftermath of France's defeat in the Franco-Prussian War and at a time when sporting activity was primarily based on military models,[4] that a group of Englishmen – businessmen working in shipping and running transit companies – got together to form a club in which they could engage in those very English sports of football and rugby. As late as 1884, a meeting of the club's members rejected the exclusive adoption of either football or rugby, preferring rather a mixture known as 'combination'. The club colours provoked an interesting response from onlookers: 'Nothing could be more suitable for the oldest club at the gateway to the Ocean than the colours sky blue and navy blue; the comical design of their shirts in these colours earned them the nickname "circus clowns".'[5]

Perhaps largely because of the dominant English influence, within individual clubs football still had to vie with rugby, which was the dominant sport of the Paris Football Club, founded in 1879. Rugby also had a head start in the school curriculum of 1888 but in the previous year, a group of young Englishmen had founded the first Parisian club devoted to football, the short-lived Paris Association Football Club; with the demise of this club, some allegiances were transferred to the newly formed Standard Athletic Club, probably in 1889. Multi-sport clubs mushroomed in France in the 1880s: for example, the «Girondins» de Bordeaux came into being in 1881, followed by the Racing Club de France (1882) and, a year later, by the Stade français (which did not adopt football until some time later). The latter two clubs in particular were at this time dominated by athletics. Football itself was – and was to remain for some considerable time – a pursuit of the middle class.

The first significant clubs devoted exclusively to football came into being in October 1891 in the Paris region: White Rovers and Gordon FC, which owed their existence to expatriate Englishmen and, in the case of the latter, expatriate Scotsmen. These clubs were followed in 1892 by the first genuinely French football club, the Paris-based Club français, whose first captain, Eugène Fraysse, did much to popularise the game amongst Parisians.

It was in 1893 and 1894 that the Paris clubs which played association football were admitted to the Union des Sociétés françaises de Sports athlétiques (USFSA), whose General Secretary was Baron Pierre de Coubertin, the founding father of the modern Olympic movement. The official bulletin of USFSA now devoted more space to reporting football matches and the following account of a match played between Standard Athletic Club (SAC) and C.A. de Neuilly-sur-Seine (CANS) at the end of January 1894, gives a good idea not only of early perceptions of the game but also of the English, pseudo-English and literally translated vocabulary which was employed in reports:

> Sur le terrain de Bécon un fort vent a gêné les matcheurs. Quelques bonnes passes des avants du Standard menacent un moment le camp du CANS. A la reprise du jeu, la plupart des équipiers de ce club, découragés de jouer continuellement contre le vent qui maintenant souffle de côté, faiblissent et, malgré une belle défense des deux backs, MM. Hutin et Caizac (capitaine) et du goal, M. Faucher, le SAC marque deux buts. A signaler quelques bonnes charges de MM. Andraud, Meslin et Beauchamp. Du côté du SAC le jeu intelligent de MM. Howatson et Tunmer est très remarqué, ainsi que les coups de pied de MM. Attrill (back) et Wynn (goal). Le match s'est terminé par 3 points au SAC contre rien au CANS.[6]

USFSA created the first (misleadingly titled) *Championnat de France* in 1894. This 'championship' took the form of a cup competition and had only six entrants: the Club français, Standard A.C., White Rovers, the International Club, C.P. d'Asnières and C.A. Neuilly. The competition took place over a period of three weeks in April and, after a replay on 5 May, was won by Standard AC (with only one Frenchman in its line-up).

The game now began to spread. We have already mentioned Bordeaux (a city most significantly with centuries-old English connections);[7] Northern France and Normandy also proved fertile ground for the eleven-a-side game, particularly in schools, in Arras, Condé and Valenciennes, for example. By the last years of the decade, according to the annually produced *Dicosport*, in addition to the clubs of the Paris region, we may list 'le Cercle Pédestre d'Asnières, le C.A. Neuilly, l'U.S. Lycée du Havre, le Stade Bordelais, la S.A. Bordeaux, l'Olympique de Marseille, le F.C. Rouen, le Red Star, le R.C. Roubaix, l'U.S. Tourcoing, etc.'[8] In 1896, the Club français won the first French championship to be contested on the basis of a league table determined by points earned for draws and wins; the nine participating clubs played one another only once and on neutral grounds. Paris's domination was broken in May 1900 when Le Havre A.C. – the northern champions – defeated the Club français 1–0 at the ground of Stade français. The Hacmen had enjoyed a hollow victory a year earlier when they were declared national champions because the winners of the Gordon Bennett trophy in Paris, the same Club français, refused to play them in what was styled the national final for the very first time.

By the end of the nineteenth century, association football was, therefore, well established in Northern France and in Paris. The country was henceforth to play a significant role in the development of what, in a few short decades, was to become the most popular global game.

The Formative Years: 1900–38

The game now went through a period of rapid expansion. The number of players rose from some 2,000 at the turn of the century to some 10,000 by 1903–4. At the same time there were 72 clubs in the Paris region alone; they were divided into several groups by USFSA. Reflecting the development of the game in the north of the country, Roubaix won the national championship for the third consecutive time in 1904, whilst in the same year the first official French international match was played (on 1 May), an away fixture in Brussels which ended in a 3–3 draw. The East and the South of France were also witnessing the foundation of clubs: the Stade lorrain, A.S Epinal, S.C. Nimes, Olympique de Cette, A.S Cannes, and so on. The game was soon being organised on an ever-broader foundation which saw the creation of various sporting bodies which in the early years of the new century tended to link the wide range of sports practised in Parisian and provincial clubs. The development of the game, though, was not without its problems: the administration of this rapidly growing sport became increasingly political as rivalry developed between the emerging groupings. The Comité français interfédéral (founded in March 1907 by Charles Simon), which was linked to other athletic, gymnastic and cycling organisations, is the forerunner of the current FFF (the Fédération française de football or Trois F as it is popularly known). In 1910, the CFI became a full member of FIFA (the Fédération internationale de football association), itself formed in 1904 under the influence of a Frenchman, Robert Guérin, the Treasurer of USFSA. The Ligue de Football Association (composed initially of only four Parisian football clubs which had abandoned the allegedly indifferent USFSA, accused of favouring rugby) was created in 1910 and joined the CFI. Other bodies which embraced football at the time were the Fédération gymnastique et sportive des patronages de France and the Fédération cycliste et athlétique de France. The formation of the former reflects a Catholic reaction to the secular educational reforms of Republican governments in the 1880s[9] and serves as a reminder of the lay–Catholic divide in educational matters which did not help to unite the rival organisations running football at the time.[10] Some clubs moved from one body to another but the CFI's competition, the *Trophée de France*, brought the winners of the championships of the various affiliated groupings together to determine on an annual basis which was the best team at national level.

As the administration of USFSA changed and at a time when Jules Rimet was elected President of the LFA, greater co-operation between the rival USFSA and the CFI was initiated as early as 1912, the aim being the reunification of the various bodies administering football. In December 1912 the CFI decided to concentrate solely on football administration and in January 1913, USFSA was admitted to its ranks – a triumph for the president, Charles Simon, whose fellow administrators now included another of France's football visionaries, the above-mentioned Jules Rimet.

A period of calm now descended on French football as internecine strife seemed, for the time being at least, to have come to an end at a time when global warfare was soon to break out. Among mixed fortunes for the (progressively unified) national team, a landmark was reached on 27 April 1913, when the final of the USFSA championship was played in Rouen: 6,923 spectators paid 8,732 francs to see Stade helvétique de Marseille beat F.C. Rouen by one goal to nil. This was but one of a number of competitions which continued to co-exist in the immediate pre-war period which also saw the national team lose its final match in Hungary (in December 1914) by five goals to one. The Great War inevitably changed the emerging face of French football.

With the vast majority of its sportsmen put on active service, the French football stronghold – the North of the country – was invaded by the Germans, causing the suspension of all competitions. Once the situation stabilised, with the establishment of the front on the Marne, some footballing activity was re-established as clubs drew on their junior (non-mobilised) members to turn out for their first teams. Such was the enthusiasm amongst the young for the game that USFSA created a 'Coupe nationale' in Paris, whilst the LFA promoted its own competition – not dissimilar to its pre-war championship and at this point known as the *Challenge de la Renommée*. Another significant competitive development of the wartime period was the inauguration of USFSA's knock-out cup competition, open to clubs of all the various federations and known as the *Coupe des Alliés*. Of greater ongoing national significance, though, are two very distinct developments: firstly, the death on active service of Charles Simon, founder-president of the CFI (15 June 1915), prompted the creation some 17 months later of the *Coupe Charles Simon* (now known as the

Coupe de France, the French equivalent of England's FA Cup on which it was modelled). This far-sighted development attracted as many as 59 competing clubs even before the armistice and the first real signs of unity in French football had now appeared. Secondly, activity in the trenches, all along the front, was punctuated by games of football between the allied forces, thereby giving the opportunity to countless Frenchmen from rural areas to receive instruction in a game which had been largely unknown to them before the war. Once again, British influence on French football was felt as the First World War gave an impromptu impetus to its greater dissemination.

Club football survived and prospered during the Great War in the form of the *Coupe des Alliés,* the *Coupe nationale* (both under the aegis of USFSA), the *Challenge de la Renommée,* the *Coupe interfédérale* (both run by the LFA), the *Challenge de la Victoire* (the preserve of the Fédération cycliste et athlétique de France), a second *Coupe nationale* and the *Challenge Esto-Vir* (competitions run by the Catholic Fédération gymnastique et sportive des patronages de France) and finally the only competition which still survives today, the *Coupe Charles Simon* (the creation of the CFI). International football was given a new lease of life when the CFI organised an unofficial meeting between France and Belgium in March 1916; this was followed by an official encounter just after the war in Brussels where some 20,000 spectators witnessed a 2–2 draw on 9 March 1919. Such wartime and post-war resilience boded well for the future of the game and in the immediate post-war period another, even more significant, milestone in the evolution of the sport was quickly reached: the unification of football under the aegis of one governing body – something which the players had long hoped for – which came about on 7 April 1919. The newly styled Fédération française de football association elected Jules Rimet as its first President and Henri Delaunay as its General Secretary. French football had finally achieved its own separate identity – something which is apparent in France today across a whole range of sports, each of which has its own federation.

French football was now established on a firm administrative footing: the Federation took up modest office space in the rue Faubourg-Montmartre in Paris in September 1919 and published the first edition of its own paper, *Le Football Association,* on Saturday, 4 October of the same year, proudly announcing the advent of a new era. Interestingly enough, the same inaugural edition of *Le Football Association* also stated, on its front page, that football 'is both the sport of the people and the king of sports'. Such an assertion may have been a little premature for, at a time when the sport was still an amateur one, and before the emergence of town clubs built around local industry and largely reliant upon the local working-class population for supporters and players alike, the players at the top level were scarcely drawn from the lower echelons of French society:

> In France, less industrialised than either the Netherlands or Germany, the working-class composition of the teams was less marked in the early 1920s, and in the Red Star team that played in the 1923 Cup Final there was only one worker, a mechanic. In the 1920s businessmen became increasingly involved in the game, and took a controlling interest in many clubs. France adopted professionalism in 1932, a reflection of the working-class involvement.[11]

If the industrial revolution in France came about much later than the industrial revolution in Great Britain, then the French working-class identification with and participation in the local town team also perhaps lagged behind the British model. What has come to be known as the 'traditional' club[12] (a club centred in a relatively small industrial town, often run by a local businessman and recruiting local talent as apprentices who later as first-teamers arouse local pride and elicit a local identity), is perhaps – as is suggested in the above quotation – a phenomenon dating from the 1930s in France. It is, of course, notoriously difficult to quantify historically the social origins and affiliations of the footballing public because 'Reliable data are lacking on the social evolution of the football crowd in France.'[13] What is perhaps clear, though, is that the professionalisation of football in France in 1932 encouraged in particular the unqualified members of the working class to seek gainful employment in a rapidly developing sport which had some 32,780 registered players in 1921 and 1,752,638 in the season 1988–89.

France's growing involvement in the sport at international level was signalled at the Antwerp Olympics in 1920 (where the football competition was won by Belgium, France having been eliminated in the semi-finals): Jules Rimet was unanimously designated as the official candidate for the presidency of FIFA (from which the English FA had resigned – temporarily in the event – in a row about the membership and status of its former enemies).

Another landmark of the 1920s was the building for the 1924 Paris Olympics of the Stade de Colombes, a stadium which could hold 45,000 spectators, 15,000 of whom were seated and under cover. For some 40 years this stadium – the forerunner of the Parc des Princes and the Stade de France – was to be the Mecca of French sport, hosting among other major events the annual Cup Final. The size of the stadium indicates the popularity, and therefore the marketability, of French sport in general and football in France was now forced to grapple with a major problem which its English counterpart had already solved: the vexed question of amateurism or 'shamateurism'. Rumours had long been circulating that top-rank players such as the legendary goalkeeper, Chayriguès, had benefited financially from the high public profile which their footballing prowess bestowed on them. At the same time, there was increasing pressure, strengthened by the perennial failure of the national team, to modify the structure of French football which, alongside its national knock-out cup, was based on regional championships. As a result of this pressure a so-called *championnat de France* was created in January 1926: open to the winners of the 15 metropolitan leagues affiliated to the FFFA who were subjected to a complex seeding system based on the performance of their league's members in the cup competition, this 'French championship' was contested in three separate groups labelled 'excellence', 'honneur' and 'promotion'. Such a complex and unsatisfactory structure could not last (1929 was its final year), and neither could the 'amateur' status of the best players.

In 1927 the French President of FIFA, Jules Rimet, and his colleagues sanctioned the payment to players of the salary they lost whilst away from work on international duty – a decision ratified after some hesitation by the International Olympic Committee and the cause of the English Football Association's 18-year resignation from FIFA, on the grounds that there was no halfway house between professionalism and amateurism. The same Jules Rimet was the driving force behind the creation of the first World Cup which was played in Uruguay in 1930; he presented the trophy to the triumphant Uruguayan captain, José Nazzazi (his side defeated Argentina 4–2 in the final), whilst his own national team – true to form – could only finish third in its qualifying group. Such international failure did not lessen the pressure to professionalise the game back in France. In addition to yet another 'glorious' French failure (it was claimed that a referee had ended a key match prematurely when the *tricolores* were pressing for the equalising goal!), the inaugural World Cup had demonstrated once more the financial viability of football: receipts were of the order of 225,000 dollars. The writer Jean Giraudoux had already commented the previous year that 'In many football teams, star players receive a financial bonus for every match-winning kick.'[14] The fact that some celebrated literary figures should take an interest shows perhaps the influence of sport in the inter-war period. Montherlant's novel, *Les Olympiques*, was part of a literary movement which celebrated physical effort, male fraternity and so on. Football was now a truly global game and the exploits of the French national team in Montevideo had been widely reported in the *Miroir des sports*, France's first sports newspaper which had been created in 1920 and was run by a former international, Gabriel Hanot.

The FFFA set up an inquiry into amateurism and professionalism in the form of a 'Commission d'étude' in 1929 and the vested interest of the regional leagues was soon to make itself felt as it was feared that a professional league would deprive the regions of their best teams and, therefore, of their major source of revenue. However, some of these very clubs got together – under the impetus of a rapidly emerging club, FC Sochaux, – to create the forerunner of the professional championship in the form of *la Coupe Sochaux*, which was contested in the seasons 1930–31 and 1931–32. In the face of such developments the footballing authorities had to act quickly and the Federal Commission, with Rimet and Delaunay often in attendance, decided to create a new category of paid player – the so-called 'statut du joueur rétribué' – in November 1930. It is not without significance that the above-mentioned former international Gabriel Hanot had long since advocated the creation of a professional game and he was to play a major role in subsequent developments. Events now followed rapidly, one after another: in January 1931 the FFFA's National Council voted, with a huge majority, for the creation of the professional player, a decision ratified by the relevant commission in June 1931. For the record, the first professional contracts fixed the players' salary at 2,000 francs per month. What should be borne in mind, however, is that 'the process [of professionalisation] did not follow the same path in France as elsewhere: French football never achieved the same status as the "People's Game" in Britain, Austria or Italy. Geographically the elite of professional clubs were found only in certain regions, and socially the first professional players often came from middle-class backgrounds and still practised other professions.'[15]

The clubs finally authorised to employ professional players were controlled by two separate bodies: the Commission de classement et de statut 'pro' run by Gabriel Hanot and the Commission du championnat de France professionnel, whose chairman was Emmanuel Gambardella. The first professional championship was launched in September 1932. As *Football*, the only French weekly newspaper then devoted solely to football, proclaimed on 8 September 1932, 'French football has reached the turning point in its history.'

The first championship, which was based on two groups, each of ten clubs, was not without its scandal: the winners of Group B, FC Antibes, were stripped of their title (having attempted to bribe their opponents before their final match) and it was left to the runners-up, Cannes, to meet the winners of Group A, l'Olympique lillois, in the final. The latter were the winners, by four goals to three after extra time.

By the start of the 1933–34 season there were 35 professional clubs in France and the newly created First Division was composed of the seven top clubs from each of the two groups competing in the 1932–33 championship; the Second Division (divided into two groups, North and South) was composed of the six clubs relegated from the two previous groups, alongside 15 newcomers. French football had adopted what is now a familiar format with its professional clubs, its national structure, the importing of foreign players and recourse to the 'transfer' system.

Another development worthy of note in the pre-war period is the founding of the (eventually) professional club in small industrial towns under the controlling influence of a local business magnate. A prime example of this was the creation in 1929 of FC Sochaux by the commercial director of Peugeot cars, Sam Wyler, with the backing of Jean-Pierre Peugeot himself. Initially in the Second Division of the Burgundy-Franche-Comté League, the club joined forces with AS Montbéliard a year later (becoming Football-Club Sochaux-Montbéliard) and was the driving force behind the above-mentioned *Coupe Sochaux*. The club won the national professional championship in 1934–35 and 1937–38. A similar Parisian success story was the brainchild of an influential and highly imaginative estate agent, Jean Bernard-Lévy: a member of the Committee of the fiercely amateur and socially exclusive (that is to say upper-middle class) Racing Club de France, Bernard-Lévy formed a new club – perhaps deliberately named the Racing Club de Paris – in February 1932. This new club, whose jerseys, like its near neighbours, were sky blue and white, won the French championship in 1935–36. Another distinguished name on the list of pre-war championship winners is that of Olympique de Marseille (OM), a club which under Bernard Tapie in the mid-1980s and early 1990s was to become the very embodiment of a new type of club which, as a strictly commercially-run operation, is capable of buying and selling players for astronomical prices and has revenue not only from gate receipts but also from television, commercial sponsorship and merchandising.[16] It is perhaps ironic that the scandal which attached itself to the notorious exploits of FC Antibes in the inaugural French professional championship was to descend on OM some 60 years later after it had been the first French 'winner' of the prestigious European Cup. The bribing of players and match officials has long been a problem of the professional game, not only in France but throughout the world, and the unsavoury side of pre-war French football clearly has its echoes in France's domestic and European exploits in the contemporary game.

One final major event of the pre-war period still remains to be examined: the staging of the World Cup in France in 1938. It was perhaps entirely fitting that a nation which, despite its own singular lack of success on the international stage, had been involved in all of the major international developments of football and which had provided an outstanding administrator in the person of Jules Rimet – whose very name will always be associated with football's ultimate international prize – should have the honour of staging what, in the event, was the last World Cup before the outbreak of the Second World War. FIFA had awarded France the privilege of staging the competition in 1936, as a sideshow to the Berlin Olympics which had been used to good propaganda effect by the Third Reich.

In a scenario familiar to the organising committee of France 98, much improvement had to be made to the chosen stadiums: Colombes had its capacity increased from 45,000 to 60,000 (the then Parc des Princes, the second Parisian venue, had a capacity of 35,000) and the grounds at Bordeaux, Marseilles, Lille, Strasbourg, Reims, Le Havre and Antibes underwent enlargement and refurbishment. Posters and commemorative postage stamps announced this major sporting event on the world stage. The 36 original entrants were reduced to 27 in the wake of a number of withdrawals; after the qualifying matches (organised geographically), the number of competitors was reduced to 16. Notable absentees were the British (still outside the fold of FIFA, as explained above), Uruguay (unable to sustain its earlier success), Argentina (which withdrew from the competition), Spain (in the throes of Civil War) and Austria (whose outstanding national team had been incorporated into the football of the Reich). Such political considerations are just one factor which make the 1938 World Cup somewhat different from France 98: politics may have played a significant part in the qualifying competition of the latest edition of the *Mondial* (including the very identity of participants in the wake of the break-up of the former USSR and of the former Yugoslavia), but it is generally accepted that the nations represented in France in 1998 include the very best national teams on the current footballing scene. The state-of-the-art Stade de France and the other all-seater stadiums, the global satellite television coverage, the merchandising, the sponsorship and advertising, the computerised ticketing and ticket allocation system synonymous with France 98 could scarcely be further removed from the 1938 World Cup.

It had been well known among FIFA delegates that France did not possess the stadiums which had graced the first two World Cup competitions, but the refurbishment of Colombes and the promised upgrading of the other stadiums were decisive factors in the awarding of the 1938 finals to France. The competition was organised under the direction of René Chevallier, the Chairman of the Organising Committee, whilst some ten sub-committees of the FFFA assumed responsibility for travel and accommodation for the visiting teams, receptions, press and publicity, finance, match organisation and so on.

In the run-up to the 1938 Finals, France was defeated in a friendly match 4–2 by England after an unusually successful run of international matches. When it came to the competition itself, France beat Belgium in its opening match 3–1, before meeting Italy in front of 58,455 spectators at Colombes (the gate receipts were 875,813 francs). On this occasion, the Italians triumphed by three goals to one and the *Azzuri* went on to beat Hungary 4–2 in the final. Total attendances were 374,937, giving an average per game of almost 21,000 spectators.

The War Years and the Vichy Régime: 1939–45

From September 1939 France's footballers were mobilised yet again at the outbreak of the Second World War and domestic competition was badly affected by the spring of 1940; Paris was occupied by the middle of June. The national competition was soon divided into three (later two) zones and the cup competition, for the next four years, reclaimed its original name, the *Coupe Henri Simon*. France itself, of course, was divided into two major zones (occupied North and 'free Vichy South) and the nation was torn between collaboration with and resistance to the German invaders. If continued competition was difficult but still possible in Occupied France (where a *zone Nord* championship was contested annually), the *zone Sud*, controlled by the collaborationist Vichy Régime, allowed greater flexibility for its own annual championship, though some encounters were ridiculously one-sided (OM beat Avignon 20–2 in 1942, for example). The *Coupe Charles Simon* remained an ultimately national affair, contested by the winners of the respective 'free' and 'occupied' zones; as many as 45,000 spectators watched the 1942 final at Colombes, but by common consent, the quality of the football could not match its pre-war antecedent.

The Vichy Régime had a very significant impact on sport in general and on football in particular. The Vichy government created a Commissariat Général à l'Education générale et aux sports, developed the gymnastic training of the country's youth and placed great emphasis on the Family, the 'Fatherland' and on Work. Vichy's Commissariat aux sports required footballers to 'to practise a trade outside football', effectively abolishing the professional game. This stemmed from the belief of Jean Borotra, the 'haut-commissaire aux Sports' (High Commissioner for Sport), that

> Sport could be used as a means of regeneration, provided that it was practised rather than merely watched, and some proficiency could be attained by everybody. Borotra saw the logical consequence of this as amateurism, so that as many as possible could compete. [He] also shunned professionalism because it was associated with financial gain, whereas sport should be 'chivalrous and disinterested'. He declared that 'shamateurism' ('l'amateurisme marron') was 'the principal cause of the moral weakness noted in recent years in some sporting circles and of the disrepute into which certain sports had fallen'.[17]

Another draconian measure imposed by the administration of Jean Borotra was the reduction of playing-time to 80 minutes. Such decrees had one particularly significant consequence: the resignation of Jules Rimet as President of the French Football Federation (his successor until the end of the war was Henri Jevain, President of the Ligue parisienne). The situation, though, was inevitably somewhat fluid. When a certain Colonel Pascot succeeded Borotra at the end of the 1941–42 season, he bowed to the pressure brought to bear by the FFFA and reinstated the time-honoured 90 minutes' playing-time whilst also re-establishing professional status (but forcing professional players to play for the club with which they were registered before the commencement of hostilities and forbidding more than seven professionals to play for a given club). Such concessions did not extend to the transfer system, which was outlawed by Vichy. The compulsory fielding of four amateur players by clubs had one major objective: to encourage the blossoming of new, younger and local players with the consequential development of truly 'regional' clubs.[18]

The aforementioned Colonel Pascot had another impact on wartime football when he played a decisive role in the *Coupe Henri Simon* in 1943: after the final between OM and Les Girondins de Bordeaux had been drawn 2–2 at the Parc des Princes, Marseille lodged a complaint about the late registration of a Bordeaux player and were awarded the trophy by the Federation. Colonel Pascot had other ideas, though, and ordered a replay which, ironically, was won by OM by the then record score of 4–0. Once again, the Vichy Régime, in the person of its High-Commissioner for Sport, had overruled the French Football Federation, though in the event the destination of the trophy did not change.

Of far greater significance, however, was the next, somewhat retrograde, initiative taken by Pascot: on 15 June 1943, he announced that henceforth all clubs would have amateur status, whilst all professionals would become civil servants (*fonctionnaires d'Etat*) and play for one of 16 federal teams, each of which would represent a region. The inevitable protestations were swept aside by Pascot and the short-lived federal set-up was administered by L. B. Dancausse who, some 12 years later, was to find himself at the helm of the revamped professional game in France. These federal teams did allow a degree of continuity for professional football and were a haven for those players who were able to avoid deportation to Germany and a spell in the Service de travail obligatoire (or STO, the compulsory labour scheme which operated whilst France was occupied). But some of the teams were scarcely 'regional' in character, the federal competition was grossly under-financed and many matches were postponed or even interrupted by the advancing allied forces. For the record, the Equipe Fédérale de Lens-Artois was at the top of the table when the competition came to a premature end in

1944. It was with the cessation of hostilities that French football was to embark on a path which would lead to the development of the game as we know it today.

The Development of the Modern Game: 1945–84

By the end of 1944 a national championship was organised for 24 clubs split into two groups, one North and one South, but the professional game adopted a more familiar format for the 1945–46 season with the establishment of a First Division of 18 clubs and a Second Division split into North and South, each with 14 clubs. The national Cup competition also continued to be staged. French football now seemed to be resurgent as the national team won ten, drew four and lost only one match in the years 1946–48. But history seemed to repeat itself in 1949 when France failed to qualify for the 1950 World Cup in Brazil.

The first French floodlit match, an evening encounter between France and Sweden at the Parc des Princes in April 1952, heralded a new era which was to facilitate the spread of mid-week club matches at national and European level, with the obvious commercial ramifications. The first real French success at club level came with the emergence of Reims in the early 1950s: the French champions won the so-called *Coupe Latine* in 1953 by beating A.C. Milan 3–0 in the final.

Club football now rapidly became a Europe-wide affair and the most powerful continental teams could see the obvious commercial advantages of European championships at club level. The European Cup, open to the winners of national league championships, was first contested in 1956 and once again French influence was paramount: the influential sports newspaper *L'Equipe* and more specifically Gabriel Hanot were the driving forces behind this initiative which was taken in Paris in 1955. The French had once again shown vision in developing the 'beautiful game' – just as they had done some 30 years earlier with the initiatives of Rimet and Delaunay. The European (Champions') Cup was soon followed by the forerunner of the UEFA Cup (1958) and by the European Cup Winners' Cup (1961). The European Nations' Cup was first contested in 1960.

With the face of football changing rapidly, success at European or World level continued to be elusive from a French point of view: the great Reims team with Kopa and Fontaine lost in the inaugural final of the European (Champions') Cup to Real Madrid in 1956 and history repeated itself in the 1959 final, except that Kopa was now playing for Real and becoming one of the most famous players in Europe. France still lagged behind its European rivals in terms of the professionalisation of the game, as Patrick Mignon has shown:

Professionalism in football was established in France in 1932, but it was not unusual up until the 1960s for talented players to remain amateurs, adding to their salary the benefits of a possible promotion within the enterprise of the local club's patron and the bonuses which he paid ... The 'soft' modernisation, French style, may take account of the lesser importance of professionalism within the working class.[19]

As Mignon shows in his study in this volume, in a period of relative economic stability, professionalism was not a live issue. The salaries offered by clubs were not high enough for qualified factory or farm workers to abandon their 'day-job'. It was immigrants who first saw football as an escape from work in the mines.

In the 1960s French football went through a particularly bad period as it was eclipsed by other leisure activities and it took the developments of the late 60s and of the 70s to put it back on an even keel: since the 1970s, as Michel Raspaud has shown, French professional football has developed greatly, and modernised its structures, in three ways:

a) by remodelling the championship into a pyramidal structure linking elite and average players, into four divisions and the regional championships, linking up amateur and professional clubs for the first time;

b) by systematic creation of training centres at professional clubs (see Eastham's chapter elsewhere in this volume), the Fédération française de football having given the lead with the Institut National de Football (first set up in Vichy in the 70s, then transferred to Clairefontaine at the end of the 80s);

c) by the establishment, after 1968, of a 'time contract', i.e. a contract of fixed length. (Previously tied to their clubs until the age of 35, players were thereafter able to sign for any club once their contract had terminated).

Raspaud goes on to argue that these developments partly explain the improved results of French professional teams. At the same time, their performances have generated interest more widely in society, in particular from financial circles, television channels, sponsors and heads of companies.[20]

Football at club and international level was soon to reach new heights in France: Saint-Etienne (*les Verts* or 'the Greens') put France back on the football map with its successful runs in the European Champions' Cup (beaten semi-finalists in 1975, beaten finalists in 1976, beaten quarter-finalists in 1977) and in the UEFA Cup (beaten quarter-finalists in 1980 and 1981). These and other club and international successes[21] heralded what, until 1998, were France's most memorable moments in football on the international scene: reaching the semi-finals of the World Cup in 1982 and 1986, and victory in the European Nations' Championship in June 1984 (a victory followed by the gold medal in the Olympic competition in Los Angeles in August of the same year).

From this fertile period in the development of French football, the events which took place in Seville on 8 July 1982 live on above all in the French collective consciousness, only to be partly eradicated by much happier memories of Euro 84. The 1982 World Cup in Spain took place just four months after France had beaten Italy (2–0 at the Parc des Princes) for the first time in some 60 years. Expectations were high when the squad left for Spain but in the very first game the *tricolores* conceded a goal after 23 seconds to their old rivals from across the Channel and eventually lost 3–1. However, three subsequent victories and a draw ensured their passage to the semi-final and a topsy-turvy, thoroughly exciting but infamous tie with West Germany in Seville. This exceptionally tense game was watched seemingly by the whole French nation on television. The match was marred by, and will always be remembered for, the cynical tackle which the German goalkeeper Schumacher made on Battiston. Despite this notorious incident, after ten minutes of extra time the French were leading 3–1, thanks to goals by their inspirational captain Platini, by Trésor and Giresse. The later introduction of the German forward Rummenigge turned the game, however, and with the score at 3–3 at the end of extra time, penalties beckoned. The outcome was a 5–4 victory for the Germans in the penalty shoot-out and arguably France's best team to date had fallen at the penultimate hurdle. Platini's men were not to be denied, though, and some two years later they reached their pinnacle on home soil.

The staging of Euro 84 in France is reminiscent of that of the World Cup of 1938 in the same country in one obvious respect: the grounds at Lens, Lyon, Marseille, Strasbourg and Saint-Etienne were enlarged and modernised; their floodlighting was also improved to conform with the highest standards. A new ground with a capacity of 52,000 spectators was built at la Beaujoire in Nantes and only the already re-built Parc des Princes remained unaltered. The competition was, by common consent, a great footballing and popular success: a television audience undreamed of in 1938 joined some 599,850 spectators for the 15 matches (giving an average of 39,990 – 80% of capacity – per game). If merchandising, ground advertising and the now familiar commercial spin-offs were marked characteristics of Euro 84 off the pitch, what happened on the field was unprecedented: Michel Hidalgo's team, captained by the incomparable Michel Platini, achieved the previously unthinkable with five victories out of five, scoring 14 goals and conceding only four in the process. On 12 June, at the Parc des Princes, the *tricolores* made a nervous start against Denmark but secured a 1–0 victory less than a quarter of an hour from the end, thanks to their captain, Platini. Their next opponents, Belgium, put up far less resistance in Nantes and were soundly beaten, by a score of 5–0, in what was one of the team's outstanding and most memorable performances. Dramatic and narrow 3–2 victories over Yugoslavia and Portugal followed (the latter game, the semi-final, was played in Marseille) and France had at last made it to a major final. It was on the evening of 27 June at the Parc des Princes that Platini's men secured the European Nations' Championship, thanks to a 2–0 victory over Spain. Both goals came in the second half and the final minutes were unbearably tense, particularly after the sending-off of Le Roux five minutes from time. It was in the very last minute that Bellone brought relief to the nation by scoring the second and decisive goal. The following day, the banner headline in the sports daily, *L'Equipe*, screamed out 'They've done it!' ('Ils l'ont fait!').

French football was at last coming of age. The country had at last shown that not only was it capable of staging a major footballing competition, but its players – Platini, Giresse, Fernandez, Lacombe, Tigana and so on – had finally shown themselves to be capable of winning a major competition whilst displaying the typically Gallic qualities of flair, improvisation and technical excellence. However, the defeat, again by West Germany, in the semi-final of the 1986 World Cup in Mexico again sowed the seeds of doubt.

Conclusion

Our survey of French football from its origins to the 1980s has demonstrated a number of fundamentally important points which may usefully be borne in mind as we move on to the contemporary game and more specifically to the staging of France 98. The game developed quickly in France in the early years after it had crossed the Channel from England and despite the internecine strife which was apparent amongst the early, rival organising bodies (strife provoked in large measure by the ideological differences between Catholic and secular organisations), France made important contributions to all the major administrative and competitive developments of the game at European and World level. At home the sport was unified under the auspices of its own national federation. Though the professionalisation and successful commercialisation of the game were slower to come into being than in some neighbouring countries, football in the *Hexagone* survived its nadir in the 1960s, modernised its structures and commercial practices and finally emerged triumphant at Euro 84. As will be seen later in this collection, French football in the 1990s has, domestically, been subject to the same influences (money, television) that have marked football in Britain, has had further success in European club competitions (Olympique de Marseille and Paris Saint-Germain) and, of course, international success. All of these developments have arrived later than for its major footballing neighbours. French football has been catching up.

NOTES

1. See, for example, J. Mercier, *Le Football*, Que-sais-je? no.1195, 3e édition (Paris, PUF, 1979), p.9.
2. N. Elias and E. Dunning, *Quest for Excitement. Sport and Leisure in the Civilising Process* (Oxford, Blackwell, 1986).
3. P. Delauney, J. de Ryswick, J. Cornu and D. Vermand, *Cent ans de Football en France* (Paris, Editions Atlas, 1994), p.10.
4. See R. Thomas, *L'Education physique*, Que sais-je? no.238, 2e édition (Paris, PUF, 1981), p.13 et seq.
5. Mercier, p.10.
6. Delauney *et al.*, p.19. The English translation of which is: 'On the pitch at Bécon a strong wind hindered those taking part in the match. A number of good passes by the Standard forwards threatened the CANS half. After the restart, most of the team members of this club, disheartened by having to play constantly against the wind which was now blowing across the pitch, began to flag and, despite the good defensive play of the two backs, Messrs Hutin and Caizac (the captain) and of the goalkeeper, Mr Faucher, SAC scored two goals. Worthy of note were a number of charges upfield by Messrs Andraud, Meslin and Beauchamp. On the SAC. side, the intelligent play of Messrs Howatson and Tunmer caught the eye, as did the kicking of Messrs Attrill (back) and Wynn (goalkeeper). The match ended with the score on three points for SAC and none for CANS.'
7. For an analysis of how anglomania and British trade connections promoted sport in Bordeaux (rugby rather than football at this time), see J.-P. Augustin, 'La percée du football en terre de rugby', *Vingtième Siècle* (April–June 1990), 97–109. Football gradually infiltrated the South West under the influence of a national championship from 1911 and especially of the work of the Catholic Church through its local youth fellowships ('patronages de quartier'), set up to regain influence over young people through organising sports activities following the secular educational reforms of the 1880s.
8. *Dicosport* (Paris, Editions Presse Audiovisuel, 1986), 217.
9. See S. Elwitt, *The Making of the Third Republic. Class and Politics in France, 1868–1884* (Baton Rouge, Louisiana State University Press, 1975), Chapter 5, 'Schools for the Republic', pp.170–229.
10. See G. Hare and H. Dauncey, 'Football in France', in G. Armstrong and R. Giulianotti, *Football in the Making: Developments in the World Game* (London, Macmillan, forthcoming 1999).
11. B. Murray, *Football: A History of the World Game* (Aldershot, Scolar Press, 1994), p.86.
12. See M. Raspaud, 'From Saint-Etienne to Marseilles: Tradition and Modernity in French Soccer and Society', in R. Giulianotti and J. Williams (eds.), *Game without Frontiers: Football Identity and Modernity*, Popular Cultural Studies: 5 (Aldershot, Arena, 1994), pp.103–18.
13. P. Mignon, 'New Supporter Cultures and Identity in France: The Case of Paris Saint-Germain', p.275 of R. Giulianotti and J. Williams (eds.), *Games without Frontiers.*
14. Quoted in Delauney *et al.*, p.119.
15. Taken from abstract of P. Lanfranchi and A. Wahl, 'La Professionnalisation du football en France (1920–1939)', *Modern and Contemporary France*, 6, 3 (August 1998), 313–25.
16. See Raspaud, p.110 *et seq.*

17. The Commissariat was responsible for sport and physical education in schools and also for 'character training' activities ('General Education'). See W.D. Halls, *The Youth of Vichy France* (Oxford, Clarendon Press, 1981), pp.138–9, and p.192.
18. See Delauney *et al.*, pp.168–70. The encouraging of truly regional or local teams is very much in keeping with 'football classicism' which has already been discussed.
19. Mignon, p.277.
20. Raspaud, p.107.
21. Other notable French successes at club level in the run-up to the 1984 European Nations' Championship were achieved by Bastia (beaten finalists in the UEFA Cup in 1978), Strasbourg (beaten quarter-finalists in the Champions' Cup in 1980), Nantes (beaten semi-finalists in the Cup Winners' Cup in 1980), Sochaux (beaten semi-finalists in the UEFA Cup in 1981) and Paris Saint-Germain (beaten quarter-finalists in the Cup Winners' Cup in 1983).

The French National Team and National Identity: 'Cette France d'un "bleu métis"'

JOHN MARKS

Between the National and the Transnational

In a recent article, Pierre Brochand argues convincingly that football now has a global status which is both national and 'transnational'.[1] Football has global significance, constantly reinforced by the media, but at the same time sport in general exerts power within relatively limited parameters, and football is no exception. In many ways it constitutes a relatively small service industry which wields little direct political power. However, as a consequence of being a genuinely global sport, transmitted around the world by satellite television, football occupies a privileged position. This privileged position means that football represents an authentically 'popular' access to the complexity of a world which is currently poised between the traditional order of the 'international' and the new order of globalisation. As far as the international order is concerned, Brochand argues that football is one of the last spheres where it is still acceptable, to a certain extent, to express sentiments of national pride and identification. This form of national identification obviously takes different forms, which are not always a 'civilised' and safe alternative conflict. As for the 'transnational' sphere, Brochand claims that the so-called *Bosman* ruling has done much to sensitise the general public to the realities of the European Union. Brochand concludes that football is a sort of 'prism', which provides a useful tool with which to examine questions such as national identity. The question of the national and the transnational will be revisited towards the end of this essay, in the context of Christian Bromberger's ethnological work on football, in order to consider the reactions to France's ultimately successful World Cup 98 campaign.

It appears, then, that football, and more specifically the French national team, may reveal useful information on the question of national identity. As J-M. Faure and C. Suaud among others argue, football frequently provides a strong affective focus for questions of identity at any number of levels, whether it be village, nation, or even continent.[2] However, before considering specific ways in which the French national team may connect with, reflect, or express, themes of national identity, it is necessary to consider some existing models for dealing with the question of football and national identity.

Football and National identity

It is obvious that national football teams can become the focus of, and a vehicle for, nationalism. As Ignacio Ramonet points out, it is not therefore surprising that international fixtures are surrounded by symbols which have military associations, such as flags, national anthems and the presence of heads of state. Ramonet also points out that football is frequently associated with martial metaphors of 'defence', 'victory', 'tactic', etc., and that these metaphors become particularly potent where national teams are concerned.[3] In short, football can function as a substitute for war. Pierre Brochand goes so far as to claim that football now represents, as an international sport, a sort of legal alternative to armed conflict.[4] As Ramonet notes, the history of football is intertwined with that of national political tensions. Mussolini recognised the potential for Fascist propaganda when Italy staged the 1934 World Cup, seeing the national team as 'soldiers in the service of the national cause'.[5] It is also possible, within nation-states, such as Spain, which contain what Ramonet terms 'local nationalisms', for club teams to become unofficial 'national' teams. This is the case with Athletic Bilbao, which is a focus for Basque nationalism, and also Barcelona, which is a focus of Catalan nationalism. Similarly, in the USSR matches between teams such as Moscow Spartak and Dynamo Tbilisi functioned as quasi-internationals between 'nations' contained within the Soviet Union. Ultimately, Ramonet is dismissive of the nationalism which is fostered and even promoted by 'nation-as-team', particularly as this conception of sport as a form of conflict frequently has recourse to tired, stereotyped images of national identity.[6]

Football as War

In a recent paper, 'War Minus the Shooting?: Jingoism, the English Press and Euro 96', Jon Garland and Michael Row are equally dismayed by the xenophobia displayed by the English tabloid press during the 1996 European Championships.[7] They show how the tabloids equated football and military victories, evoking previous military conflicts between 'Britain' and Germany. They go on to argue that, whereas in Victorian Britain sport was seen as a metaphor for war, it is now the language of war which informs sport.

It is undeniable that the French team is also a focus for nationalism, whether benign or jingoistic. However, in general, it is hard to see the French national team as a focus for jingoistic nationalism. Michel Samson's article 'Cocorico ball', which deals with some of the press coverage of France's World Cup qualifying game against Yugoslavia in 1986, does identify nationalistic tendencies, such as the way in which the French press concentrates on the game almost exclusively from the perspective of the French team.[8] However, this particular brand of 'chauvinism' seems particularly mild when compared to the excesses of the English tabloid press in recent years. It seems, therefore, that it is necessary to look for other ways in which the French national team might tell us something about national identity.

This relatively non-chauvinistic attitude towards the national team is also emphasised by Olivier Villepreux, who acknowledges that the atmosphere within stadiums during France's games in 1998 has lacked the 'festival ardour' of South American supporters or the passionate 'devotion' of Anglo-Saxon supporters.[9] He argues that French football supporters find their natural habitat in bars and cafés, which become places where football can be discussed and celebrated. Here, the football fans can enjoy the 'beautiful game' whoever is playing. According to Villepreux, the typical French supporter is not chauvinistic, or at least feels a little better about celebrating victory after having intellectualised about 'le foot'. French supporters may, tentatively, be acquiring from other nations the wearing of team colours, but there is a reluctance to associate 'the colours of the Republic' with football. (It should be noted that Villepreux is writing before the extraordinary fervour which surrounded France's victory against Brazil.) In fact, although he does not think that French supporters are chauvinistic, Villepreux does suggest some fairly complex links between football supporting and French national identity. Those who follow the national team would like it to express a sense of style, of 'emotive perfection', which would provide relief from the constant demands of efficiency and profitability which constrain national life. Of course, it might be argued that Villepreux is actually speaking to, and about, the educated middle-class readership of *Libération*, who would presumably be flattered to be described as convivial football connoisseurs.

However, two points seem particularly important here. Firstly, the question of a national 'style' of play, and, secondly, the notion of this style of play providing a point of identification for French supporters. The important point is that this style, football as an 'ambassador' for an innate French sense of style, provides a relief from, and a contrast to, the contemporary 'transnational' value of economic efficiency with which France is so ill at ease. What cannot be denied is that the success of the French team, as the World Cup 98 tournament progressed, became the catalyst for an expression of national feeling which had very little direct connection to football as 'war'. In fact, several commentators argue that the

French public were, in expressing their pride in a victorious 'multiracial' team, rejecting the racist politics of Le Pen *and* the 'politically correct' dismissal of football as crudely nationalistic.[10]

National Styles of Play

The question of national styles of play has frequently been seen as a way of making connections between any national football side and national identity. As Christian Bromberger points out in a recent publication, the concept of a style of play is one important way in which identities are constructed.[11] Bromberger argues that a local or national style is obviously not necessarily linked to the actual performance of a given team. It is rather a question of a 'stereotyped image', built up over time, which becomes associated with the side. The notion of a style of play springs from narratives of national identity as much as from what actually happens on the field of play.[12] Bromberger draws attention to some fairly sophisticated examples of notions of national style. Firstly, R. Da Matta finds connections between style of Brazilian football and the Brazilian social system. According to Da Matta, the 'golden rule' of Brazilian society – and football – is to give the illusion of ease, however much dissimulation this may entail.[13] Similarly, R. Grozio argues that the Italian national team, from the 1930s to the early 1980s, provided a metaphor for the 'Italian way of life'. The balance between defensive players ('braccianti del catenaccio') and attacking players ('artisti del contropiede') symbolises two poles of the Italian national psyche: the negative tendency of an absence of organisation and preparation, combined with the positive tendency of creativity and selfless teamwork.[14]

Perhaps, then, it might be possible to identify a specifically French style of play, and to make some connections between that style of play and national identity. We have seen already that, according to Villepreux, French supporters want a style of football which is something more than 'efficient'. Certainly, the term 'football-champagne' has been associated with the French team, particularly in the Platini era. Nusslé attempts to identify this style, looking primarily at the period 1978–86. One of the main elements of this style of play, according to P. Nusslé, is a spirit of improvisation, the capacity to react to situations in ways which go beyond the stereotypical. This spontaneity is combined with a sort of Latin 'vivacity'. In this way, the passing game of the French team at times approaches a sort of 'euphoria'.[15]

However, it is hard to reconcile this notion of a national style of play with the French team which competed in the 1998 World Cup. Shortly before the tournament, following France's 1–0 defeat of Belgium in a friendly in Casablanca, *France Football* was generally optimistic, regarding the team as capable of performing at a high level. However, the team was perhaps a little 'pedestrian'. In short, 'football-champagne' was no longer the order of the day. A few days before the beginning of the 1998 finals *France Football* assessed the essential characteristics of the French team as, 'a very strong physical presence, a good defensive base, overall awareness, but also rather pedestrian and stereotyped in attack'.[16]

It would seem, then, that the question of a national style is an unpromising subject from which to draw conclusions about national identity. Of course, as Bromberger points out, the notion of a style of play is largely imaginary, drawing on tradition rather than contemporary reality. However, there appears to be a strong consensus that football is currently undergoing a process of homogenisation. As L. Ravenel notes in a recent doctoral thesis on the 'geography' of football in France, the economic changes which are currently at work in football, particularly the *Bosman* ruling, are arguably undermining the existence of regional or national styles. Ravenel quotes from a 1996 editorial in *France Football*, where G. Ernault emphasises this process of homogenisation. Interestingly, Ernault seems to be expressing a widespread French anxiety concerning the processes of globalisation and homogenisation, when he claims that football is increasingly controlled by the logic of a certain 'pensée unique' (an exclusive consensus around neo-liberalism).[17] Ravenel draws attention to the tactical uniformity of teams in Euro 96,[18] and argues that club teams, such as Juventus, who now have the economic power to attract international players, have in many ways ceased to be an 'Italian' side.[19] It is, then, necessary to look at football in a wider political and social context in France in order to make connections between the national team and national identity.

Sport and Identity: Metaphor or Index?

In a recent article, N. Blain and H. O'Donnell argue that questions of sport and national identity, particularly as they are dealt with in the media, function in a specific way in the UK press.[20] In short, it is common in the UK press, particularly in the 'tabloids', for sport to be seen as a subject which is closely and, to a certain degree, unproblematically, linked to wider issues of culture and identity. In this way, they argue, sport has 'an indexical relationship' to other forms of cultural life. So, for example, 'a German football performance is felt to be truly an aspect of a wider German identity which has to do with organisation, energy, commitment and aggression'.[21] Similarly, England's victory over Holland in Euro 96 is discussed on *Newsnight* in the context of contrasting difficulties with European Union partners concerning the ban on British beef.[22] The assumption is that sport, politics and culture are 'continuous and deeply interlocked'.[23] In countries like France, Germany and Spain, however, Blain and O'Donnell claim that sport has a function which is chiefly symbolic or metaphorical. In simple terms, they argue convincingly that sport is somehow overdetermined in the British press, reflecting perhaps the multiple problems of identity in the United Kingdom, whilst sport functions as a more self-contained world in countries such as France. The national football team is not seen as being synonymous with national pride, and is not frequently linked with other cultural and political themes.

It is difficult here to corroborate Blain and O'Donnell's thesis definitively, since this present study does not pretend to provide an exhaustive content analysis of French press sources. It should also be pointed out that football *is* linked to questions of national identity in European nations other than Britain. For example, A. Sonntag traces some of the ways in which the performance of the West German and now German national sides has been discussed coextensively with questions of national identity.[24] In fact, Helmut Kohl received a good deal of criticism when he associated Germany's Euro 96 victory with 'traditionally' combative German values.[25] However, it does seem that football in France occupies a position which would bear out Blain and O'Donnell's argument. Firstly, it is obviously important to recognise that the very existence of a serious, 'quality' sporting press in France means that football, when discussed in publications such as *France Football*, is not related to general social and political issues as frequently as it would be in the British, particularly tabloid, press. Further to this, Faure and Suaud emphasise the fact that sport is conventionally seen to be a 'restricted universe' in France. In Germany, Italy and England professional football exists in the private sector but is assumed to have a responsibility to engage with the interests of the wider community. However, in France the FFF is an amateur structure which comes under the supervision of the State.[26]

It is also extremely important to understand that in France the national football team is often seen as a separate entity from the concept of 'le football français'. The national team might achieve a certain amount of success (three times losing semi-finalists in the World Cup, and now World Cup winners), but a constant anxiety exists concerning 'le football français'. So, following France's World Cup success in 1958, Jacques Ferran reminds the readers of *France Football* that this success should not be taken as proof that 'le football français' is in a generally healthy state.[27] In a way, this anxiety remains 40 years later, with French club football frequently compared unfavourably to the perceived passion and commitment of the English club scene. In the editorial of the edition of *France Football* which immediately preceded the 1997–98 French domestic season, Jean-Jacques Vierne assesses the deficiencies which hold France back from becoming 'a great footballing nation'. He acknowledges that the national team, whilst not the best in the world, is certainly among the front runners. However, France lacks the 'religion' of a domestic championship, such as those in England, Germany and Spain, where every weekend the passion and commitment of these leagues is physically evident.[28]

French Football: 'Russian Salad' or 'Cultural Mosaic'?

As far as the French national team is concerned, one particular issue connects football to wider social and political matters. This is the general question of immigration, and the 'racial' composition of the national team. As will be seen, the 'multiracial' nature of the team in Euro 96 and World Cup 98 was much discussed in both the sporting and general press. However, the question of immigrants, or the sons of immigrants, within the French side has been an important issue throughout much of its history.

French Football and Immigration

In 1958 Jacques Ferran expressed uncertainty concerning French football and the national team. It was, he claimed, possible to say just what constituted English or Soviet football. However, for Ferran, the crucial elements of the French national team – Raymond Kopa, the son of Polish immigrants, Just Fontaine, born in Marrakesh to a Spanish mother, and Roger Piantoni, the son of Italian immigrants – did not constitute a coherent identity; French football was 'a Russian salad, a jumble', 'a hotchpotch of doctrines'.[29] In some ways, it might be argued that Ferran's concern over the heterogeneity of the French team relates solely to the world of football. The team lacks cohesion, and is really only a collection of talented individuals. However, it is also possible to detect a certain wider anxiety concerning French society, which was voiced by others in the sporting press. For example, in February 1958, a few months before the World Cup in Sweden, Gabriel Hanot urged the French to play as a team. He accuses the team of 'individualism' and 'inconstancy', faults which he claims are shared by the French people as a whole.[30] Echoing a common theme in the French sporting press, Hanot argues that French football should take note of one of the virtues of the English game. The French game should concentrate on producing 'triers' – he uses the English term – rather than 'star players' (for which, presumably, we might read Kopa). Hanot continues in a similar mode in June of the same year, when he produces a brief assessment of each of the finalists in the World Cup. French football is, he says, 'unstable', but this only reflects a general instability in French society. French football is excessively introverted, and relies too heavily on individual talents such as Raymond Kopa. Interestingly, it seems that Hanot is not actually opposed to immigration within French football. In fact, on the contrary, he appears to feel that the official policy of the football authorities to prohibit foreign players between 1955 and 1961 (and again between 1963 and 1966) is detrimental to the French game. However, although he acknowledges Kopa's talent, a certain hostility – he describes Kopa as 'overly celebrated as a Messiah' – is obvious.[31]

S. Beaud and G. Noiriel agree that the question of immigration has been an important area of debate in the French sporting press.[32] They argue that, particularly since the 1960s, immigration has largely been seen as an element which has enriched the national game in France. According to this point of view, French football is a sort of cultural 'melting pot'.[33] At the same time, they note the existence of a contrasting point of view, which corresponds closely to that of Ferran: the heterogeneity of styles in French football – in part due to the presence of immigrants, but also accentuated by a diversity of regional styles – leads to a chronic weakness in the national game. (It should be noted that the existence of heterogeneous regional styles of play was evoked by the football authorities in France as far back as the 1920s as a reason for the lack of success of French teams.)[34]

Raymond Kopa

Raymond Kopa, widely acknowledged as one of the greatest ever French players, and certainly a crucial part of the French team which performed so well in the 1958 World Cup Finals in Sweden, provides a useful focus for debates concerning the national identity. These debates bring together questions of immigration and modernisation.[35] As P. Lanfranchi and A. Wahl point out, Raymond Kopa was arguably the greatest French player of the 1950s. His style of play, characterised particularly by good dribbling ability, also made him the most popular footballer of this era.[36] He was the son of Polish immigrants, born in the mining community of Noeux-les-Mines (Pas-de-Calais) in 1931, and he established himself as a star player with Reims in the early 1950s, playing for them when they lost in the final of the European Cup to Real Madrid. He then went on to join Real Madrid, with whom he won three European cups. In the 1958 World Cup he established a great striking partnership with Just Fontaine. Kopa returned to Reims to continue his partnership with Fontaine at club level, winning the French championship in 1960 and 1962. The significance of Kopa and Fontaine might be measured by the fact that they are evoked in match reports even today.[37]

Alfred Wahl shows how Kopa as a sporting hero was at the centre of a series of issues which went beyond the purely sporting arena. Kopa's first symbolic act occurred before his stardom as a footballer, when he changed his name from Kopaszewski to Kopa. In his 1958 autobiography, in a chapter entitled 'Kopaszewski est mort, vive Kopa' ('Kopaszewski is dead, long live Kopa') he describes his feelings as he flies over Poland. He claims that he realises at this point that Poland is simply a 'foreign' country like any other to him. The fact of being recognised in France as 'Kopa' provides him with his real identity. For Kopa, it was this symbolism which cemented his sporting success and made him 'French'.[38] In many ways, this choice set the pattern for the various ways in which Kopa would be viewed throughout his career. Firstly, the two syllables, 'Ko-pa', already seemed to mark him out as a star. In some quarters, however, it was his distinctive talent which marked him out as being too individualistic, perhaps too concerned with his own stardom. At the same time those who wished to see him as a symbol of the modernisation of France claimed him as a well-integrated immigrant.

Wahl examines at some length the 'controversy' which accompanied Kopa throughout his career. Among France's sporting press he was particularly admired by the journalists at *Miroir-Sprint* and *Miroir du Football*.[39] As Wahl and Lanfranchi point out, these publications were sympathetic to the Communist Party.[40] For these journalists, football was to be admired as a spectacle, 'a kind of relaxation and an idealised expression of social harmony; a festival for the players and the crowd'.[41] Another group, however, primarily linked to *L'Equipe* and *France Football*, had more reservations about Kopa. These proponents of the 'modern' game were suspicious of Kopa's flair and individualism. Wahl sees their conception of the game as a reflection of an inflexible conception of modern liberal economics, which emphasises values of efficiency and profitability above all else.[42] If Kopa was to succeed as an 'immigrant', they would rather that he were a symbol of the 'New France', which was becoming modernised and efficient. As Wahl and Lanfranchi point out in their articles on Kopa, Gabriel Hanot, a contributor to several sporting journals and a technical adviser to the French football authorities, was one of the main representatives of the 'New France' lobby. It is as if Kopa, the son of a miner who opted for French nationality at the age of 21, had to prove himself capable of integration. Wahl argues that Kopa's journey from humble origins to national glory has a symbolic function in reinforcing the values of a modernising post-war France. Kopa became more than a sporting idol: he became for some a symbol of liberal economic values of the 'cult of hard work'. The very fact that Kopa began his life towards the bottom of the social ladder only served to emphasise these values.[43]

At the same time, Kopa's immigrant origins had been the focus of what amounted to racist abuse in some quarters following France's poor performance in the 1954 World Cup Finals in Switzerland. Kopa bore the brunt of the criticism, often characterised by the cry 'Kopa, retourne à la mine!' ('Kopa, go back to the mine!').[44]

It seems, then, that one of the main ways in which the national team intersects with wider questions of national identity is in the field of immigration within French football, or what might be termed the 'racial' composition of the side. It is also the case that footballing issues become inflected with general concerns over national identity and social cohesion, such as the demands of economic modernisation.

Euro 96 and France 98

The question of the racial composition of the French national side became a subject of wider political debate during the European Championship of 1996, played in England, when Jean-Marie Le Pen declared the French team to be 'artificial'. He claimed that players such as Lamouchi, Zidane, Djorkaeff, Lizarazu, Pedros, Angloma, Karembeu and Lama had chosen their nationality as a matter of expedience, enabling them to play international football. Le Pen went on to pledge that he would investigate closely the status of these players in the event of coming to power. *Le Monde* reported the story in its sports pages on 25 June 1996. Le Pen declared that it was 'artificial' to bring 'foreign' players into the French side. He also claimed that several players did not sing the *Marseillaise* 'or visibly did not know the words'.[45] Le Pen followed up his remarks of 23 June with an interview given to *France-Soir* on 25 June. Here, he reiterated his point that several players in the French team had taken on French nationality as a matter of convenience, singling out Desailly who was born in Ghana, and Martins who, Le Pen claimed, held dual French/Portuguese nationality before opting for French nationality. He also drew attention to players who were the sons of immigrants, such as Loko, Zidane, Lamouchi, Madar and Djorkaeff.

Players, politicians and journalists were swift to condemn Le Pen, sometimes invoking the notion of inclusive Republican values, and also notable players from the past such as Kopa. In this vein, Lionel Jospin pointed out that Le Pen would do well to remember that Guyana, the French West Indies and New Caledonia were actually part of France, and that if Le Pen's objections had been put into practice, France would have been deprived of major talents such as Kopa, Platini and Fernandez.[46] Several members of the team refused to comment, although Christian Karembeu stated that he did not sing the *Marseillaise*, but that it meant a great deal to him, and that he reflected on his family and his 'people' whilst it was sung. Bernard Lama, born in Guyana, also offered a terse rejoinder to the effect that he had not asked to have ancestors who were sold into slavery.[47] In an editorial entitled 'L'anti-France' *Le Monde* attempted to turn the tables on Le Pen by showing how he plays on two themes which actually undermine the national identity he seeks to protect. Firstly, *Le Monde* claims, Le Pen wishes to show that France is in decline, 'going from bad to worse', and

1. Young *beur* fans support the national team.

2. Zinedine 'Zizou' Zidane, *beur* and French national hero, in an Adidas advertisement.

consequently he is disturbed by success of any kind, including success on the football field. Secondly, if any success is achieved, it cannot be attributed to the 'the "real" France'. *Le Monde* is unequivocal in linking Le Pen's promised reassessment of nationality laws to the racist policies of the Vichy regime.[48]

Only weeks before Le Pen's controversial claims, *France Football* published an article by Jean-Marie Lanoë which emphasised the diverse origins of the members of the French squad for Euro 96.[49] The tone of the article contrasts strongly with Le Pen's comments, arguing that such diversity is frequently an element of great teams, and suggesting that this team reflects the 'cultural mosaic' of contemporary France. Firstly, several players were born outside of metropolitan France: Lama was born in Guyana, Angloma in Guadeloupe, Karembeu in New Caledonia and Desailly in Ghana. Several others come under the category of 'descendance directe', with parents who were born outside metropolitan France: Thuram's mother was born in Guadeloupe, Loko's father in Congo, Zidane's parents are Algerian Kabyles, the parents of Lamouchi and Madar are Tunisian, Pedros' father Spanish, Martins' father is Portuguese, Djorkaeff's mother is Armenian and his father is of 'Kalmouk' origin (a Mongolian minority from the former Soviet Union), and Di Meco's father is Italian. Two players come under the category of 'descendance indirecte': Barthez has a Spanish grandmother, and Lizarazu has three Spanish Basque grandparents. (Of these players Karembeu, Lama, Zidane, Thuram, Djorkaeff, Desailly, Lizarazu and Barthez were in the 1998 World Cup squad.) Lanoë points out that the presence of players of diverse origin is nothing new for the French team. The 'ethnic diversity' of the French side has reflected different eras of immigration: it is simply the case that the origin of the 'immigrants' has changed.[50] Whereas players such as Kopa, Cisowski, Ruminiski, Gianessi and Piantoni in the 1950s were the sons of Polish and Italian immigrants, the current team is made up of players whose origins are the French DOMs and TOMs (overseas departments and territories), or Africa. The 'Russian salad' has apparently lost its negative connotations of incoherence, and has now become 'cultural mosaic'.

As mentioned before, Lanoë emphasises the advantages offered to French football by this 'cultural mosaic', and in this way connects football, largely by implication, with the wider issue of immigration. However, during and after World Cup 98, the issue of the ethnic composition of the French side became one of the most talked-about aspects of the finals, moving from the sports pages in both France and Britain, to become a significant object of discussion.[51] The French squad was the most ethnically diverse of all the competing countries. Apart from Karembeu, Lama, Zidane, Thuram, Djorkaeff, Desailly, Lizarazu and Barthez, the squad included Henry (parents from Guadeloupe), Diomède (parents from Guadeloupe), Boghossian (Armenian extraction), Trezeguet (Argentinian father) and Patrick Vieira (born in Senegal). France's victory quickly became associated with the possibility of new, positive developments, particularly towards acceptance of a multicultural society. Zinedine Zidane in particular was much discussed as a symbol of 'successful integration'. In short, the French team became associated with intense, but perhaps somewhat unfocused, feelings of national pride which went well beyond the realm of football. Laurent Joffrin's editorial in *Libération*, entitled 'Illusion utile', on 10 July, two days before the Final, portrays the French team in lofty tones as a shining example of the Republican model of integration. In this way, they represent Renan's model of citizenship as a permanent plebiscite, rather than Barrès' ethnic model. That is to say, an inclusive notion of French citizenship as a conscious choice which is not dependent on ethnicity. Joffrin knows that, in practical terms, the World Cup will not change French society, but he is satisfied that it will help to change ideas. Joffrin is yet another commentator who evokes the notion of the French 'mosaic'. As far as he is concerned, this French team, and its victory in the World Cup, reflects a way in which France may, finally, be coming to terms with the challenges of globalisation, of Europe, and is acknowledging the presence of the 'children of immigrants'.[52]

One obvious point to be made here is that the 'cultural mosaic' of the national side emerges as a relatively unproblematic symbol of a generally Republican model of integration. In practice, of course, the notion of the Republican model and multiculturalism are seen by some, such as Alain Finkielkraut, as incompatible.[53] In fact, in order to understand this outpouring of national sentiment which accompanied France's victory, it is perhaps most useful to draw on Christian Bromberger's speculations on 'football as metaphor'.[54] Bromberger argues that, from an ethnological point of view, football is intimately connected with the values of contemporary democratic societies, which are both meritocratic and also recognise the importance of collective endeavour and teamwork. Football represents a 'demo-meritocratic' conception of society. Football, and particularly a competition like the World Cup, represents a rich series of metaphors which seem to express the texture of our everyday lives. In particular, football offers a way of understanding and negotiating the sometimes contradictory demands of individual achievement and collective effort which underpin contemporary liberal democracies.[55]

It is not, therefore, surprising that the French team and its historic victory should be a stimulus to talk about the sorts of choices a contemporary democracy is faced with in a world which is poised between the national and the transnational. It seems that international football in the

1990s in France has increasingly taken on an analogous role to sport in Victorian Britain. That is to say, quite simply, sport becomes a metaphor for life. This contrasts to the situation in the British press, where sport is infused with metaphors from other areas of life. In Victorian Britain the metaphor was that of war, whereas in France in the 1990s the metaphor is the problematic question of integration. In short, discussion of the French national team is intimately linked to two subjects which impinge on the general question of national identity: firstly, and most obviously, questions of immigration in post-war France, secondly, and less obviously, the ability of France and the French to adapt and modernise in this post-war era. Of course this second area of concern inevitably touches upon the problem of whether France can, or needs to, maintain distinctively 'French' values which may appear to be at odds with these processes of modernisation and globalisation.

Conclusion: 1958–98, from Kopa to Zidane

This essay has attempted to make some tentative connections between French national identity, and the French national team. The World Cup finals of 1958, when France finished third, and 1998, when France defeated the pre-tournament favourites Brazil 3–0 in the final, frame the discussion. It can certainly be argued that the 1958 team was not seen, by the public and the press, as being intimately connected to a sense of national identity. During the 1998 finals in France *Le Monde* contained an article by Benoît Hopquin on Just Fontaine, who scored a record 13 goals in Sweden.[56] In the summer of 1958 France was preoccupied with the momentous political events of the Algerian War, de Gaulle's return to power and the creation of the Fifth Republic. Little was expected of the squad after 1954, and they departed for Sweden a full month before their first match set up an intimate training camp in the rural setting of Kopparberg. Here, the players played a handful of undemanding friendlies and trained a little, but spent most of their time fishing or playing cards and *pétanque*. They were accompanied by a few journalists, and 200 fans. Even the French footballing authorities were reluctant to associate themselves with the team. Far from embodying national aspirations, the 1958 team was in some ways cut off from the rest of France, in their rural idyll of Kopparberg. The preparations of the French team isolated them from the dying moments of the Fourth Republic.[57] Crucially, it should also be remembered that, shortly before the finals in Sweden, two players who were shortlisted for the French squad – Rachid Mekloufi and Mustapha Zitouni – had left France to join a team set up by the FLN, the Algerian National Liberation Front.[58]

In 1998, however, the situation was very different. Although lacking top-class strikers, France, the hosts, were seen as a 'solid', well-prepared outfit. Expectations were enormous, and several matches were attended by President Jacques Chirac, who wore a French *Allez les Bleus* scarf to the Final, and held aloft a French shirt in celebration. In short, the success of the French team was closely associated with the contemporary situation of France. The 'multiracial' composition of the side – and consequently of supporters – was widely seen as signifying a new, potentially positive development in French society. This team was seen to represent the Republic as a positive force of integration. On the Sunday of the World Cup Final *Le Monde* noted a national mood which was helping the French to forget temporarily the 'dominant discourses' of unemployment, economic crisis and racial tension.[59] This 'bonheur précaire' ('fragile happiness') will not change French society fundamentally, but it does seem to represent some sort of positive statement of identity, which temporarily silences the voice of Le Pen and his like.[60] It is interesting to note that, caught up in the euphoria of a remarkable victory, relatively few commentators pointed out that ethnic diversity of the French team is nothing new, with Kopa, Fontaine and Piantoni *et al.* replaced by Zidane, Djorkaeff, Desailly *et al.* The main difference is that this diversity of origin is now embraced in the positive light of multicultural integration.

If the theme of French football and immigration transforms itself into something like a tentative celebration of a putative new multiracial Republic, the theme of the national team as a mirror of French society, although now couched in different language, articulates what are in some ways surprisingly similar preoccupations across the 40-year interval. Although commentators such as Joffrin and Villepreux do not advocate the thoroughgoing adoption of modernising principles of economic efficiency and profitability, they are still preoccupied with the capacity of France and the French to adapt to a changing world. Now, the team is seen as a symbol of the nation: teamwork is equated with the tasks facing the nation. Here the tone in 1958 and 1998 is ambivalent: success in Sweden in 1958 is applauded, but the suspicion remains that France as a nation is too individualistic. Similarly, in 1998, victory in the final and the explosion of national rejoicing across gender, race and class barriers – which is compared to the Liberation – offers a moment of grace to what is in many ways a fundamentally 'depressed' nation. Again, the French need to reject individualism, division and corruption, in favour of what *Le Monde* talked of as Jacquet's 'traditional' values.[61]

NOTES

1. P. Brochand, 'Entre le national et le transational', *Le Monde diplomatique: Manière de voir*, 39 May–June 1998, 24–6.
2. J.-M. Faure and C. Suaud, 'Les Enjeux du football', *Actes de la recherche en sciences sociales*, 103 (June 1994), 3.
3. I. Ramonet, 'Le football, c'est la guerre', *Le Monde diplomatique: Manière de voir*, 39 May–June 1998, 17.
4. Brochand, p.25.
5. Ramonet, p.17.
6. Ibid., p.18.
7. J. Garland and M. Rowe, 'War Minus the Shooting?: Jingoism, the English Press and Euro 96', *Scarman Centre Crime, Order and Policing Series*, Occasional Paper No.7.
8. M. Samson, 'Cocorico ball', in J. Bureau and J. Chancel (eds.), *L'amour foot: une passion planétaire* (Paris, Éditions autrement, 1993), pp.243–50.
9. O. Villepreux, 'En France, le foot se vit plus au bar qu'au stade', *Libération*, 9 July 1998, 25.
10. See R. Castro, 'Allez la France Mondiale!', *Libération*, 10 July 1998, 7.
11. C. Bromberger, *Football: la bagatelle la plus sérieuse du monde* (Paris, Bayard Editions, 1998), esp.'Le style: une manière d'être', pp.77–85.
12. Ibid., p.77.
13. See R. Da Matta, 'Notes sur le *fuetbol* brésilien', *Le Débat*, 19 (1982), 68–76. Cited in Bromberger, p.77.
14. See R. Grozio, 'Credono gli Italiani alla Nazionale?', in R. Grozio (ed.), *Catenaccio e contropiede. Materiali e immaginari del football italiano* (Rome, Antonio Pellicani, 1990), pp.139–48. Cited in Bromberger, p.77.
15. P. Nusslé, 'Jouons "à la française"', in Bureau and Chancel, *L'amour foot*, p.33.
16. *France Football*, 2, 720, 29 May 1998, 2.
17. G. Ernault, 'Le style c'est l'homme', *France Football*, 2, 631 (1996), 19. Cited in L. Ravenel, 'Le football de haut niveau en France: espaces et territoires' (unpublished Ph.D. thesis, University of Avignon and Pays de Vaucluse, 1997), 299.
18. See R. Williams, 'Reasons to be cheerful and a blueprint for the future', *The Guardian Sport*, 2 July 1998, 2. Williams makes a similar point about the World Cup, arguing that tactics in France 98 were no more important than technique and an inherent understanding of the game, borne out of a long footballing tradition in nations such as Brazil, Holland and Argentina.
19. Ravenel, p.299.
20. N. Blain and H. O'Donnell, 'European Sports Journalism and its Readers during Euro 96: "Living Without the Sun"', in M. Roche (ed.), *Sport, Popular Culture and Identity*, Chelsea School Research Centre Edition, Volume 5 (Meyer and Meyer Verlag, 1998), pp.37–56.
21. Ibid., p.43.
22. Ibid., p.44.
23. Ibid., p.43.
24. See A. Sonntag, 'Un miroir des vertus allemands', *Le Monde diplomatique: Manière de voir*, 39 (May–June 1998), 60–2.
25. Ibid., see note 18.
26. See Faure and Suaud, p.5.
27. J. Ferran, 'Ne pas confondre: l'Equipe de France et le football français', *France Football*, 643, 8 July 1958, 3.
28. 'Le bon tempo', Editorial, *France Football*, 2,678, 5 August 1997, 3.
29. Ferran, p.3.
30. G. Hanot, 'La France exprimera la valeur véritable de son football si chaque sélectionné a la volonté de faire plus qu'il ne peut faire', *France Football*, 620, 4 February 1958, 13.
31. G. Hanot, 'Le talent argentin, la méthode anglaise, la fierté suédoise, la sûreté yugoslave', *France Football*, 637, 3 June 1958, 12.
32. See S. Beaud and G. Noiriel, 'L'Immigration dans le football', *Vingtième siècle*, 26 (April–June 1990), 83–96. On the general question of immigration in French football see

also M. Barreaud, 'Elite sportive et immigration: les footballeurs professionnels étrangers en France et leur intégration dans la société, 1945–1992' (unpublished Ph.D. thesis, University of Reims Champagne-Ardenne, 1996).

33. *Football Magazine* (January 1961), 27. Cited in Beaud and Noiriel, p.95.
34. See A. Wahl, *Les Archives du football: sport et société en France (1880–1980)* (Paris, Gallimard/Julliard, 1989), p.206.
35. See A. Wahl, 'Raymond Kopa: une vedette du football, un mythe', *Sport Histoire*, 2 (1988), 83–96. See also P. Lanfranchi and A. Wahl, 'The Immigrant as Hero: Kopa, Mekloufi and French Football', in R. Holt, J.A. Mangan and P. Lanfranchi (eds.), *European Heroes: Myth, Identity, Sport* (London and Portland, OR, Frank Cass, 1996), pp.114–27.
36. Lanfranchi and Wahl, 'The Immigrant as Hero…', p.114.
37. See for example, R. Williams, *The Guardian*, 29 June 1998, 1: 'Forty years ago France met Paraguay in the World Cup and beat them 7–3. Just Fontaine scored a hat-trick, prompted by the genius of Raymond Kopa. Here, just a couple of goalkicks away from the mining village where Kopa was born, France again beat Paraguay but their victory came at the end of a performance that did no honour to the tradition of French football.'
38. R. Kopa, *Mes Matches et ma vie* (Paris, Editions Horay, 1958), p.21.
39. Wahl, 'Raymond Kopa', 87.
40. Lanfranchi and Wahl, 'The Immigrant as Hero', pp.115–16. See also Wahl, 'Raymond Kopa', p.87.
41. Lanfranchi and Wahl 'The Immigrant as Hero', p.116.
42. Wahl, 'Raymond Kopa', p.87.
43. Ibid., p.91.
44. B. Hopquin, 'Just Fontaine, le héros parmi les héros de 1958', *Le Monde*, 19 June 1998, 21.
45. *Le Monde*, 25 June 1996, 22.
46. *Le Monde*, 26 June 1996, 8.
47. Ibid., 8.
48. 'L'anti-France', Editorial, *Le Monde*, 26 June 1996, 16.
49. J.-M. Lanoë, 'Cette France d'un "bleu métis"', *France Football*, 4–10 June 1996, 36–9.
50. Ibid, 36.
51. See for example J. Lichfield, 'For Once United', *Independent on Sunday*, 12 July 1998, 19. See also 'Hommes, femmes, blancs, blacks, beurs', *Libération*, 10 July 1998, 2–5.
52. *Libération*, Editorial, 'Illusion utile', 10 July 1998, 2.
53. See A. Finkielkraut, *La Défaite de la pensée* (Paris, Gallimard, 1986).
54. See C. Bromberger, with A. Hayot et J.-M. Mariottini, *Le Match de football: ethnologie d'une passion partisane à Marseilles, Naples et Turin* (Paris, Editions de la Maison des sciences de l'homme, 1995), particularly Chapter 2, 'Le football comme métaphore'.
55. Ibid., p.199.
56. B. Hopquin, 'Just Fontaine, le héros parmi les héros de 1958', *Le Monde*, 19 June 1998, *Mondial*, V.
57. Ibid., *Mondial*, V.
58. See P. Lanfranchi, 'Mekloufi, un footballeur français dans la guerre d'Algérie', *Actes de la recherche en sciences sociales*, 103 (June 1994), 70–4. See also Lanfranchi and Wahl, 'The Immigrant as Hero'.
59. *Le Monde*, 12–13 July 1998, 11.
60. Ibid.
61. See *Le Monde*, Éditorial: 'La parabole Jacquet', 14 July 1998, 1 and 14.

The Organisation of French Football Today

JAMES EASTHAM

Sport as a Public Service

The 1998 World Cup took place in France at a time when the financial and economic climate of football was undergoing great change. An explosion of commercial interest in the 1990s, through increases in broadcasting rights, sponsorship and merchandising sales, had created a booming industry and generated unprecedented sums of money in the sport. In France, State involvement and regulation has carried a strong influence on the historic progression of football and remains a feature of the domestic game. French football has therefore struggled to accept and adapt to the onslaught of commercialisation in recent years. The concept of French exceptionalism is threatened by the globalisation of football and the burgeoning power of individual clubs over authorities and federations.

By hosting the 1998 World Cup, France had an opportunity to make a significant contribution to football in a sporting and financial sense, to strengthen its own football infrastructure and to generate funds for the sport in France. It also gave the French football authorities a chance to assess France's position in the world game, examine the recent financial evolution of football and decide how best to survive and flourish in the new economic era.

State Intervention and Football as a Non-profit-making Activity

Of Western European countries, France has the strongest State intervention in sport. The Republican state justifies its high level of involvement in terms of the need to 'ensure that the general interest of sport prevails over the multitude of private interests that traverse it'.[1] This statement seems at odds with the modern attitude towards sport and particularly football as a commercial enterprise, yet France still adheres to its principal belief that sport should act as a public service.

The involvement of the State in French football is perhaps best exemplified by drawing a comparison with its English equivalent, which during the 1990s has become the epitome of *laissez-faire* economics. In England, football is essentially dependent on individual initiative and its organisation and regulation are left to autonomous bodies which operate independently of the State. The British government has even handed over the duty for awarding grants to sports clubs and associations to a non-governmental body, the National Lottery. English football clubs are run outside local government control as profit-making organisations, they are proprietors of their own stadiums and are free to enter the stock market as public limited companies. The State possesses almost no influence over football in England.

What a contrast with France. Funding for French sports clubs and associations is allocated by a public body, the National Fund for Sports Development (FNDS), which obtains some of its money from two major public organisations, the Loto Sportif (National Football Pools) and the National Lottery. In France the development of sport is seen as a public service for which the State accepts some degree of responsibility. As a consequence of this sense of obligation, the Ministry for Youth and Sports delegates the organisation and regulation of football in France to the French Football Federation (FFF), equivalent of the English FA. The tutelage exercised by the State is real and allows supervision of the legality and fairness of the Federation's decisions, for example in respect of disciplinary measures. In theory, the State has the power to withdraw official approval of the Federation, since authority has simply been delegated by the State to the FFF on behalf of the French citizens.

The development of football and sport in France has been influenced by another specifically French institution: the 'association 1901' or 'association à but non-lucratif' (non-profit-making association). The law of 1901, which established freedom of association, was seen in France as a major advance in democratic rights. For the first time in its history the French State authorised any group of citizens to come together legally in order to undertake a common activity of their choice. In France, where professionalism in sport developed much later than in England, the 1901 law was the natural statute under which to create small town amateur football clubs like the Association de la Jeunesse auxerroise sports club in 1905. When such clubs turned professional, founder members realised that the 1901 law still provided all the necessary legal protection while allowing them to trade on behalf of the club and pay employees. In the spirit of the French non-profit-making sporting ethic, it was unknown for the *Société anonyme* (Limited Company) model to be adopted by professional clubs. The 1901 law guaranteed that, in principle, elected administrators did not profit personally nor distribute dividends to members and that the club be run according to open democratic principles.[2]

Local Municipal Involvement

Another aspect of public sector involvement resides in the financial support provided for local teams by municipalities. Town councils see it as part of their public mission to subsidise sports activity. This remains the case today: even at D1 level, French football clubs are still supported financially by local authorities through the 'subventions' system which nowadays represents 14 per cent of the clubs' cumulative budget. Town halls make these annual payments to their local football clubs simply as part of their obligation to promote and develop sport. They do not attain any managerial role within the club as a result of their financial input, except insofar as they are represented on the Board of the 'association 1901'.

This sense of public mission under the 'association 1901' extends to French clubs making use of the municipal stadium. Stadiums (with the single exception of Auxerre) still remain the property of local municipalities who are required to pay for maintenance and reconstruction. For example, funding for the redevelopment of the ten World Cup venues came from a mixture of private and public sources, but the football clubs themselves (who are essentially tenants) did not have to pay a single franc.

Recent Evolution of the 'association 1901'

The loi Avice of 1984 forced professional sports clubs with an annual turnover of more than 2.5m francs to constitute themselves into SAOS (Société anonyme à objet sportif) or SAEMS (Société anonyme d'économie mixte sportive) – both sporting limited companies. A modification to the law in 1987 allowed them to legally remain under 'association 1901' on condition that the club was not in the red for two consecutive years. These changes were introduced as compromises to help football adapt to the reality of modern economics. The broad consequence of these changes in statute was that football clubs were obliged to conform with the basic principles of commercial enterprise. In an SAOS the association must hold one third of the shares in order to have a blocking minority. In an SAEMS the municipality must hold 50 per cent of the capital and voting rights. Neither of these statutes allows profits to be paid out to shareholders. One consequence of these regulations is that it still remains impossible for club chairmen or directors to make direct personal profits from the success of their clubs. Thus very few investors enter football in order to make financial profit. Although other gains are on offer from involvement with football, it is rare to find businessmen holding court at the head of French football clubs for purely financial reasons.

Despite these changes to the financial statute of football clubs, the structure of the game in France still reflects a view of sporting activity as part of the public mission of the State and of local authorities. This may be traced back to Coubertin's Olympic ideal, seeing sport as a philosophical and ethical approach to life: as 'promoting the development of the physical and moral qualities that are the basics of sport'.[3] Although State intervention in sport is by no means restricted to France, the peculiarities of the French football system certainly set it apart from other major European leagues.

Free-market Economics and the 'Exodus'

The prominent regulatory role of the State makes it extremely difficult for individuals to profit from administrative positions. However, certain exceptions have (in)famously broken through the barriers and exploited football for their own financial and political advantage.

Football as Business: Lagardère, Tapie and Financial Affairs

The case of Matra Racing is perhaps the finest illustration of French football as a failed business venture. During the 1980s Jean-Luc Lagardère, one of France's most successful businessmen and owner of the Matra-Hachette-Europe 1 company (a high-tech arms, transport, publishing, radio and media conglomerate), saw an opportunity to associate his firm with a top sports brand in Paris for personal gain. He bought into Racing Club de Paris, an historically famous and much-loved club which was languishing outside the professional divisions. He spent 50m francs to launch the club in 1984 and freely admitted the promotional advantage he intended to achieve. In addition to publicity in France, Lagardère attempted to use the multiracial character of the team to promote his companies in Africa.[4]

Racing won a D1 place in 1984, were immediately relegated and then promoted back to D1 in 1986. At this point they began investing heavily in international players. World Cup stars Enzo Francescoli (Uruguay) and Pierre Littbarski (Germany) arrived for expensive fees while French midfielder Luis Fernandez was symbolically poached from city rivals Paris Saint-Germain. Racing Club adopted the name of Lagardère's company in 1987 to become Matra Racing and finished seventh in D1 the following season.

However, the club failed to attract large crowds and it soon became clear that Lagardère's flimsy financial foundations would lead to ruin. He had started building the club from the top and neglected to put in place a firm structure built on regular income through the gates or a proper youth system. Matra Racing simply did not have the money to realise their grand ambitions. The Littbarski transfer was an expensive disaster, Francescoli moved on to fellow big-spenders Marseille in 1989 and the club was relegated as Racing Paris in 1990. They reformed under the name Racing FC in 1992 after the Matra partnership fell apart. Lagardère has not returned to football since.

The most astonishing example of football being used and abused for financial and political purposes dates back to the notorious Bernard Tapie era at Olympique de Marseille. Tapie, a high-profile businessman with political ambitions, became the media-friendly chairman of a major football club and transformed it into one of Europe's most successful teams. Tapie led 'OM' to five consecutive French championships (1989–93) and the European Cup (1993) before receiving a jail sentence in 1995 for bribery of players and corruption, which left his business career bankrupt and his political career in ruins.

The ageing long-term mayor of Marseille and influential socialist minister, Gaston Defferre, invited Tapie to become chairman of Olympique de Marseille in 1986 with a view to improving the fortunes of the club. Tapie was happy to accept and put aside 500m francs per year from his business group to invest in OM.[5] With no local political base, here was a golden opportunity for Tapie to put down political roots and eventually succeed Defferre as mayor.

Tapie the businessman had specialised in taking over firms in difficulty and turning them, temporarily at least, into going concerns. Stories of his previous incarnations as a 1960s land owner and a singer and songwriter (he allegedly wrote the music for the John Wayne film *Green Beret* under the name Bernard Tapy) added to his larger-than-life appeal. Tapie was a man of the people, who dared to take on Jean-Marie Le Pen for the socialists in television debates and struck a chord with the citizen viewer-voter. He became a favourite with President Mitterrand (eventually winning a place as a minister in his government) and knew he could use his political protection to persuade the nationalised banks to back his speculative ambitions.

Tapie's dream was to win the European Cup, something no French club had ever done before. He created his own commercial structure for OM and became majority shareholder but retained, as part of the structure, the 'association 1901' in order to remain within the FFF rules. Tapie's thirst for success broke all precedents: he destabilised the transfer market by hiring high-profile managers (Hidalgo, Beckenbauer) and buying star players (Allofs, Mozer, Waddle, Amoros, Stojkovic, Tigana, Völler) and paid unheard-of wages in French football. Tapie's massive investment destroyed the opposition and by the start of the 1990s Marseille were clearly the best and most popular team in France.

Tapie had built an international reputation for himself as a dynamic football club president and Marseille became known across the world as one of the most exciting teams in Europe. Thanks to the success of OM and his use of the media, Tapie was able to realise the profile and celebrity he yearned for. Their first European Cup final followed in 1991 but Marseille were beaten on penalties by Red Star Belgrade. Two years later, Marseille defeated the mighty AC Milan in the 1993 European Cup Final. On that night, 26 of May 1993, Tapie was recognised globally as the man who had built France's finest ever club side.

However, it soon emerged that bribes had been offered to fix the result of a league match against Valenciennes a few days before the final. Valenciennes player Jacques Glassman (who, among others, was offered a sum of money to 'throw' the match) revealed the affair and it passed through the football authorities to the courts. This initial revelation proved to be just the tip of an iceberg: financial irregularities dating back several seasons, and it became clear that Tapie had used illegal practices throughout his reign at the club. He found himself in court on several different charges. Nobody was able to establish where 88m francs had gone after leaving the club accounts – Tapie claimed that all but four or perhaps six million had benefited the club. Marseille's 1993 French championship was taken away by the FFF although they retained the 1993 European Cup triumph since (despite persistent rumours) no match in that competition was found to have been fixed. Tapie was condemned to eight months' imprisonment for match fixing and a further three years (18 months suspended) for fraud concerning the club's accounts. Five other members of his management team (including national hero Michel Hidalgo, who coached France during the Platini era) received jail sentences. Olympique de Marseille were punished with two years of enforced relegation in 1994 and the club went bankrupt in 1995. As investigations widened into Tapie's business affairs he also received an 18-month prison sentence (12 of which suspended) for tax evasion. His financial empire collapsed like a house of cards.[6]

Olympique de Marseille have slowly recovered from the financial ruin of the Tapie era. They won promotion back to D1 in 1996 and Robert Louis-Dreyfus (head of Adidas) is now installed as president. The club finished fourth in D1 in 1997–98 and qualified for the UEFA Cup.

Other cases of financial irregularities in French football during the same period prove that Lagardère and Tapie were not isolated examples. Bordeaux president Claude Bez received a jail sentence for fraud after illegal payments were made to members of his family following construction work on the club's headquarters during the late 1980s. Saint-Etienne were punished in the 1970s for an illegal slush fund which involved club officials and players. PSG president Daniel Hechter was banned from football for life after a double-ticketing scandal in the mid-1970s. A culture of corruption and fraud appears to have survived in French football throughout the 1970s and 1980s without any real action being taken to stop the rot permanently. Indeed, many football observers believe that Tapie was simply made a scapegoat for the crimes of others and that his severe treatment at the hands of the football authorities served more as a warning to others to clean up their act rather than as retribution simply for his own misdemeanours.

The Exodus: Small Turnovers, High Social Costs, and the Bosman *Ruling*

Following the 'money madness' era typified by Lagardère and Tapie, French football has entered a period of financial prudence. Clubs no longer spend fortunes on foreign stars: in 1997 the only major arrivals from abroad were Marco Simone to Paris Saint-Germain (essentially an AC Milan substitute) and Fabrizio Ravanelli to Marseille (desperate to escape Middlesbrough). However, the most striking financial and sporting development of this post-Tapie phase has been an unprecedented trend referred to by press and fans alike as the 'exodus'.

Prior to 1996 it was unusual to find French footballers playing for foreign clubs. In the 1980s Platini was the only star to move abroad. During the first half of the 1990s a handful of players chose to leave France (Cantona, Papin, Desailly, Deschamps) but these remained firmly exceptions to the rule. It is hard to explain why French players remained with French clubs, since better salaries could be found elsewhere in Europe, French clubs did not fare well in European competition and it was a generation of considerable talent: men like Tigana, Giresse and Rocheteau would have proved great assets to clubs anywhere in the world. For whatever reason, though, French clubs always managed to hang on to their best players. Which makes the 'exodus' of French players since 1996 all the more astounding. Over half of the French 1998 World Cup squad play abroad, including nearly all the key players (Thuram, Desailly, Deschamps, Zidane, Djorkaeff). Nowadays most French clubs accept that their brightest prospects will sooner or later move on to a foreign club.

Perhaps more worrying than the now inevitable sale abroad of top internationals is the second layer of departures which has further damaged the fibre of French football. This involves the loss of solid D1 footballers (usually non-internationals) who provide the foundations of a competitive premier division and help to cement the standard of the French league within a domestic and European context. Examples of this latest wave of departures include Jocelyn Blanchard (Metz to Juventus), Laurent Charvet (Cannes to Newcastle United), Stéphane Ziani (Lens to Deportivo La Coruña) and Christophe Sanchez (Montpellier to Bologna).

This astonishing and rapid loss of the nation's best footballers has thrown into doubt the ability of French clubs to compete with their European rivals and poses two questions about the sporting and financial power of French football: firstly, why are French clubs no longer capable of retaining their best players? Secondly, what development policies have allowed France to produce such good players in the first place?

Clubs have been open to widespread loss of players since the *Bosman* ruling in 1995 which transformed the European transfer market. The ruling also served to highlight the financial weakness of French football, linked to small crowds and high labour costs. Yet French clubs continue to produce good players thanks to their highly developed national coaching structure. These factors, which have provoked the exodus, are worth looking at in greater detail.

French clubs have small turnovers and budgets when compared to rivals in Italy, Spain, Germany and England. This is primarily a result of low attendances in the French league, which results in less regular income through gate receipts. This perceived lack of interest dissuades sponsors, television broadcasters and advertisers from making substantial investments. Hence smaller sums of money circulate in the French game and, consequently, all areas of the sport are affected: club profits, player wages, transfer fees, and so on. In effect, all financial transactions in French football are down-sized in comparison with other major European leagues. So when it comes to competing for the most expensive players or paying the biggest salaries, French clubs are at a marked disadvantage.

High labour overheads or 'social costs' (*charges sociales*) are a general constraint for French companies in relation to their European counterparts. The whole of the French national health and social security system plus the retirement pension system is financed not from the central State budget but from contributions paid by employers and workers as a percentage of salary. These costs apply to football clubs just as to any other employer. Studies comparing the tax and national insurance overheads for players and clubs in the five major European leagues reveal that France is at a considerable handicap. The figures show that a net monthly salary of about 50,000 francs costs a French club over three times as much due to social costs. A similar salary is much less of a financial burden for clubs in Italy, Spain, Germany and England.

TABLE 1

COMPARISONS FOR PLAYERS WITH GROSS MONTHLY SALARY
OF 100,000 FRANCS[7]

	UK	Italy	Spain	Germany	France
National Insurance deductions	1,440	1,740	960	5,085	15,937
Employer's contributions	10,200	3,610	5,158	5,085	55,150
Net income before income tax	98,560	98,260	99,040	94,915	84,063
Monthly income tax payable	36,084	41,395	47,870	49,030	34,130
Player's net monthly income after income tax	62,476	56,865	51,170	45,885	49,933
Total cost of above salary to club	110,200	103,610	105,158	105,085	155,150
Net salary as percentage of total cost to club	56.7%	54.9%	48.7%	43.7%	32.2%
Total cost to club as percentage of net salary	176.4%	182.2%	205.5%	229.0%	310.7%

These high social costs are considered the biggest financial restriction for French clubs and the single major factor for France's inability to compete with rivals elsewhere in Europe. During 1997–98 Youri Djorkaeff earned 12m francs with Inter Milan while fellow international Robert Pires earned just 1.5m francs with Metz.[8] By moving from a French club threatened with relegation (Strasbourg) to an English club threatened with relegation (Crystal Palace) in January 1998, Valérien Ismaël gained an 800 per cent salary increase.

In April 1997 the Gaullist French Minister for Sport, Guy Drut, announced his intention to amend the laws affecting football clubs in order to render them more competitive. In order to allow the highest-paid players to keep more of their salaries, Drut wanted to ensure that, beyond a certain level of salary, social costs would no longer be applied. However, the plan fell foul of the change of government in May 1997 and was dropped as unrealistic by Socialist Prime Minister Jospin and his Communist Minister for Sport, Marie-George Buffet. So social costs remain the major scourge of French clubs.

In the above financial context, changes in European law in 1995 had important consequences for French football: the so-called *Bosman* ruling opened up the football transfer market and made it easier for EU nationals to move freely between European clubs after Belgian footballer Jean-Marc Bosman opposed the traditional transfer system and took his case to the European Court of Justice. The European Court ruled in September 1995 that the transfer system for out-of-contract players and the limitation on the number of EU players were both in contravention of article 48 of the Treaty of Rome on the freedom of movement of workers and article 85 on the freedom of competition. The consequence of the *Bosman* ruling was that football could no longer claim to be outside the law. More directly, the two immediate effects were: a) players at the end of their contract could move freely within the EU without a transfer fee, and b) EU clubs could sign as many EU nationals as they wished.

It is the second of these two rulings which has provoked the exodus of players from France. Some players have taken advantage of freedom of movement at the end of their contracts, but most of the players who have left France have done so while still under contract with a French club and therefore the selling club has received a fee. However, the abolition of restrictions with regard to EU players means that clubs are now free to stockpile internationals from France or any other EU nation without having to keep count. Clubs are no longer required to calculate the risks as carefully as in the past, when the arrival of a footballer from abroad took up a valuable 'foreign player' slot in the squad.

The problem is compounded by the financial superiority of foreign clubs, who can make bids which are well within their means, safe in the knowledge that the selling French club will have to accept since no larger offer will be forthcoming from within France. This weak internal market makes French clubs an ideal source of cheap, quality players for more powerful foreign buyers.

This combination of weak financial structures and the 1995 *Bosman* ruling explains why French clubs are no longer capable of retaining their best players. This begs the question of course as to how France was able to produce the sheer number and quality of footballers during the 1990s. This can only be accounted for by looking at the French attitude towards and organisation of youth development over the last 25 years.

'Centres de Formation' and the 'Youth Exodus'

French football is widely credited with the invention of *centres de formation* or training centres. The seeds were sown in 1974 when it became compulsory for all professional clubs to run training centres for promising young players. At the same time the FFF created the National Football Institute at Clairefontaine (also used as a base for the national team) which trains 40 young footballers (from 16 years old) for professional careers. A national technical Director of Coaching was also appointed and one of his major responsibilities is to oversee the organisation of youth training.[9]

France's carefully structured system of youth development begins for youngsters aged 6–8 (known as Débutants), who then become Poussins (8–10), Pupilles (10–12), Minimes (12–14), Cadets (14–16) and Juniors (16–19). Responsibility for coaching youngsters, even at an early age, is accepted by local clubs rather than schools in order to ensure that they are trained by qualified coaches and instructors. Some of these clubs are funded by local municipalities while others may be affiliated to the local professional club. At junior level, the best players are accepted into clubs' training centres as *stagiaires*. This nation-wide scheme of youth training is underpinned by a rigid national coaching structure. France has a highly developed set of coaching qualifications which must be attained before coaches can move on to operate at a higher level.[10]

As a result of the money and energy invested in the organisation of its youth training schemes, French football now produces arguably the greatest depth of high-quality young footballers in Europe. Nantes, for example, has produced the likes of Desailly, Deschamps, Karembeu and Loko in recent years, while it is not uncommon for six or seven first-team players at Auxerre to be products of the club's training centre.

A further worry to French clubs is the disastrous combination of their own prolific training centres and the *Bosman* ruling, which creates a 'youth exodus'. Arsenal manager Arsène Wenger was the first to realise that the breakdown of the traditional transfer system in 1995 means that it is now legal to 'poach' young players from France, without a fee, as they come to the end of their apprentice contracts. Such a practice is outlawed within France, since a young apprentice is obliged to sign his first professional contract with the club who trained him, but these rules do not apply across Europe. Thus Wenger captured Nicolas Anelka from the PSG training centre. PSG were outraged but, under European law, had no rights to stop Wenger taking one of France's most promising young players.

Since this initial precedent was set, further cases of 'apprentice poaching' have occurred. Although FIFA stepped in to deem both of these moves illegal, no rule has been put in place to protect French clubs from losing star *stagiaires* in the future or to ensure that a fee is paid. In the summer of 1998 Rennes youngsters Michaël Silvestre and Ousmane Dabo announced they were leaving France and would sign their first professional contracts with the Italian club, Internazionale. Rennes called on the FFF and FIFA to halt the moves but (at the time of writing) seemed powerless to prevent the two players moving to Italy.[11]

This is potentially the most damaging consequence of the *Bosman* ruling for French clubs. If they are not provided with a guarantee that the youngsters they train so proficiently will actually play for their professional teams, or at least that a fee will be received on the departure of a player, regardless of their age or status at the time, then there is a risk that clubs will no longer feel the need to invest in their *centres de formation*.

The combination of their prolific training centres and weak financial structures (small budgets, high social costs) makes French clubs ideal prey for richer European rivals. In effect, France has replaced former cheap breeding grounds like Yugoslavia as a country where clubs can be relied on to develop talented footballers who are available for sale at low prices. The ease with which most French players adapt to life abroad, plus their general good discipline and professionalism which is allied to their carefully monitored development at a young age, mean that in the post-*Bosman* era of freedom of movement they have become heaven-sent additions to teams all over Europe.

New Sources of Income: The Success of Paris Saint-Germain

The one French club which appears to possess the sporting and financial capacity to compete with rivals across Europe and protect itself from the consequences of the exodus is Paris Saint-Germain. During the 1990s they have established themselves as France's most successful club on and off the field. It is important to study how PSG positioned themselves at the top of French football and examine whether they are part of the European elite, in order to see the new economic factors which are influencing football. The changing nature of football and the growing influence of business and sponsorship in sport have allowed PSG to emerge from nowhere and grow into a European force in a very short time. This would not have happened without the involvement of the French television subscription channel Canal Plus.

PSG

Founded in 1970 as a business consortium, PSG immediately won the D2 championship and have remained in the top division ever since. A brief spell under couturier chairman Daniel Hechter (1973–77) came to an end after a ticketing scandal and the club was taken over by chairman Francis Borelli and a board of businessmen. It was Borelli who built up the finances and reputation of the club and in the 1980s PSG started to win trophies: they claimed the French Cup in 1982 and 1983 and won their first championship in 1986. However, PSG failed to advance in European competition and began to lose ground to Bordeaux in the French league. Meanwhile, Bernard Tapie was starting to turn Marseille into a powerful club. Borelli left the club in 1991 with debts of 51m francs[12] (and he would receive an eight-month suspended jail sentence in May 1998 for financial irregularities during his time at the club). It was five years since PSG had won a trophy and at this point they had fallen well and truly into the shadow of Tapie and Marseille. However, PSG was about to be saved by the single major change in the financing of French football during the 1990s: the new influence of commercial television.

The year 1991 marked the beginning of a new economic period for PSG and French football when Canal Plus announced their intention to take over PSG. Canal Plus was founded in 1984 as Europe's first terrestrial subscription television channel, which concentrated on sport and films. Their strategy was to turn PSG into a big team capable of rivalling OM (Paris and Marseille being geographically and culturally the biggest potential rivals in French football). Canal Plus had realised that a company with a vested interest has a better chance of influencing future relations between football and television from the inside as owners of a major football club.

Canal Plus presented a rescue plan for the club in association with the City of Paris and its mayor Jacques Chirac. The take-over co-ordinator was PSG club president Bernard Brochand, an advertising specialist. On 31 May 1991, PSG was reborn with a new structure. The Association sportive PSG (with Brochand as president) held 51 per cent of the capital, Canal Plus held 40 per cent of the capital and the remaining 9 per cent was taken by individuals. Free reign of the club was handed to *président délégué* Michel

Denisot, a television presenter, who had football credibility from being the successful chairman of the small Châteauroux club he had been steering through the regional leagues into the second division. The Paris municipality cleared the 51m franc debt and contributed 30m francs to an annual budget of 120m francs (30m francs came from Canal Plus and the rest from season tickets, gate receipts, sponsorship and broadcasting rights). This initial investment from Canal Plus and the local municipality provided the foundations for PSG to compete on a domestic and international level. Pierre Lescure, Director General of Canal Plus, later confirmed that his company would not have dared undertake such a challenge if Tapie had not been so (apparently) successful at Marseille.[13] It was in Canal Plus's interest in covering French domestic football to have a more competitive French league.

During the next seven years PSG became the most powerful club in France and a considerable force in European football. They won the French championship in 1994, the French Cup in 1993, 1995 and 1998, the French League Cup in 1995 and 1998 and reached five consecutive European semi-finals from 1993 to 1997, including a victory in the 1996 Cup Winners' Cup. Only Juventus played more matches in Europe during the same period. On a financial level, the downfall of Tapie and Marseille left PSG head and shoulders above the competition in France. Their budget rocketed from 120m francs in 1991 to 345m francs in 1997 (Monaco were their nearest challengers with a budget of 245m francs, followed by Bordeaux with 210m francs).[14] The average attendance swelled from 14,000 to 35,000 (easily the largest in France) and the club signed a long-term sponsorship deal with Opel, which made PSG part of the same publicity stable as European giants AC Milan and Bayern Munich.

Despite their apparent success at home and abroad, though, PSG remain well behind Europe's major clubs. The reduced sums of money involved in French football (low crowds, television rights and sponsorship deals) means that even PSG struggle to compete, in a financial sense, with clubs from Italy, Spain, Germany and England. In a 1996 survey into club finances, PSG's budget placed them 22nd in Europe, way behind Manchester United, Juventus and Barcelona.[15] During the last three years PSG have failed in their attempts to buy some of France's most promising footballers (Karembeu, Vieira, Zidane and Ba), who all chose instead to move abroad. During the same period the club also lost the likes of Ginola, Weah, Djorkaeff and N'Gotty to foreign rivals. In short, PSG are clearly the richest club in France but, despite the best efforts of their Canal Plus administrators, they have not managed to join the 'super rich' élite of European football.

In order to match the financial power of rivals across Europe, French clubs have realised that modern methods of making money must be learned and adopted. Thus belated efforts are being made to copy the examples of trend-setting clubs like Manchester United, Bayern Munich and Barcelona, who enjoy vast incomes from sources like merchandise sales, television rights and sponsorship. French clubs, who appear uncomfortable with the commercialisation of football, have been slow to exploit these potential sources of revenue but are currently striving to make up for lost time.

Television and Merchandising

Football across Europe is no longer solely reliant on fans through the gate for its income, largely due to the increasing influence of television. Although France may not benefit from the huge sums of money on offer in Italy and England, the marriage between French football and French television (particularly pay-television) was in some ways a precursor for the type of relationship which can nowadays be found all over the continent.

Since the creation of Canal Plus in 1984, television revenue has exploded as a means of income for football clubs. As a new pay channel specialising in football coverage, Canal Plus provided competition for the State television market leader, TF1. The rivalry became more acute after the privatisation of TF1 in 1987. Television exposure for football increased as a result, which in turn allowed greater income from sponsorship and advertising. Canal Plus and TF1 have shared the coverage of football during recent years and between them these two stations have largely priced the public service channels out of the market. And the money has just kept flowing: television rights distributed among D1 and D2 clubs leaped from 161m francs in 1991–92 to 621m francs in 1996–97.[16] Estimates for 1997–98 were set at 700m francs. While these figures are only approximately a third of the television revenue received by clubs in England, they have rapidly become a principal source of income for French clubs.

A further development in televised football was set in motion at the start of the 1996–97 season, when Canal Plus launched its specialised pay-per-view service. The subsequent opening of its digital satellite transmissions has widened the options for television football fans in France. Canal Satellite's pay-per-view service offers every single French D1 match simultaneously live on nine digital channels at a cost of 50 francs per match, 75 francs for access to all nine matches on a given evening or a 'season ticket' for 950 francs (28 francs per match payable in ten instalments). The French League signed a five-year exclusivity contract with Canal Plus for pay-per-view coverage from 1996 to 2001. Fears that the chance to watch all D1 matches in your living room would reduce match-day crowds subsided as a result of the pre-World Cup record attendance during the 1997–98 season. Early figures for the 1998–99 season suggest that attendance would increase even further thanks to record season ticket sales at many clubs. The high figures can be explained by improved stadiums and an explosion of interest in football following France's World Cup triumph.

It is likely that the sale of official club products will always remain a secondary source of income for French clubs, since the selective French fan has rarely shown willing to purchase his team's latest shirt, let alone aftershave or duvet covers. Nevertheless, several clubs are currently seeking ways to broaden their merchandising appeal. PSG opened their first superstore in Paris in May 1998. Marseille enjoy the greatest income from merchandising and plan to open a string of shops across their region before targeting other major cities in order to make the most of their nation-wide popularity.[17]

But perhaps the French model in this field will be current champions Lens. On 15 May 1998 Lens opened the biggest club shop in France next to their Félix-Bollaert stadium. They plan to set up a mail order service and intend using their wide fan base and sporting success to boost their merchandising income from 10m francs to 60m francs in the next three years. This represents a profit increase which, proportionally at least, even Manchester United would struggle to match.[18]

Club-sharing

In February 1998 it was reported that FC Barcelona were on the point of taking control of AS Cannes. The reasons behind the proposal were clear: Cannes, like many French clubs, were in financial difficulties. Furthermore, Cannes have an extremely fruitful youth system (they produced Zidane and Vieira). In return for their investment, Barcelona would receive first pick of graduates from the Cannes youth system while also using the club as a testing ground for new recruits. When this reciprocal agreement did not materialise, Cannes opened negotiations with other interested parties, notably Arsenal.[19]

In June 1998, however, Arsenal entered into a formal agreement with former French champions Saint-Etienne, who are now struggling in the French second division. The two clubs signed a five-year deal with the principal aim of exchanging ideas about *centres de formation* and the coaching of *stagiaires*. Arsenal agreed to invest 3.5m francs annually into the French club in return for expert advice from Saint-Etienne, who boast wonderful youth facilities and an excellent recent record at youth level (they won the national under-17 championship in 1997 and France's most prestigious youth trophy, the *Coupe Gambardella*, in 1998). With a daily flight direct from Saint-Etienne to London, trainees will be sent on 'work-placement' style exchanges to benefit from the specialist training on offer in France and the winning mentality so apparent at Arsenal. At the end of every season, Arsenal will be allowed to take out an option on a Saint-Etienne youngster of their choice and will occasionally send a player to the other on loan. The first transfer took place immediately, with 18-year-old David Grondin leaving Saint-Etienne for Arsenal for 5m francs (yet another example of the 'youth exodus'). The money may well keep Saint-Etienne alive and their formal involvement will also act as a deterrent to other foreign clubs tempted to steal Saint-Etienne's best youth products. It also offers French youngsters a chance to get their foot in the door of a major European club and may therefore attract promising young players to choose Saint-Etienne over other French rivals. Meanwhile, Arsenal hope to gain a regular supply of talented, professional and well-educated young footballers at low cost which could ensure their long-term success.[20]

As French clubs fight to survive in a European market where financial differences are becoming more marked, club-sharing, in theory, unites richer and poorer clubs, often across national boundaries, for the common good of both parties. It appears likely that more French clubs will become targets for richer European rivals as a result of their excellent *centres de formation* and relatively weak financial positions.

While club-sharing may provide a means of survival for some clubs, it also illustrates the growing disparity between the rich and the not-so-rich of European football. French clubs are finding it increasingly difficult to maintain their own traditions and methods in the face of cross-European competition and the fading of international boundaries.

The Changing Financial Climate

The clearest example of French exceptionalism remains the 'subventions' system of municipality funding for football clubs. However, it appears that the financial climate of European football has changed to such a degree that even subventions no longer have a place in the sport. French clubs are having to face the reality of local authority withdrawals, finding private sources of finance and launching themselves on the stock market.

The Pasqua Decree

French football will soon be forced to relinquish one of its most traditional sources of financial support. The French 'subventions' system of local government funding has been deemed illegal by European competition law which guarantees the free working of competition and the raising of all trade barriers on the internal market. Specifically, article 92 of the Treaty of Rome bans help given by states where such help creates unjustified competitive advantage. This applies to professional football clubs.

It was French interior minister Charles Pasqua of the right-wing

1993–95 Balladur government who declared subventions illegal. A decree from the subsequent Juppé government on 24 January 1996 called for the gradual phasing out of all town hall subsidies by the end of 1999. Recently amended by the left-wing Jospin government, this law now permits subventions until 2002. It is rather ironic that local authority funding, granted historically as a means of image promotion, reinforcement of local identity and out of a sense of public obligation, is now seen as a form of discrimination which destroys fair competition.

As a consequence of the Pasqua decree, football clubs in France will lose roughly 15 per cent of their budget, which will damage the financial structure of French football and force clubs to find fresh sources of income. Although subventions have been reduced in recent years, they still provide a reliable base on which to build a budget and often have a crucial stabilising effect on the overall balance sheets. French clubs are appealing, wanting the law to be amended to allow subventions to continue as a specific source of funding for training centres. However, even if this appeal is won, there is little doubt that the Pasqua decree will come into force.[21]

The DNCG and Financial Regulation

The Direction nationale de contrôle de gestion (DNCG) is an independent body of financial experts who analyse the accounts of all professional clubs in France. It places strict regulations on clubs before they are allowed to enter into any financial transactions. For example, it is not unusual for the DNCG to place a club under temporary suspension and ban all transfer activity if it is not satisfied with the state of the club's finances. No club is allowed to over-stretch itself or spend money it does not have. Since 1991 the influence of the DNCG has radically altered the financial health of French football, demonstrated by the figures in Table 2.

However, such a financial regulator only exists in France and Germany. Most clubs in Italy and Spain have working debts. While French clubs are constrained to work within the boundaries set by the DNCG, their supposedly 'rich' rivals in Italy, Spain and England are free to speculate and accumulate on the transfer market, which allows them to have first pick of the best players and meet wage demands.

French clubs want conformity. In order to compete equally with other countries they would like football's governing bodies to set up a pan-European financial regulator along the lines of the DNCG to monitor the accounts of all football clubs in Europe, who would be compelled to meet an agreed set of financial requirements. French officials would prefer something like their own French DNCG model, rather than allowing themselves to be swallowed up into the free market system which operates nearly everywhere else.

TABLE 2

EVOLUTION OF FRENCH D1 CLUBS' FINANCIAL POSITIONS
(expressed in multiples of 1,000 francs)[22]

	1990–91	1991–92	1992–93	1993–94	1994–95	1995–96	1996–97
400,000							
300,000							343,663
200,000							
100,000						165,343	
0					60,402		
-100,000				-118,477			
-200,000			-195,175				
-300,000		-308,263					
-400,000							
-500,000	-451,676						

La Bourse

The French government is currently considering allowing French clubs to become *sociétés anonymes* or public limited companies. Such a change promises to revolutionise the finances and economics of French football since it would enable clubs to be quoted on La Bourse (the French stock market) and pay dividends to shareholders.

The political aspect to La Bourse is provided by a sports law being drawn up by the French government and expected to pass before parliament in October 1998. The aim of the law is to give a new dimension to the financing of football clubs by allowing clubs to float on the stock market. However, the whole process will take some time. Clubs first need to convert into limited companies and the Jospin government has made clear its objections to the philosophy behind limited companies. If and when football clubs become legally permitted to enter La Bourse, they will remain under the control of the sport's governing bodies and still be subject to certain conditions. It will probably be four or five years before French clubs float on the stock market.[23]

Very few French clubs are currently fit for a stock market entry. A maximum of five or six clubs have the financial strength and administrative structure to support the change in statute (conservative estimates say just two or three). Indeed, several clubs are still *associations* and some (like Montpellier) have no intention of floating on the stock market at all. Municipal ownership of stadiums places French clubs at a distinct disadvantage and their merchandising and sponsorship departments still require further development in order to make a flotation worthwhile. In short, the weak level of investment in French football would make playing the stock market game a serious gamble for all but the very richest clubs.

Nevertheless, three in particular are keen to join: Marseille, PSG and Strasbourg. It is no coincidence that all three clubs are directed by businessmen of international companies: Robert Louis-Dreyfus (Adidas), Charles Biétry (Canal Plus) and Patrick Proisy (IMG McCormack). They have studied the enormous success of Manchester United, who used their stock market flotation to transform themselves into the world's richest football club, and are aware of imminent flotations in Italy. In their opinion, the only way French clubs will be able to survive on the international stage is if the French State and football authorities hand control over to individual clubs to compete on the free market. The worry for the rest of French football is that, if a small minority of clubs successfully enter La Bourse, will they not pull away from the rest of the pack and create an unhealthy gap between the élite and the also-rans? Is La Bourse not destined to destroy the traditional French ethos of sport as a public service?

Conclusion

As the 1997–98 season drew to a close, the financial climate of French football appeared to be on the point of further change. The highest D1 crowds in history indicated a clear potential for economic growth within the sport. Olympique de Marseille broke the French transfer record in May 1998 by signing Robert Pires from Metz for 60m francs. The additional arrivals of Florian Maurice (37m francs), Peter Luccin (37m francs) and Jocelyn Gourvennec (23m francs) threatened to price smaller clubs out of the market. Determined not to be outdone, PSG set about scouring Europe for top international players in order to continue their assault on European competitions. German defender Christian Wörns arrived out of contract from Bayer Leverkusen and Brazilian Adailton came on loan from Parma, while a total of 70m francs was spent on French players Ouédec (Español), Goma (Auxerre), Laspalles (Guingamp), Carotti (Nantes) and Leroy (Cannes). In July 1998, just before the start of the new French season, PSG astonished French football by signing Nigerian World Cup star Augustine 'Jay-Jay' Okocha from Turkish side Fenerbahce for a fee of 100m francs, breaking all previous French transfer records in the process. The huge sum of money paid out by PSG appears to be a response to the burgeoning activity of Louis-Dreyfus at Marseille and underlines their intention to compete on a wider scale with clubs in Italy, Spain, Germany and England.

This wheeling and dealing is set against a promise of greater financial freedom in the years to come. An increase in merchandising sales, plus growing sums of money from television, the expectation of improved sponsorship deals for success in Europe and blossoming interest in football thanks to France's victory in the World Cup, is encouraging a new wave of spending. French clubs enjoyed record season ticket sales during the 1998 close season (up 30 per cent), with Marseille attracting 40,000 *abonnés* or season-ticket holders, and a sell-out 60,000 crowd for their first home match of the new season.[24] The prospect of an entry into La Bourse within the next few years has provoked an awareness of the need to strengthen financial structures in preparation for becoming European 'super clubs'. As a result, French clubs are using the World Cup success and its positive consequences to maximise their financial potential.

Are Louis-Dreyfus and Biétry merely hoping for an opportunity to pull away from the rest of France? Or can they provide the ambition required to drag the whole of French football up towards the financial heights seen in Italy, Spain, Germany and England? On the other hand, will the continuing financial restrictions of French football render futile any attempts to compete with European rivals?

For the majority of clubs, surely Lens and Metz are models to follow. They seem set to use their current success as a platform for long-term prosperity on and off the field (albeit on a smaller scale than OM or PSG) through better understanding of areas of growth like merchandising and sponsorship. Their ability to compete in a sporting sense provides evidence that, for now at least, money is not a necessity in order to succeed in French football.

Outside France, however, the boundaries are somewhat different. French football is having to come to terms with a European market free from barriers. Money is pouring in and profits are multiplying. television is paying higher and higher sums and sponsors are desperate to attach themselves to football all over the continent. The *Bosman* ruling has shattered the traditional transfer system and players are now commanding huge salaries. The Champions' League provides an annual guarantee of cross-European competition with huge jackpots for the biggest clubs. And now, Europe's most powerful chairmen are meeting in secret and drawing up plans for a breakaway 'super league', which may be in place as early as the year 2000. As the dash for cash gathers speed across the continent, French clubs have to face the challenge: adapt to survive or be trampled and crushed in the stampede. Who knows, perhaps French football will even manage to use the current feel-good factor provided by high attendances and the World Cup triumph to boost its financial power, keep pace with the rest and move into a new economic era.

NOTES

1. C. Miège, *Les Institutions sportives* (Paris, PUF – Que sais-je?, 1993), p.68.
2. See J.-C. Bardout, *Les libertés d'association: Histoire étonnante de la loi 1901* (Paris, Juris, 1991).
3. Miège, ch.1, *passim*.
4. J.-F. Bourg, *Football Business* (Paris, Olivier Orban, 1986), pp.73–7.
5. Ibid., p.78.
6. M.-E. Lombard, 'Tapie: l'addition s'alourdit', *Le Figaro*, 6 July 1997, 9; J. Lichfield, 'Sport: Cup plans proceed despite scandal', *Independent*, 4 January 1997, 23.
7. The figures combine an Arthur Andersen study and a French study by Bérard ('Clubs professionnels et football: une comparaison', *Problèmes économiques*, 2513, 15 January 1997, 29–31, first published in the French players' union newsletter in October 1996. Figures are for an unmarried player with no dependent children, and are expressed in francs.
8. E. Wz, *Capital Magazine* (April 1998), 92.
9. R. Thomas, J.-L. Chesnean and G. Duret, *Le Football* (Paris: PUF – Que sais-je? 1195, 1991), pp.71–2 and 87–9.
10. Miège, pp.70–2.
11. F. Verdenet, *France Football*, 26 May 1998, 38.
12. G. Sitruk, *France Football*, 24 April 1998, 17.
13. C. Michel, 'Le PSG version Canal Plus capitalise sur le football', *Sport's magazine*, 20 (March 1996), 88–9.
14. P. Ferré, *France Football*, 17 April 1998, 4.
15. R. B., 'PSG, premier club français et premier client de JCD', *Les Echos*, 26 November 1996.
16. *Capital Magazine* (April 1998), 74.
17. F. Deschamps, *France Football*, 28 July 1998, 5.
18. J. Domenighetti, *France Football*, 17 April 1998, 2–3.
19. P. Aguilar and K. Natton, *France Football*, 6 February 1998, 8–9.
20. F. Verdenet, *France Football*, 30 June 1998, 65.
21. J.-P. Bouchard and J.-M. Lorant, *France Football*, 27 February 1998.
22. Figures circulated by Montpellier's Director General, Philippe Peybernes at meeting of D1 clubs' financial directors in Paris in April 1998, and given to the author.
23. Bouchard and Lorant.
24. F. Deschamps, *France Football*, 21 August 1998, 13; T. Collins, 'Opening night draws 60,000 as France head for big time', *Observer Sport*, 9 August 1998, 2.

Fans and Heroes

PATRICK MIGNON
(Translated by John Roach)

The Surprise of 12 July

More than a million people gathered on the Champs-Elysées the night of France's victory in the World Cup 1998. The scenes were repeated all across France as people congregated to celebrate the triumph of the French football team. This public outburst of joy surprised more than one observer. Before the competition, a number of foreign journalists considered that France was hardly worthy of staging the event given the weakness of its football culture. For the French, even if there was some enthusiasm among the young for players such as Zidane, the general feeling was one of doubt about the chances of the national team, and about the interest for the event among the French public.

Do the collective manifestations of celebration refute the analyses which stress the tepid commitment to football among the French?[1] Or, on the contrary, do they highlight the special place which the French national team holds in French football culture in contrast to the situation in Britain or Italy or Spain, where football culture is founded on support for club teams rather than the national team?

Forms Taken by French Football Culture

Whereas in England, Italy or Argentina there is an excess of passion for the game, it would seem that in France there is a lack of it. The figures are eloquent about the moderate commitment of the French. In Germany during the 1996–97 season, the gates for first division games averaged just over 30,000. The figures for Italy were 29,775 and in England 28,434: in France the average was 17,000 for the 1997–98 season, itself a record since the advent of statistical records of attendance. If one considers percentage of capacity, leaving aside Marseille and Lens, who often play to full houses, French club teams play to 50 per cent of capacity at best, even a club like Paris Saint-Germain. In France spectators represent 16 per cent of clubs' revenue, and a French club's commercial director will note that few supporters wear the club strip. It can also be pointed out that it is difficult to imagine that several thousand supporters would organise themselves to follow the national team to away games from the start of a competition. The fact is that few French supporters went to Euro 96 in England to follow the national team and similarly support for the French team in the World Cup 98 grew only as the French team progressed from round to round. It should also be noted that there are few French equivalents of the British fanzines, that few supporters go to away matches and that the French 'ultras' are far fewer in number and tamer in their behaviour than their Italian role models, whom some estimates number at 200,000, while there are barely 50,000 French equivalents. Finally, the French police will testify that French hooligans are far easier to control than their foreign counterparts. Has this always been so?

In his book on sport in France during the 'Belle Epoque', Richard Holt quotes an English traveller being astonished that 'the French excel at a number of sports', either new English sports performed by the wealthy classes or traditional French sports performed by the working classes, especially in rural areas.[2] In 1914 in the Pas-de-Calais department, there were more gymnastic clubs, more archery and cycling clubs than there were football clubs, and it is recognised that football only really established itself in rural areas during the 1920s.[3] Just before the First World War, rugby, which had already established itself in the major cities among students, became popular in the countryside and in the small industrial towns of the Languedoc as well as the Rhône valley and the Alps region. The same was true a little later for basketball and more especially cycling. From the first track and road competitions in 1870, cycling became a popular sport, and with the creation of the Tour de France in 1903 it became part of the popular imagination.

But football soon won a place of honour in the sporting landscape. Three phases in the history of supporters in France can be distinguished.[4] There was at the outset a phase of growing popularity, roughly between 1900 and 1950, during which football established itself throughout France. Records show sizeable crowds in the 1930s, for example, over 10,000 spectators for cup games at Le Havre and Lille, and over 60,000 for certain finals, as well as over 50,000 for international matches against England or Belgium. In the championship, at Lens (where a supporters' club was created in 1926) the average attendance was 5,000–7,000, not much less than in Paris, where, generally, 10,000–12,000 spectators came. There are also reports of pitch invasions, especially in the 1920s, and of the pursuit of players through the surrounding countryside following matches between Marseille and Sète during the 1920s. All this is evidence of a balance in French football culture between support for the local club, spectacularly so in the French Cup, and the national team.

The period from 1950 to 1980 was characterised by a steady decline in attendance figures which reached a nadir in 1968 with an average gate of less than 7,000, and gates were only to return to the 1950 levels (12,000) in the 1987–88 season. Until then the average was 9,000–11,000 with the good years marked by the success of clubs like Reims and then Saint-Etienne, Marseille, Lens and Paris Saint-Germain. But over the same period there was a noticeable upsurge in enthusiasm for the national team sparked off by the 1958 World Cup and for the success as representatives of France (that they came to represent) of clubs like Reims (1956–62) and Saint-Etienne (1974–80) in European competitions.

Finally, there is a third phase which starts from the 1987–88 season when there began to be a marked upturn in attendances culminating in the highest average of 17,000 for the 1997–98 season. At the same time there is a growing commitment among supporters with the growth of the traditional fan clubs and the advent of the 'ultra' groups and even of hooligans. One clear sign of this is the fact that football attracts a vast television audience. More than 17 million watched the European Cup final between Marseilles and AC Milan and 24 million watched the France v. Brazil World Cup final. Furthermore, the television company Canal Plus has had considerable success with its pay-per-view football channel. For the regional press the success of local teams is a sales advantage. *L'Equipe*, which devotes most of its space to football, is the most widely read daily in France with a readership of over 400,000; the day after the World Cup Final it printed one and a half million copies. Above all, one might point to the fact that there are over two million players registered with over 20,000 clubs. The popularity of football is therefore not in dispute, but the situation remains that only two clubs can be compared in terms of popular support to British or Italian clubs, that is Marseille and Lens, and a metropolis the size of Paris has only one top-flight team. A football culture does exist, but it is a football culture where open commitment is only manifested by a minority, where people will show their support only conditionally (if the team plays well and if they can associate themselves with a style of play, as happened progressively in the case of the national team during the 1998 World Cup); where club teams, despite the advent of supporters exclusively attached to their club, are worth supporting because they represent a national cause. In 1993, for the European final against AC Milan, Olympique de Marseille was supported by the great majority of football fans.

Football and Urban Culture

The People's Game

If one compares France with the situation in England or Germany one might conclude that differences come from the place of the working class in French society. No enclosures which brutally drove millions of people off the land and into cities at the end of the eighteenth century, no large industrial conurbations as in the Rhur. The presence of cheap areas for 'workers' in stadiums in the 1930s and the development of clubs in the industrial regions after the First World War show that football quickly established itself as a working-class sport without ever excluding players or spectators drawn from other social classes, as is evidenced by the fact that the two major areas for football are the North East, which might be attributed to the size of the industrial working class, in so far as it is the industrialised part of the country, and the South East which is not very industrial.[5] Today the football public is young and working class: together with students and secondary-school children (who constitute 25–40 per cent of supporters depending on the club), the blue collar and white collar working class represent up to 50 per cent of the attendance, the rest being middle-class, professional people and the self-employed.[6] Other than for the presence of students and schoolchildren, the rest of the public must have been very similar in previous years. In general a club's support reflects the demographic structure of the city and region in which it is located, with the exception of the highly educated who are under-represented. The industrial working class predominates when a club is in an industrial area, while in the Paris region the majority of the supporters are drawn from white collar working class and lower management. Football in France is thus 'popular' in the republican sense of the word, that is, it draws its support from the whole of society, defined in less restrictive terms than in Britain, and closer to Italy, though without the same degree of local atavism or the same level of precocious commitment to a team.

French Football, its Towns and Cities

The aspects which characterise French football culture are attributable more to the slow development of cities and urban cultures than to the absence of any appropriation by a specific social class.

The development of football in Europe was based on the existence of large cities determined to be rivals on the national scale. The French centralist tradition (Jacobinism) and the concentration of power in Paris denied this role to French football. Setting aside its modest size compared to London, Paris was not only a centre of population, it was a place where political power was concentrated. Paris was also more a city of politics and administration, a city of office workers and civil servants who believed in self-discipline and in respect for bourgeois values, in the capital's centralising mission, and rather more in the virtue of education than of sport. What is more, until the 1970s the mayor of Paris was not elected but appointed. There was therefore no competition among the local notables to seek popular support by developing popular leisure activities. There was no Parisian *haute bourgeoisie* such as that in Milan or Barcelona, ready to use football clubs as a means of mobilising the populace. For a long time the clubs were the product of volunteers or the extension of social clubs dating from the introduction of English sports. A further point is that Paris was not a city peopled by true Parisians, the majority of its inhabitants were recent arrivals and retained close links with their places of origin. Thus the sports club as the expression of one's roots had little reality; roots were elsewhere and Paris was the place of modernity and of social advancement, not the place where one sought to establish new roots. There was therefore no strong, let alone passionate commitment towards Parisian football teams. There was only the attraction of the spectacle which drew the spectator to the Parc des Princes or to the Six Day Cycle Races, more as an ironic observer than as a committed fan. There was support for the national team, and in the championship as many Parisians supported visiting teams as they did the home team. This was the consequence of internal migrations and of the ambivalent relationship which uprooted provincials had with the capital where they lived and worked.[7]

At the time when football was introduced, France was a largely non-urban society and was to remain so up to the 1970s. In 1911 France counted far fewer than the 36 British cities with populations of over 100,000 and was still a long way off in 1960, when children at school were still learning the names of the ten French cities with more than 100,000 inhabitants; until the 1950s the majority of French citizens lived in towns that were agricultural or administrative centres, rather than in major industrial conurbations or in cities. French football is in great part the product of small and medium-sized towns, as exemplified at the present time by such teams as Auxerre, Guingamp, Sochaux, Saint-Etienne, or Reims and Sedan in the 1950s, and Sète and Alès in the inter-war years.[8] Big city clubs from Marseille and Paris have only dominated for brief periods and have frequently languished in the lower divisions, some have even dropped out of professional football or have disappeared altogether, as was the fate of clubs from Lille, Toulouse, Bordeaux and Paris. Before the last war there were a number of clubs in what is now the Lille-Roubaix-Tourcoing conurbation, but they did not survive the 1950s and the same was true in Paris with Red Star, the Stade Français and the Racing Club, or more recently with Paris Saint-Germain and Matra Racing, the latter having disappeared following poor results and poor support.

The Working Class and Football

Let us return to the issue of the relationship between the working class and football. This raises the question of size, of the existence of a large market for football, and that of cultural heterogeneity, the obligatory sharing of common leisure activities. Thus in Lorraine or in the Pas-de-Calais, which until the 1970s were the most industrialised regions of France, there were few large working-class cities; most people lived in small towns and even villages.[9] In Lorraine, the major town was Metz, which was not really an industrial city, while at the smaller Forbach there was a professional club until the 1960s. In the Nord-Pas-de-Calais region there was Lille but there were also Roubaix, Tourcoing, Lens, Noeux-les-Mines, Auchel. In such places the clubs had strong local support and a good source of players, but they did not have the resources to win promotion or to stay up once promoted, nor were they able to draw support from across the whole region. The distribution of clubs across numerous small or medium-sized towns went against the growth of large urban support such as existed in Britain and Italy. As a consequence the small number of supporters and their limited ability to recruit players meant that these clubs were vulnerable, unless some wealthy sponsor supported the club, as in the case of Peugeot at Sochaux,[10] the coal industry at Lens and the textile magnates at Sedan and Roubaix, but at the same time the clubs were then at the mercy of changes in the industries that supported them.

As everywhere else in Europe, football has undoubtedly helped to forge links between people who had no cultural or social identities other than the fact of belonging to a certain urban space. But in France this process of creating collective identities has frequently taken place in a context of communities which had not severed their links with the traditional rural environment. Given the slow pace of the rural exodus, throughout the nineteenth century the working class remained very heterogeneous socially, culturally and politically, and perhaps, as a consequence, little inclined to engage in community building through participation in urban leisure activities such as football. The establishment of football in France, which was complete by the end of the 1920s, took place during a phase of the development of a modern working class when it was only slowly detaching itself from its rural or artisan roots. In large cities like Lyon or Paris the industrial working class only represented part of the workers, many of whom were still employed in small workshops and were distributed across the urban space, mingling with other social groups. In the suburbs of Paris or Lyon the workers lived alongside other social groups with whom they shared a common experience, namely that of having been uprooted. Few workers were the sons of workers. In the steel industry the workers, from father to son, worked alongside the children of farm workers who from time to time still worked on the land and who maintained close contacts with the rural society of their origins. In cities like Paris or Lyon, those who settled in the suburbs and bought or built a house on a new estate, probably spent most of their time working on their property rather than going to watch the local team. There were also many differences within the working class of any area with regard to political beliefs, sociability and leisure activities.

Thus at a time when in Britain there occurred a considerable rise in the standard of living of the working class (better housing, better wages and more free time at weekends) which provided the time and resources for leisure activities, the French experience was much more marked by a greater instability linked to the changes in traditional forms of employment and the practical constraints imposed by the process of settling into cities, as well as the means by which individuals moved out of the working class, into shopkeeping or self-employment. Where the working-class community was more homogeneous it was in rugby that it often found the best means of expressing its values of strength and solidarity. This is what happened in the industrial valleys of the Alps and the Jura, or in the case of the Burgundian steelworkers and the miners of the Midi.

Popular Culture and Republican Passions

A further dimension is the fact that over many decades these potential supporters were engaged in a passionate struggle to achieve citizenship and the recognition by the state of their rights, as well as being engaged in the defence of the nation. One might say that football was subsumed into these struggles. In republican France, people found a strong sense of citizenship in entities such as villages or small towns and retained close links with them because it was comforting to do so, hence the passion for the French Cup (*la Coupe de France*) which enabled places like Bourg-Peronnas or Raon-L'Etape to figure on the map of France. But this bond was relativised with the emergence of a sense of the nation, a sentiment inculcated in the population by wars and the republican school system. The relativisation of football within French society has therefore probably been due to this republican construct of a society composed of autonomous individuals, not reducible to any common category (class, region, sex or age). If football has a significance, it does so only within that tension between community and society, within the fact that 'being in public' means manifesting that one belongs to some 'natural' group (region, culture, age, gender) but through forms of action, in the sphere of politics, which bring to the group a national dimension and inscribe it as a policy of participation in the community of citizens.[11]

Political passions have had a significant impact on the place of football in French society because at the time when it was establishing itself it was ideologically associated, for example in the 1900s, with the struggle between Church and State.[12] This had an impact on the choice of sport. In the Midi, for example, secular primary teachers formed rugby clubs when the Catholic sports federation (FGSPF) set up football clubs. Similar considerations also had an impact on the organisation of common competitions and on professionalisation, and thus on the possibility of a rapid expansion of football in so far as the public interested in football was faced by a multiplicity of competitions and champions. The first *Coupe de France* was organised in 1917, and only in 1919 was a French Football Federation established; even more striking is the fact that there was no national championship until 1932, following the official recognition of professionalism. One should also note the efforts made to create an industrial working-class sport before the First World War in an attempt to break dependency on paternalistic employers and to create a socialist ethic for sport. There was also an attempt to organise working-class sport more widely, which struggled in the face of the rivalries between Socialist and Communist federations with the consequence that there was a fragmentation of competitions and thus of supporters until the unification in 1934.

Furthermore, the working-class parties and republican parties held the belief that the progress of the working class depended on access to culture, that this was one of the factors of its emancipation and of its accession to true citizenship, and that it was an essential means of enabling it to accede to wider universal culture. It was therefore not a priority to develop a working-class culture. There was, of course, a working-class culture which developed in the 'red' suburbs of Paris and in the steel-making valleys of Lorraine, especially through sports teams. But, if this culture was valued for its unpretentiousness, its solidarity and its virility, it was nevertheless not an end in itself. Class as a cultural unit, the 'ethnicity of class',[13] was alien to the way in which the working-class parties projected themselves. The Socialist and Communist organisations fought for access to the universal, just as much as they struggled for political power. Such ideas were welcomed by the élite of skilled workers. For them, emancipation also required the rejection of conventional sports, which were seen as alienating, and the notion of football, indeed of all competitive sport, as the opium of the people extended beyond intellectual circles.

Football's National Heroes

One example of this relativisation of football may be seen in the slow progress of professional sport, which took a long time to be perceived as a means of social advancement among the working class. The French professional player, more often than not semi-professional, usually had a middle-class background, such as being a student, for whom football was an agreeable and lucrative pastime. From the 1950s professional football became a working-class 'job' but right up to the 1960s it was not unusual to see talented players choose to remain amateur, thereby adding to their salaries the possible benefits and bonuses distributed by the sponsor's business.[14] The industrialisation of France which, though difficult for some, was on the whole slow, may account for this attenuation of professionalism in the working class; in other words, becoming a professional was not the only means of escape. The wages offered by clubs were not sufficient to tempt a skilled worker to give up his job or for a semi-rural worker to give up his work on the farm. For many, school, the hope of becoming a civil servant, or of taking over the family farm, or of following their father into the steelworks, or of gaining a qualification, represented realistic dreams of social promotion. The move to professionalism in the 1950s, which corresponds with a massive influx of players of working-class origin, to the point of their becoming dominant, is in large part due to immigrants.[15] Only the immigrants, initially the Poles and Italians, then the Spanish and North Africans, could envisage football as being the best means of getting out of the mines, as in the case of Kopa, for whom professional football replaced work as an electrician, which in any case was made difficult due to anti-Polish prejudices.[16] Generally, for a long time, football appeared to be something of an extra income and other sports such as rugby and, even more, cycling (with all its intermediary stages between amateur and professional), were just as attractive as football, if not more so, in tune with a society in which social promotion is seen as being essentially an individual matter rather than as one for collective strategy.

In the collective imagination, football appeared more as the symbol of integration in a national identity rather than a sign of belonging to a particular social class or region. French peasants learned French and football in the trenches of 1914–18,[17] in the same way that the Polish and Algerian immigrants who played for France were the proof of republican universalism. The heroes of French football are heroes because they enabled France to win or to put up a good show. They are people like Kopa and Platini more than Cantona or Ginola, since the latter two's great successes were at club level.

The Decline of Football

After 1945 France underwent great transformations.[18] Most notably in the 1960s and 1970s France became an urban society and this urbanisation went against the football culture that had grown up. One can explain the crisis which afflicted French football in the 1960s as a consequence of the scale of the urban change which then took place. Between 1960 and 1968 some of the most prestigious French clubs disappeared or dropped into the second division never to come back up, for example, Sète, Red Star, Le Havre, Alès, the CAP, the CORT (Roubaix-Tourcoing), and they did so amidst an almost total indifference on the part of the local public. The cost of running a professional club cannot be covered by gate receipts, its only source of income other than municipal funding. The small and mid-sized towns which lost their economic vitality could not sustain a professional club and those towns which were expanding were peopled by families who were preoccupied by the business of making a living in their new locality, or who were more interested in new forms of leisure pursuit. The poor quality of the football and its failure to enthuse spectators could not resist competition from other forms of leisure. In fact the process of urbanisation was also a process of diversification in life styles, which became structured more by generational differences or more individualistic as a consequence of the improved quality of life. This phenomenon was replicated in all European countries, where there has been a marked drop in attendances at games, but was more dramatic in France no doubt because of this great geographic and cultural upheaval. For people wishing to explore the modern experience of life, football was less exciting than the cinema, travel, shopping, television, DIY, buying a car or a property. The family bonds which persisted among those who settled in the new estates and their parents still living in the countryside led to an exodus from these areas in the big cities at weekends. For young people a new means of meeting their needs emerged: pop music, both as a part of the rise of mass consumption and as a means of challenging the massification of culture by developing a militant counter-culture. For such young people it would be unacceptable to be associated with a sport which was both nationalistic and male chauvinist. For those who wanted to be modern, football was 'old'. It was one of those institutions like the Church, political parties and trades unions that suffered a serious crisis of recruitment in the period following 1968. Under the tutelage of the State, which was widening its areas of intervention, individuals attending to their own affairs and building their own independence felt no need to identify with a football team.

From One Mode of Supporting to Another

Tradition and Innovation among Supporters

Throughout the dark days of French football, supporters still got themselves talked about, especially during the *Coupe de France*, although such events were localised. In the cultural context of the period reports tended to represent the supporters in a bad light like the drunken narrow-minded chauvinist in the film *A mort l'arbitre!* (Kill the Ref!).[19] Newspapers reported violence at matches such as that in Lens in 1972 between the local team and Bastia when the Lens fans hurled missiles at the Bastia players and invaded the pitch. Their passion was a subject of astonishment, as was the intensity of the Saint-Etienne supporters in their home ground, the Geoffroy Guichard Stadium, known as the 'green furnace'. With Saint-Etienne, and before the whole of France, there appeared the phenomenon of the public as the 'twelfth player'. But in noting such factors the reports were noting anachronisms rather than identifying new social phenomena: they were noting the particular intensity of the Corsicans, the local chauvinism of the mining communities of Lens and Saint-Etienne. Today, the key areas of football fervour are still Lens and its old mining basin, Saint-Etienne and the memory of 'les Verts', Metz and the Lorraine steel industry, or even clubs which represent strong cultural identities that have been 'rediscovered' in the 1970s, like Bastia and Corsica, or the Breton clubs of Guinguamp or Lorient, not forgetting towns whose specificity is founded on the feeling they are looked down on by the rest of France, like Marseille. But since the mid-1980s, there is also Lyon, and Bordeaux, or Paris.

Today virtually all professional clubs have at least two supporters' clubs, Marseille has eight and Paris Saint-Germain up to 15; in all there are some 200 such clubs. These supporters' clubs have very variable numbers of members, some as few as a dozen while the largest have over 6,000. The size of these clubs is such that they can represent some 20 per cent of spectators at certain away games. Duringthe 1997–98 championship, 3,000 Lens supporters regularly travelled to away games. As for the 'ultras' and the hooligans they have created in people's minds the idea of football matches as danger zones in the same way as their English and Italian counterparts have done.

Some of these supporters' clubs are 'official', that is recognised by the club, and their members act as volunteer stewards or sell programmes and other products associated with the club. The supporters' club is judicially independent of the football club but acts as a means of promoting the latter's commercial interests. In such cases they receive financial support and are affiliated to the Federation of Supporters' Clubs (Fédération des associations de supporters – FAS). They can be called 'Official', along Italian lines, or identify with the slogan 'Helping not hindering' of traditional British supporters. Such supporters are generally socially and economically integrated in society. The Marseille Central Supporters' Club, founded in 1945, is made up of adults, manual workers, artisans, office and shop workers or shopkeepers, who meet in cafés to play cards and discuss football. Another club is made up of young executives and managers fascinated by the success of Bernard Tapie.[20] In the Pas-de-Calais, depending on where they are located, the supporters of Lens meet in working-class cafés, or in somewhat more upmarket places in the case of executives and company directors who consider the running of the club an indication of social success.[21]

Alongside all these official associations, new groups have evolved since the mid-1980s, making up the world of the 'ultras'. They are characterised by a determination to be independent of the club authorities, to be highly visible in their participation at matches and to be much more militant. They organise the spectacle in the stadium (drums, banners), travel to away games and sometimes produce fanzines. From 1992 to 1995 there was a magazine, *Supmag*, which acted as a sort of official newsletter for the various groups, allowing them to assess their impact within the 'ultras', to exchange views and information about their activities and their significance.

Among the 'ultras' one finds a cause, which swings between being a commitment to the club and a wish to participate in the life of the club, and a strong desire to remain independent of the official aspects of the club. Located in specific parts of the ground the 'ultras' express through their chants and actions their commitment to the team, their authenticity as supporters and their collective identity. Their talk is of respect for the shirt, pride in their city and their team, honour, territory, solidarity, autonomy, of collective effort, of being part of history and of participating in the creation of legends, as well as of the heroic nature of being a supporter. In this way they seek to distinguish themselves from the average supporter, who is seen as passive and fickle. They continually call on club and players to honour their duties to the game in general and to the supporters in particular. They rail against those who denigrate, abuse, betray or ignore them. They consider themselves to be victims of the commercialisation of football, the power of the media and the policy of all-seater stadiums. They are committed to the cause of football, and to their cause as active participants. Some 'ultras' cross the thin line, as in Italy, separating them from those who reject all contact with the official world of football, the 'hools' or 'casuals' of Britain and Northern Europe, with their cortège of confrontations between rival supporters, or with the police, or displays of Fascist symbols and the chanting of racist and xenophobic slogans, although their actions cannot be attributed solely to the influence of the extreme Right.

Urban Identities and the Democratisation of Youth

The first reason for this renewal of football support and supporters is that all these new town-dwellers are now settled into their new environment. In Paris, for example, the partisan commitment to Paris Saint-Germain is also related to a new problematic in defining Parisian identity. Why do people want a major club in Paris? To share the experience of great exploits with a crowd of others, 'to be as proud of football as of the Eiffel Tower, not to be different from others: the Bretons have their pride, the Milanese have theirs, we want to have ours'. Being Parisian is no longer at all special. The fact is that during the crisis years of its football, the Parisian urban space underwent profound changes. Paris became peopled more and more by Parisians, but they were more and more suburban Parisians; a phenomenon which was indeed replicated in all major French cities. The public's growth in numbers and social diversity signifies being settled in a new urban identity: the supply of football has met the demand of being able to participate in a shared routine where individuals' horizons are no longer defined only by mobility within the big new metropolises, and where allegiance to a club becomes a legitimate means of self-definition. To have your own space on a football ground means being able to meet people like yourself, to have a good time with them and to fix regular meetings so as to mark out the week with activities and places to go and, possibly, becoming a football activist brings a little more meaning to one's leisure activities.

Increase in crowd numbers is also linked to the democratisation of young people's experience. In the Parc des Princes, 60 per cent of spectators are under 35, and 40 per cent are under 25 (at Marseille 50 per cent). These new supporters are young people and not-so-young people from various social backgrounds. The age range of the 'ultras' is more precisely between 15 and 25, students, older secondary school children, unemployed, or young people scraping along on temporary jobs, or people in their first job. People quit between the ages of 22 and 25, to set up a home, to be in regular employment or to take up their studies again. Those few who stay beyond the age of 30 do so because they have a position of responsibility in a supporters' club or because they are having trouble finding a place in society. The phenomenon of 'ultra' supporters corresponds to the prolongation of youth called post-adolescence,[22] which is linked both to the democratisation and lengthening of studies, and also to difficulties in finding a job and becoming integrated into society. Post-adolescence is linked to the lightening of social constraints which itself goes hand in hand with the increased importance of generational groups, which brought young French people closer to their British or German neighbours in the 1970s and 1980s when the model of youth as founded on the experience of social indetermination and participation in mass popular culture was tending to spread to all young people. These two decades saw young people escaping from the tutelage of school and family in the sense that the 1970s and 1980s pointed away from a model of socialisation founded on identifying with the parental model towards a model based on experimentation. To be young no longer meant adhering to a course set by parents. The young worker, just like the student, could no longer be sure of being able to reproduce the parental context. Because of unemployment, the transition into work and into society tended to require everyone to construct strategies based on the trial-and-error principle until individuals achieved a satisfactory definition of self in their own eyes as well as for others. Anti-institutional attitudes are no longer only the privilege of students; and most students are no longer familiar with high cultural models but with mass popular culture, rock, rap and football, which are no longer beneath them, but elements of shared experience now common to all. Being a supporter thus constitutes a field of self-discovery and offers a field of experimentation through a search for differentiation and inclusion in something wider, in the shape of a cause or a movement in which they can participate. And sometimes the functions which are attributed within the supporters groups seem to lead to the acquisition of socially useful transferable skills, for example, learning to manage groups, negotiation skills, being enterprising, plus the experience of travelling across France and going abroad, and of participating in national and international networks. Football, and belonging to a supporters' group, has provided the opportunity to acquire status, and a reputation, and to make a career out of it.

However, differences of social status explain the differences which exist between various 'ultra' groups. At Metz there is a difference between one group made up of teenage schoolchildren and students, and another composed of young workers, blue collar or white collar working class, mostly in temporary employment. In Paris the 'Auteuil End' is younger and more 'studenty' than the 'Boulogne End',[23] while in Marseille the various 'ultra' groups recruit from significantly different social and geographic sections of the city. For example, in the more middle-class southern districts for the 'Commando Ultras', or in the more working-class and immigrant northern districts for the 'North Yankee Army' as it was, or the 'Winners' (including more students perhaps) today. As in Paris, they occupy different parts of the ground.

Influences on Supporters

We can, however, discern three limitations on this expansion of the public for football and of new types of supporter. Firstly, in terms of numbers, the phenomenon remains a minority experience, with the exception, again, of Marseille and Lens. The case of Paris need not be dwelt on: a town of more than two million inhabitants allowing only one big club to survive and filling the Parc des Princes only for big occasions. It may be noted at this point that the domination in almost every French stadium of the highly organised Italian style of supporter is explainable less by reference to the shared Latin cultural model than by the facilities offered by the technologies of mobilisation and collective expression that are not offered in France by the traditional British model based on common shared references (songs, chants and sheer numbers of supporters). In France the underdevelopment of the supporter phenomenon is linked to the underdevelopment of clubs and societies (*le mouvement associatif*) compared to other European countries.

This raises a second question, to do with the independence of supporters, in so far as the underdevelopment of supporters' clubs makes them dependent on those football clubs which can allocate resources to them and seek to orient their activities. The new football culture in France should be seen as the result of a conjunction between football itself, the clubs and their management, and the worlds of finance, politics and the media, each of them seeking to mobilise a public, voters, staff or audiences. The work of promoting football, which is linked to the effort to promote cities, regions and even firms, connects from the 1980s with the militancy of the 'ultras', who project their own brand of support and reinvent the definition of 'supporter'. For the triumphs of Saint-Etienne in European competitions, from 1974 to 1980, then the achievements of the national team in Argentina in 1976, and then in Spain and Mexico, and finally the emergence of major clubs like Bordeaux, Marseille and Paris Saint-Germain, are the consequence of the major transformations in professional football in the 1970s and 1980s. The policy of centres of excellence improved the quality of French players, the money from television, the arrival of ambitious club presidents like Bernard Tapie, Claude Bez, or Canal Plus, the decentralisation reforms which make mayors powerful allies when they seek to associate their city with the success of the football team, all of these factors explain the improvement in results, but also explain the wider concern to mobilise spectators both as an economic resource and as a means of heightening the profile of a club and its city. Hence the creation of dedicated supporter networks, the help given to supporters' clubs, and the attempt to control them, be they 'ultras' or otherwise. A number of these associations receive some funding from the clubs which allows them to buy equipment for the fans and to organise special demonstrations of support for their team at certain games. They may benefit from the loan of a place to store their equipment or receive help with travel. Thus in Lens, the 'Sup-R-Lens' are closely controlled by the club, as a superimposition of the paternalism of the Nord-Pas-de-Calais's old social democracy, made up of a network of local economic interests. At Le Havre, the 'ultras' supporters' clubs are recognised provided they join the federation of supporters' clubs recognised by the club and participate in social activities aimed at supporters. At Paris Saint-Germain, on the other hand, in order to gain supporters, between 1980 and 1994 the club tolerated the presence of extreme right-wing groups, but when Canal Plus associated itself with the club, the latter developed a policy of negotiating with supporters and allocated funds in order to develop new supporters' clubs, at the Auteuil end, so as to create a new image for the club. Of course, others refuse to accept funding so as to remain independent of the club authorities, though they will participate in the various meetings organised by the club, as is the case for Paris Saint-Germain. They raise money through the sale of fanzines, photo of matches, the sale of team scarves, tee-shirts, badges etc. which then funds travel to away games and social gatherings, but this remains a minority activity, and these associations are under threat, as in Marseille, Lens or Paris, from clubs' plans (on English lines) to develop season tickets, recruit a better-off audience, and transform the supporter into a spectator-consumer.

Finally, the question of extreme-right politics must be addressed, or, more generally, the issue of xenophobic attitudes of a section of the new supporters.[24] This concerns only a minority of supporters' groups but it set the tone in the stands for a long time and is linked to the fact that supporters' groups mainly, except in Marseille and partly in Paris at the Auteuil end, represent white youth and not really the youth of immigrant communities. The rediscovery of football is happening in a society which is no longer perceived as offering a path to citizenship, a higher standard of living and modernity, the factors which had characterised the movement from the countryside to the cities. Society is now perceived as a central locus which seems more and more remote and from which there is a growing risk of exclusion. All this generates the social conditions for a redefinition of a sense of identity and of territory as well as providing new reasons for being committed to football, reasons that feed on the crisis of the French model of integration and the French model of definition of identity.

The fact that France has become a more and more urbanised society means that there are more and more people who can express their discontent about where they live, and therefore about their social status. This new urban geography is a spatial manifestation of a tendency to dualism in French society. The hooligans and 'ultras' do not necessarily come from areas characterised by social disintegration, but they feed on a sense of dereliction and the fear of social decline. For some, their presence on the Boulogne 'Kop' at the Parc des Princes is determined by street rivalry between 'white' and 'French', and 'black' and 'North African' (*beurs*), especially when the white youths come from the more affluent suburbs or the 'good' council housing estates (*habitation à loyer modéré* – HLM), or when some of them have been forced to move into council housing as a consequence of a decline in economic and social circumstances, a family breakdown, failure at school or parental unemployment. In the suburbs the apparent freedom of young African and North African males is felt, by some white youths, be an unjust constraint on the right to express their own experience of society and to control the streets. At that time of life (adolescence and post-adolescence) when young men have an uncertain sense of masculinity, the North African and African gangs give the appearance of being much more macho and of belonging to a community, and this appears to be what gives them strength. That is how football appears to provide an answer. Alongside the traditional mode of support, the pleasure of the game and local pride, there grows up, among those individuals who feel most keenly that their social integrity is threatened, a mode of supporting which enables them to define themselves against what appear to be communities by proclaiming themselves to be part of a community as well. Their presence in a stadium is the expression of the relationship between the centre and the periphery, of their appropriation of the centre in response to the appropriation of the suburbs by ethnic enemies. A whole section of the Boulogne 'Kop' bears witness to this logic: the creation of a territory against other territories and the creation of a gathering place for those who are like-minded.

Conclusion: after 12 July?

What light do these different elements cast on the events of 12 July? Initially, these events were analysed, very ambitiously and at the risk of overinterpretation, as the manifestation of a new state of mind in French society and in its direct effects on this. There was talk of a victory for integration, since the crowds, like the French team, were made up of members of all component parts of French society; there was talk of rediscovered national pride, and of a non-aggressive and non-exclusive nationalism; some stressed the effects of a football victory as one element in a nation's improved image of itself; others stressed the new values symbolised by Aimé Jacquet and his team, the work ethic, solidarity, discretion and modesty, the opposite of what Tapie stood for, the opposite of glitz, said some, as a lesson aimed at politicians and leaders; finally, it was made to mean a defeat for the Front National, and the emergence of new attitudes towards immigrants and the issue of the deprived suburbs.

It may indeed be thought that those who experienced the events and who in so doing experienced a peaceful crowd, a city where people no longer feared one another, have lived through an experience that will help give them a new perception of society. But the crowds on the Champs-Elysées or those who watched the scenes on television, in their heterogeneity, were no different from the crowds in the stadiums on a Saturday: within them coexisted different understandings of what the victory of the French team means, as well as different understandings of what France means. Did we therefore have a celebration of a multicultural France, or the celebration of a France of integration, or even of assimilation? The team was just like previous French teams since the 1930s which were also made up of players of Polish, Moroccan, Spanish, or Italian etc. origin. And what meaning can we give to the fact that on the day of the final many young people from the suburbs were wearing Brazilian colours? It is interesting to note that the same issue of *L'Express*[25] which carried an article on the crowds on the Champs-Elysées and the French team symbolising integration, also carried an article on the attraction that the Front National exerts on the unskilled and socially excluded under-thirties. The celebrations of 12 July were indeed symbols of a call for unity precisely because that unity is far from real. The multiracial nature of the French national team exemplified a diversity which is not accepted by everyone, in particular not by those for whom the experience of life in society is not one of successful integration, but the experience of the difficulties young people have, whether 'white', 'black' or *beurs*, in integrating themselves in society. If the victory celebrations do underline the importance of the national dimension in French football culture, they also stress that, to be realised, the promises held out by the celebrations require political measures to be taken regarding the school system, employment, the fight against racism, new urban policies, but also in football.

For in terms of football culture, what did we see and what can we expect? No doubt a considerable increase in the number of young and very young players joining clubs. But it is not certain that the event will result in an increase in the attendances at First Division games. If indeed people can follow the World Cup and support the French team for all the good reasons that have been rehearsed, it is because the French team belongs to everyone, but clubs and their terraces can still represent habits that people are not about to lose and territories that still seem hostile. Thus it may be thought that the expressions of support for Front National ideas on the terraces will not suddenly abate, nor will North African or Black African spectators (who are still under-represented on most French grounds, though more numerous than the 1–2 per cent representation of the minorities in English grounds) suddenly find themselves accepted at Paris Saint-Germain or the Racing Club de Strasbourg. The future of a second Parisian club, based in the Stade de France, is assured neither in terms of financial resources nor in terms of support it can command. Similarly it is not certain that the female interest recorded during the World Cup (40 per cent of viewers were women, and in the later rounds of the tournament women represented some 20 per cent of the spectators in grounds) will persist in league games, since the routine of the league reflects the routine of the sexual division of leisure pursuits. What needs therefore to be watched in this context is how football's governing bodies, the clubs, the government and supporters' groups put into action policies that match up to the hopes expressed on the night of 12 July.

NOTES

1. P. Mignon, *La Passion du football* (Paris, Odile Jacob, 1998).
2. R. Holt, *Sport and Society in Modern France* (London, Macmillan, 1981).
3. R. Hubscher (ed.), *L'Histoire en mouvement. Le sport dans la société française* (Paris, Armand Colin, 1992), p.50.
4. For information towards a social history of football in France, see A. Wahl, *Les Archives du football. Sport et société en France (1880-1980)* (Paris, Archives Gallimard-Julliard, 1989).
5. For the geography of French football clubs, see L. Ravenel, *La Géographie du football en France* (Paris, PUF, 1998).
6. From data gathered in surveys in Saint-Etienne by P. Charroin, 'Il pubblico del Geoffroy Guichard di Saint-Etienne', in P. Lanfranchi (ed.), *Il Calcio e il suo pubblico* (Edizioni Scientifiche Italiane, 1992); in Lens, by Y. Maerten, W. Nuytens, P. Roquet, *Le Peuple des tribunes. Les supporters de football dans le Nord-Pas-de-Calais* (Musée d'Ethnologie Régionale de Béthune, 1998); in Marseille by C. Bromberger, *Le Match de football. Ethnologie d'une passion partisane* (Paris, Editions de la Maison des Sciences de l'Homme, 1995); in Paris and in Metz by P. Mignon (Ligue nationale de football, unpublished document).
7. In A. Wahl, pp. 226–7.
8. The hypothesis of J. Marseille, 'Une histoire économique du football en France est-elle possible ?', in 'Le Football, sport du siècle', *Vingtième Siècle*, 26 (April–June 1990).
9. See G. Noiriel, *Les Ouvriers dans la société française* (Paris, Le Seuil, 1986).
10. P. Friedenson, 'Les ouvriers de l'automobile et le sport', special number on L'Espace du sport, *Actes de la Recherche en Sciences Sociales*, 79 (September 1989).
11. D. Schnapper, *La Communauté des citoyens. Sur l'idée moderne de nation* (Paris, Gallimard, 1994).
12. For these issues, see A. Wahl or B. Dumons *et al.*, *Naissance du sport moderne* (Paris, La Manufacture, 1987).
13. The term used by P. Cohen in 'We hate humans', special number on Violence et politique, *Lignes*, 25 (1995).
14. A. Wahl and P. Lanfranchi, *Les Footballeurs professionnels des années trente à nos jours* (Paris, La Vie Quotidienne-Hachette, 1995).
15. S. Beaud and G. Noiriel, 'L'immigration dans le football', in *Le Football sport du siècle*, *Vingtième Siècle*, 26 (April–June 1990).
16. Ibid.
17. E. Weber, *La Fin des terroirs. La modernisation de la France rurale* (Paris, Fayard, 1983).
18. For the major transformations of French society, see P. Mendras, *La seconde révolution française, 1965-1984* (Paris, Gallimard, 1988); G. Lipovetsky, *L'Ere du vide* (Paris, Gallimard, 1983); A. Ehrenberg, *Le Culte de la performance* (Paris, Calmann-Lévy, 1991).
19. Film directed by Jean-Pierre Mocky, 1975.
20. In C. Bromberger.
21. In Y. Maerten *et al.*
22. See J.-C. Chamboredon, 'Adolescence terminée, adolescence interminable', Colloque national sur la post-adolescence, 1984, and O. Galland, *Sociologie de la jeunesse* (Paris, A. Colin, 1991).
23. P. Mignon, survey of Parc des Princes spectators in November 1996 (Ligue nationale de football, unpublished).
24. On Paris Saint-Germain supporters, see Mignon, *La Passion du football* and 'Supporters et supportérisme au PSG, une identification problématique', in *Sociétés et Représentations* (forthcoming 1998).
25. *L'Express*, 16–22 July 1998.

Building the Finals:
Facilities and Infrastructure

HUGH DAUNCEY

Providing the facilities and infrastructures required by FIFA for staging the 64 Finals matches was a primary concern of the Comité français d'organisation de la Coupe du monde (CFO), French government and French football authorities. France's bid to host the World Cup had promised a national stadium seating 80,000, and FIFA required the other grounds to be able to safely seat 40,000. When the organisation of the Finals was originally awarded to France in July 1992 none of the regional club grounds were of a capacity or quality meeting FIFA requirements, and the proposed national stadium was still no more than the latest chapter of planning in a saga of sporting and political indecision dating back to the 1920s. The eventual success of France 98, during which Stade de France and regional grounds provided excellent facilities for teams, spectators and media, was enabled by frenetic activity during 1992–98 by CFO, the Fédération française de football (FFF), government and the clubs and towns whose grounds were selected (the bid was approved by FIFA in July 1992, and the CFO was created in November 1992).

Safety, seating and other improvements to regional grounds – most of which were relatively old and in need of modernisation – and the building from scratch of the Stade de France in Saint-Denis were thus the two major strands in France's material preparations for the World Cup. They can usefully be located within the context of two features of French football, sport, politics and society. The first of these is the nature of French football as a semi 'public service', an implication of which has been the traditional links – political and financial – between clubs and local authorities: municipalities are responsible for the upkeep of stadiums, and therefore renovating World Cup grounds unavoidably involved local, departmental and regional politics. The second feature combines the long-standing French psychodrama of indecision over building a national stadium and the traditional recourse in France to monumental architecture as a buttress to national prestige and identity. In the 1980s and 1990s President Mitterrand's Parisian *grands travaux* ('great works') – most famously the Grande Arche at La Défense, the Bastille Opéra and the Grande Bibliothèque – have illustrated the continuing temptation for the State to foster national identity and pride through monumental architecture.[1]

Building the 'Grand stade' (as it was long known) was controversial at every stage of selecting location, design, contractors and operators. Where and how the Grand stade was located was determined by politics, finance and national symbolism, and even naming the stadium provoked dispute between modernists favouring 'Stade Michel Platini' and traditionalists advocating 'Stade Charles de Gaulle', in reflection of the emotional symbolism of national monuments. The final choice of Stade de France seemed a compromise.[2] Politically and economically, design and location of the ground opposed Left and Right, central and local government, Prime Minister and Mayor of Paris, and catalysed debate over the profitability of hosting the World Cup in straitened convergence-criteria France. Occasionally, the Finals were used by national politicians as an electoral instrument, firstly by presidential-candidate Jacques Chirac in 1988 when he announced France's (and Paris's) bid for the competition, and secondly, by candidates Chirac and Balladur during the 1995 Presidential elections, when both attempted to monopolise the glory of bringing the Finals to France and the Grand stade to Paris. Now that the stadium is built and has served its (initial) purpose, controversy continues over its future role. Firstly, however, we shall examine the ways in which the regional stadiums were selected and renovated to host the World Cup.

Regional Stadiums: Where and What?

Ten stadiums were used for the 64 matches of the Finals. In addition to the Stade de France at Saint-Denis (nine matches), games in Paris took place also in the Parc des Princes (six), and in the provinces eight towns and cities hosted the remaining 49 fixtures. Bordeaux, Lens, Lyon, Marseille, Montpellier, Nantes, Saint-Etienne and Toulouse provided the locations for the regional dimension of France 98. Over half the stadiums were originally built in the 1930s and 1920s, and only the Stade de France was entirely new and purpose-built (in one sense) for France 98. Stadiums and the role they play in the lives of cities and of spectators are often the subject of interesting socio-cultural analyses of crowd behaviour, architecture and symbolic values.[3] Here, however, we restrict ourselves to a consideration of the economics and politics of how the regional grounds were chosen and improved.

Renovating and Improving Stadiums

The Stade de la Mosson in Montpellier is the next most recent construction, having been built only in 1987, whereas the Stade de la Beaujoire in Nantes was erected in 1983 in order to serve in the European Championships of 1984, hosted and won by France. The Parc des Princes in Paris, until the creation of the Stade de France, was the serving national stadium for football, rugby, other sports and major pop concerts. It was built in 1972 and hosted the final match of Euro 84. The table below lists these ten sites.

TABLE 1

THE TEN SITES OF MATCHES IN FRANCE 98

Town/city	Stadium	Capacity (matches)
Saint-Denis	Stade de France (1997)	80,000 (9)
Paris	Parc des Princes (1972)	48,275 (6)
Bordeaux	Stade du Parc Lescure (1935)	36,500 (6)
Lens	Stade Félix-Bollaert (1934)	41,275 (6)
Lyon	Stade de Gerland (1920)	44,000 (6)
Marseille	Stade Vélodrome (1937)	60,000 (7)
Montpellier	Stade de la Mosson (1987)	35,500 (6)
Nantes	Stade de la Beaujoire (1983)	38,500 (6)
Saint-Etienne	Stade Geoffroy Guichard (1931)	36,000 (6)
Toulouse	Stadium municipal (1934)	36,500 (6)

Total costs of improving these mostly rather old stadiums and of furnishing infrastructures around them were shared by central government, cities and regions. The *collectivités locales* (city, metropolitan, departmental and regional authorities) contributed overall over 1 billion francs simply to the renovation of grounds and the improvement of general urban facilities. This sum represented some two-thirds of the total costs. In offering to stage the matches of the preliminary rounds of the Finals, the regional host cities were aware that they would be able to use the event as international publicity, not only for purposes of future tourism, but also as a means of showcasing special industrial, scientific, educational or other strengths in the different French provinces. Another advantage for the regional cities in hosting the fixtures was that some of the funding from the state for stadium improvements and ancillary infrastructures could be used to finance improvements to other sporting facilities only tangentially of use to the World Cup. Moreover, French stadiums are traditionally multi-use, and thus sports other than football benefited from France 98.

The following table indicates how overall funding for stadium renovation and infrastructure development was shared between central government and the various city, departmental and regional authorities.

In some cases, the different tiers of municipal, departmental and regional government were happy to share relatively equally the costs of renovation and improvement not covered by central government funding. Thus in Bordeaux the city, the *Communauté urbaine* (metropolitan area), department and region were basically agreed to divide the expenses of

TABLE 2
STADIUM AND INFRASTRUCTURE DEVELOPMENT: SHARED COSTS

Town/city	Cost of Renovation (FF.)	State	City	Metrop. area	Dept.	Region
Saint-Denis	10m	–	10m	–	–	–
Paris	45m	–	45m	–	–	–
Bordeaux	75m	16.5m	14.3m	14.3m	14.3	14.3
Lens	145m	?	25m?	?	?	?
Lyon	213m	28m	114m	25m	25m	20m
Marseille	355m	107m	188m	–	30m	30m
Montpellier	130m	25m	82m	–	9m	14m
Nantes	42m	16m	17m	–	5.5m	4m
Saint-Etienne	98m	34m	28m	–	16m	20m
Toulouse	147m	37.5m	68m	–	10.35m	10.35m
TOTAL	1440m					

Source: 'Dix villes mobilisées pour la Coupe du monde 1998', La Gazette des communes, 9 June 1997.

uprating the Stade Lescure's safety, sound and floodlighting systems, installing extra seats, building a press centre and improving the players' quarters. In Lyon, similar but more expensive improvements were deemed more the responsibility of the city than of the metropolitan area, department or region. In Marseille, where the ageing Stade Vélodrome was important to the CFO and FIFA as a semi-final host ground, the state contributed more towards the high costs of increasing capacity, still leaving the city of Marseille with a very high bill.

Selecting Host Cities

The choice of the locations was made from an original list of 14 cities which had answered a call for bids launched by the CFO and the French government in consultation with FIFA. Throughout the process of selecting stadiums and improving their facilities, the CFO/DICOM (Délégation interministérielle à la coupe du monde) under Michel Pernier (responsible for infrastructures) and FIFA monitored the progress and quality of preparations, culminating in a final check of the grounds by FIFA a few weeks before the start of the competition. To a great extent, the possible host stadiums and cities were self-selecting, given the nature of French top-flight professional football where only a restricted number of top teams attract the followings to warrant large grounds, and FIFA's requirement that the ground should provide seating for 40,000 spectators. France's hosting of the 1984 European Championships and the infrastructure development that had then occurred also favoured some grounds, such as the Stade de la Beaujoire in Nantes, purpose-built in 1983.

From among the initial group of candidate cities, Rouen, Lille and Nancy soon withdrew because their regional authorities realised that the costs involved – even with subsidies from the State – would be too great. In the cases of Rouen and Nancy, new stadiums would have had to be constructed, and although Normandy and Lorraine were anxious not to be excluded from the 'tour de France' of French regions promised by the World Cup, in the financially straitened period of 1992–93 when submissions were being considered, it seemed that initial costs would exceed future benefits. In the case of Lille, a city as keen to host the World Cup matches as it was to stage the Olympic Games of 2004, planned enlargement and modernisation of the Villeneuve d'Ascq stadium was estimated at 300–400m francs, too much for the ambitions even of the influential former Socialist Prime Minister mayor of Lille Pierre Mauroy, and the sizeable Lille conurbation.

Proceeding alongside the imbroglio of choosing a site for the Grand stade, the selection of the regional stadiums seemed by contrast to be almost without controversy, although the case of Strasbourg illustrated various problems which eventually led to the city's self-exclusion from hosting any World Cup matches. Although in general, Strasbourg's Stade de la Meinau was considered to be of high quality, having been much renovated for Euro 84, it could only provide 17,000 seated places in contrast with the 40,000 still required by FIFA and the CFO. The cost of rebuilding the stadium to provide the extra seats was estimated at 200m francs, and another study budgeted the expenses of increasing capacity to only 36,000 at 160m francs. Even had Strasbourg been able to benefit from the eventual reduction in required seating capacity to 35,000, these costs would still have been considered too great by the city, departmental and regional authorities, who struggled with the government and CFO over their desire to host World Cup matches, but not at any price.[4]

Combined with the withdrawal of Nancy, Strasbourg's failure to comply with requirements meant that no World Cup matches would be hosted in the East of France, an omission which was viewed by the highly centralised French political and sporting establishments as sufficiently regrettable to warrant attempts to encourage Metz (D1) to submit a bid, in order that Republican equality of treatment for citizens of all regions could be guaranteed. When Metz was unable to produce a credible package for staging matches, the government had to accept the nine remaining cities (along with Saint-Denis and the Stade de France). Although this choice of sites was eventually made only in October 1994, for three of the stadiums concerned – in Lens, Marseille and Nantes – the agreement with the CFO was still ultimately dependent on the provision of a satisfactory financial framework.

Throughout the process of choosing appropriate stadiums, CFO and government struggled with attempts by the cities concerned to reduce the minimum seating requirement, and to persuade the State to provide more money for ground improvements. The initial offer from the Bérégovoy government in November 1992 was to finance 30 per cent of renovation and improvements, but as Rouen, Lille, Nancy and then Strasbourg successively ruled themselves out of France 98 and as the remaining candidate-cities realised the expenses involved, calls arose to raise state funding to 40 per cent or more. Despite different scales of works required in different stadiums, host cities argued that the state should contribute up to 44.5 per cent of costs, reflecting government financing of the Albertville Winter Olympics in 1992; another argument was that regional stadiums should receive the same proportion of central government funding as the new Stade de France (approaching 50 per cent). The final figure fixed in March 1996 was 36 per cent, when Prime Minister Alain Juppé agreed to raise total State funding of stadium renovations to 305m francs.[5]

Local politicians in the candidate cities were united in their desires to see the state contribute as high a proportion of costs as possible, and in general, local and regional political opinion supported their bids to involve the cities in France 98. In some cases, however, political difficulties in the provinces made bids more complicated to bring to fruition than others. In Strasbourg, conflict between the Ville de Strasbourg, the Conseil général and the Région Alsace over the costs to the city, department and region of rebuilding the stadium caused the withdrawal of the application, as mayor Catherine Trautmann (Parti socialiste – PS) insisted on demonstrating cost-efficient Socialist administration of public money to the centre-right Balladur government (1993–95).[6]

Elsewhere, in Lens, Marseille, Nantes and Saint-Etienne the campaign for the June 1995 municipal elections gave rise to disagreements between Left and Right at different levels in local and regional politics over details of funding, although some commentators saw overall consensus in the shared belief that hosting matches would focus attention on the cities.[7] In Lens, the Socialist mayor André Delelis criticised the centre-right government for refusing further State funding for the Stade Félix-Bollaert, arguing that the North of France, severely hit by recession, needed special treatment and 'national solidarity' (region and department were both prepared only to match state funding, thus leading to further conflict). In Marseille the Conseil général of Bouches-du-Rhône and the Conseil régional of Provence-Alpes-Côte d'Azur disagreed with the Town Hall over the validity of two different costings as various politicians (including Tapie) manoeuvred to prepare future electoral campaigns.[8] In Nantes, although planned changes to the La Beaujoire stadium were amongst the least expensive of all infrastructure improvements, negotiations were delicate between Town Hall (PS) and Conseil général (Rassemblement pour la République – RPR) over the funding package most convincing to the CFO. In Saint-Etienne, in contrast to near neighbour Lyon's unanimous support for World Cup matches, centre-right mayor Michel Thiollière (Union pour la démocratie française – UDF), although having successfully negotiated with PM Balladur to increase State funding for ground improvements, was in conflict with local Communist and Green politicians. Subsequently in 1997, after his defeat in the general election, when Prime Minister Alain Juppé returned to Bordeaux to devote himself full-time to his job as mayor, the Socialist Conseil général reacted badly to his complaints that the city was contributing too much in comparison with department and region, further complicating progress of renovations to the Stade Lescure, whose cost was gradually increasing.[9]

Why Montpellier but not Strasbourg?

The final list of cities hosting matches was in some other senses predictable. The history of football in France, itself linked to industrialisation and the demography of French towns and cities, combined with political traditions of centralism and contemporary moves towards more responsibility for the regions, created a complex of forces favouring regional capitals. The French urban hierarchy is characterised by the pre-eminent position of the Paris conurbation (almost 10 million inhabitants) and an almost perfectly logarithmic rank-size distribution of regional centres marked by small populations compared with the primate Paris. Table 3 demonstrates the relative populations of the host cities and their conurbations in comparison with other urban centres in France.

Such a comparison reveals a number of initially perhaps surprising anomalies. Although Montpellier is low in the urban hierarchy, it was ambitious to host World Cup matches as part of its long-term strategy of self-promotion whose proud slogan is 'Montpellier la surdouée'. The local city and regional authorities have invested heavily in football over the last 20 years which have seen the club rise from the Division d'honneur (Third Division) to European competitions, and the mayor and the president of the Regional Council undertook a regional tour as early as 1996 to publicise the city's hosting of the World Cup among the local population. They were able, before the end of 1997, to measure economic effects, in terms of jobs, with many local firms working on the renovations to the stadium, the smallest of the ten, its capacity being enlarged by 50 per cent to turn it into a 35,500 all-seater stadium. The Montpellier conurbation has grown rapidly over the past 20 years, fuelling the ambitions of its long-term mayor Georges Frèche.

TABLE 3

POPULATION OF HOST CITY CONURBATIONS

Rank	Urban centre	Conurbation	City/town
1	**Paris**	9m	2.2m
2	**Lyon**	1.26m	422,000
3	**Marseille**	1.1m	807,000
4	Lille	0.9m	364,000
5	**Bordeaux**	0.69m	214,00
6	**Toulouse**	0.6m	365,000
7	**Nantes**	0.5m	245,000
8	Nice	0.48m	342,000
9	Toulon	0.44m	167,000
10	Grenoble	0.4m	150,000
11	Strasbourg	0.39m	252,000
12	Rouen	0.38m	102,000
13	Grasse-Cannes-Antibes	0.34m	222,000
14	Valenciennes	0.34m	58,000
15	**Lens**	0.32m	35,000
16	**Saint-Etienne**	0.31m	199,000
17	Nancy	0.31m	100,000
18	Tours	0.27m	230,000
19	Béthune	0.26m	49,000
20	Clermont-Ferrand	0.25m	136,000
21	Le Havre	0.25m	196,000
22	Rennes	0.24m	197,000
23	Orléans	0.24m	105,000
24	**Montpellier**	0.23m	210,000
25	Dijon	0.23m	147,000

Considering Strasbourg's ranking in the urban hierarchy and the success of its football team (recently taken over by an ambitious business consortium led by IMG), its absence from the list of host cities seems all the more regrettable, whereas the early failure of bids from Rouen and Nancy seems easily explicable, given their populations and the fact that Nancy was playing in Division 2 and Rouen competes in the lowly Championnat de France amateur (CFA) division. The collapse of Lille's candidature seems intriguing given the city's status as the major northern population centre and a team in Division 2, but the presence nearby of Lens and its highly successful D1 team (1997/98 champions) with the excellent facilities of the Stade Félix Bollaert and good regional support undermined support for the application. Grenoble (CFA), Nice (CFA) and Toulon (D2) did not submit bids, partly because of their lack of sufficiently developed local footballing tradition and facilities, but also because of Marseille's domination of football in the South East; Nice in particular has an image as a resort which fitted ill with staging fixtures for the Mondial. Cannes, similarly overshadowed by Marseille in football (despite AC Cannes playing in D1) is arguably more preoccupied with its status as a centre for culture than with associating itself with the World Cup. The position of Saint-Etienne, geographically close to Lyon and relatively low down the urban hierarchy, would normally suggest that it would lose out to its much larger neighbour; although doubts were expressed over fixtures occurring in closely located sites, the great footballing tradition of Saint-Etienne (despite currently being in D2) and the facilities available at Stade Geoffroy-Guichard outweighed such concerns.

All regional host cities were anxious to use the World Cup as another element in their image communication. French regions often see themselves in competition with each other for inwards investment, state subsidies, tourism and media attention. Bordeaux and Toulouse, for example, historical rivals as capitals of the Aquitaine and Midi-Pyrénées regions, are still competing in industry, science and technology. As the regions, regional cities and departments gradually gain measures of greater autonomy from Paris under decentralisation and as interaction with European partners intensifies, peripheral urban centres such as Bordeaux, Toulouse and Strasbourg are becoming increasingly aware of the need for a European image, with Bordeaux and Toulouse turning towards Spain, and Strasbourg exploiting historical links between Alsace-Lorraine and Germany.

Hosting the Olympics was also a privilege for which French regional cities were competing. Lyon and Lille were vying to become France's candidate to stage the Olympic Games of 2004. Paris was not in the competition, despite having narrowly lost the Games of 1992 to Barcelona, and despite the prospect of a newly-completed Grand stade, Mayor Chirac was reluctant to risk adding the costs of the Olympics to France 98.[10] Lille and Lyon were convinced that their strategies would benefit image communication and development of sporting and urban infrastructures, but there was also concern – mirroring that of Paris – that the eventual cost to the State of the Albertville Olympics implied a need for caution. Lille was eventually selected by the French Olympic committee (Comité national olympique et sportif français – CNOSF) to be France's candidate.[11]

Paris: The Parc des Princes

The Parc des Princes stadium, sited in a well-to-do area in the west of Paris, provides an interesting link between consideration of 'provincial' infrastructures and those to be renovated or created *ex nihilo* in Paris and Saint-Denis. The Parc, ground of the top-flight Paris Saint-Germain (D1) club is maintained by the Ville de Paris, who financed stadium renovations for France 98, and although owned by the pay-per-view TV channel Canal Plus since 1991, PSG receives some 30m francs annually from the Town hall. Constructed in 1972 as a replacement for the ageing Colombes stadium and now run by a company wholly owned by Canal Plus, the Parc has been a successful venue for international soccer and rugby matches and has provided a useful home to PSG during the 1980s and 1990s.[12] The stadium has always suffered however from problems of congestion linked to its site at the Porte de Saint-Cloud and from concerns over its effects on the quality of life in a politically sensitive area of Paris. Too small to host the World Cup Final (48,000 capacity after renovations) although it staged the final of Euro 84, the Parc saw itself relegated to a supporting role in the Paris area to the Stade de France, the successful future exploitation of which – as we will see – is closely linked to whether PSG will continue to use their traditional ground, or become the resident-club of the new national stadium.

The Stade de France: Political Football?

In December 1995 the controversial 'Grand stade' under construction at Saint-Denis was officially named the Stade de France. In November 1997, after 26 months of work, the stadium was completed at a cost of 2.67bn francs, 53 per cent financed by the private sector and 47 per cent by the French State. Each French citizen had thus contributed 20 francs to the national stadium, in an innovatory contract between the State and the Consortium Stade de France which for the first time entrusted design, funding, building and running of a large sports facility to the private sector.[13] Since the 1920s France has faced the dilemma of whether and how to create a national stadium, and building the Stade de France for France 98 was a complicated dossier for government.

Not Choosing a National Stadium (1924–98)

In 1924 the specially built Colombes stadium in the Paris suburbs hosted the Olympics, and in the 1930s and 1940s national stadiums of 80,000–100,000 capacity were proposed in Passy (1936), Montesson and Vincennes (1945). In 1936 the announcement of France's hosting of the 1938 World Cup, given the 60,000 capacity of Colombes, heightened French ambitions to create a stadium comparable with Berlin's Reichssportfeld; moreover, the 1937 Paris Exposition Universelle offered further opportunity to demonstrate French genius. Architects Pingusson and Mallet-Stevens proposed developing a sports quarter in Paris with a huge horse-shoe shaped stadium on the Quai de Passy (near the Parc des Princes vélodrome, Stade Jean-Bouin, Roland Garros and Molitor baths). Le Corbusier proposed a 100,000 capacity 'National Centre for Celebration' ('Centre national de réjouissance') in the Bois de Vincennes, but despite desires to rival German architectural and sporting achievements, the Popular Front remained true to improving the lot of ordinary French citizens, and faithful to its creation of a secrétariat d'Etat aux Sports et aux Loisirs in 1936, funded local sports facilities and *sport de masse* rather than *sport d'élite*.[14] The 1938 World Cup Final was played in Colombes before a crowd of only 58,000.

The Vichy régime accorded great importance to sport in maintaining national moral and physical fitness, and in 1943 plans were initiated to create a 'Parc olympique national' of 100,000 places in the Bois de Vincennes, but the Liberation, and creating the Fourth Republic shelved discussion until 1949, when returning social, political and economic stability and healthy attendances at matches (such as France 2 – England 1 at a capacity Colombes in 1946) suggested to Parisian politicians and businessmen that a new stadium could be profitable. Between 1949 and 1956 the SIPECS business consortium (Société immobilière parisienne d'études et de constructions sportives) considered plans for a stadium honouring Resistance hero Jean Moulin (or boxer Marcel Cerdan), but despite plans to stage France's 1952 Cup Final, bureaucratic difficulties and a competing project proposing an enlarged Colombes eventually caused plans to be frozen.

Under the Fifth Republic, renewed government interest in sport (the Haut commissariat à la Jeunesse et aux Sports was created in 1958) encouraged interest in 1960 for a national stadium, and the old Stade Pershing was chosen for a 100,000 capacity ground. Despite efforts to create a mixed public-private sector company to build and run the stadium, usual problems of rival projects and concerns over urban planning in Vincennes meant that only after President de Gaulle's final appeal did PM Pompidou decide (in 1962) to locate the ground there, funded and managed in partnership between the Ville de Paris and the public-sector bank la Caisse des dépôts. A stadium design was chosen by competition in 1965, only for further concerns over its impact on Vincennes to lead to its cancellation.

With the transformation of the old cycling stadium in west Paris into the new Parc des Princes in 1972, providing an arena for national rugby and football matches of about 45,000 capacity, thinking about another national stadium was shelved until the early 1980s and France and Paris' applications for the 1990 World Cup and 1992 Olympics. After the 1990 World Cup went to Italy, and France's Olympic bid lost to Barcelona in 1987, the 1988 Presidential election witnessed Mayor of Paris and right-wing presidential candidate Jacques Chirac's call for France to host the 1998 World Cup, necessitating the construction of a high-capacity stadium in Paris or the Paris region. The current chapter in the saga of a national stadium began in 1988, and in the decade of preparation leading to France 98 its planning became a political and social-cultural puzzle. The why, where, how and what of the Grand stade are questions encompassing many typical issues of French politics. In the following sections, we trace these different issues as they have interacted in the voluminous dossier of the national stadium.

Choosing the Site

How the site for the Grand stade was chosen revealed how competition between areas on the outskirts of Paris, in the Paris suburbs and in the Paris region responded to motivations of prestige for local politicians as well as to the desire to develop infrastructures and to attract economic activity. More tangible than advantages derived on a national level in terms of image and tourism are the infrastructure development and commercial activities which accompany the construction, initial use and afterlife of stadiums. In discussing the choice of site for the new stadium it is useful to consider what became known in debates over the Grand stade as its two principal *logiques de développement,* or rationales.

The first rationale conceives the construction and use of a stadium to be principally informed by the French tradition of *aménagement du territoire* (regional development), whereas the second considers primarily commercial profitability. For the first rationale, World Cup and building of

3. Michel Platini (Co-president of the French Organising Committee) and Blatter (President of FIFA).

4. The Stade de France.

the Grand stade were linked with infrastructure provision and urban renewal, placing France 98 in the context of post-war regional development. For the second rationale, constructing and running the Grand stade were seen as catalysing local business, linking national prestige with commercial rejuvenation.[15] The extent to which purely sporting factors were absent from the debate indicated how 'political' the issue of the national stadium became. The logic of *aménagement du territoire* saw the Grand stade as an element in the existing overall plan for developing the Paris region (the 'schéma directeur d'aménagement de la région parisienne') using transport and other infrastructures necessary for the new stadium to reduce East–West inequalities in the Paris area. Since the 1960s and before, the State has created new towns and new axes of development in order to compensate the east of Paris for the concentration of facilities and prosperity in the West, and the Socialist governments of 1988–91 were committed to this equality through their White paper on the Paris area (the *Livre blanc de la région parisienne*). Taken to its extreme, as critics pointed out, this rationale would lead to 'a national stadium in a field of sugarbeet', whose construction would bring infrastructures, but where the subsequent operation of the stadium would be economically impossible because of distance from Paris.

Conflicting rationales for the Grand stade were compounded by conflict between Matignon and Mairie de Paris for control of the project. Initially in December 1988, oversight of planning the stadium was entrusted by Chirac as *Maire de Paris* to his Director of sports Jacques Perrilliat, who became the first 'Monsieur Grand stade' when he considered the feasibility of sites at Vincennes and Colombes, both soon rejected because of local concerns about the environment and quality of life, and political fall-out from these worries. In October 1989, central government responsibility for the Grand stade was attributed to Jean Glavany (later interministerial delegate for the preparation of the Albertville Olympics), appointed from Matignon by Prime Minister Rocard, whose government was apparently giving full support to the World Cup bid. In parallel with Glavany's planning, discussions involving interested ministries such as Transport, Equipment and Housing, the Ville de Paris continued to sound public opinion and prepare possible legal statutes for the stadium. Both Glavany and Perrilliat listed potential locations, illustrating the division (and conflict) of responsibilities created by rivalry between left-wing Matignon and the right-wing Town Hall.

'Stade urbain' or 'Stade champêtre'?

More than a simple choice between *Urba* and *Rus,* where, in what form and how the stadium was to be built depended on the equilibrium reached between the different logics and the competing political ambitions of local and national politicians. As the final selection of the Grand stade site eventually revealed, a kind of balance between commercial viability and development was possible, but even when the logical compromise had been reached, competition between rival sites lengthened the selection process, already made unwieldy by tension between Matignon and Ville de Paris. Significantly, as an indication of the increasing political importance of the dossier, the sole contributions to the debate of French sports movements were preferences expressed by the CNOSF for a stadium in Vincennes, which was one of the first locations to be ruled out (not for sporting reasons but because of its electoral sensitivity) and for Nanterre, a site in the West of Paris also quickly eliminated. The 26 sites initially considered by Glavany were reduced in September 1990 to only seven still maintaining their applications, or entering late bids.[16]

The candidates remaining were Cergy-Pontoise, Massy, Nanterre-La Défense, Tremblay-en-France, Vigneux-sur-Seine, Melun-Sénart, and Saint-Quentin-en-Yvelines, but the selection procedure was still far from complete. From September 1990 until end-1992 bids were gradually rejected through Rocard's preliminary choice of Melun-Sénart in February 1991, doubts in Melun-Sénart about the financial viability of the project, the launch of a new bid from Nanterre backed by the (unusual) left-right team of politicians Michel Sapin and Charles Pasqua, and final confirmation of Melun-Sénart by Socialist Prime Minister Pierre Bérégovoy in December 1992. In May 1993 a new centre-right government inevitably reopened the dossier, attracting new bids from Rosny-sous-Bois, Marne-la-Vallée and Gonesses (Val-d'Oise) but Prime Minister Edouard Balladur then rejected the new town of Melun-Sénart, and chose the old *banlieue* of Saint-Denis. Saint-Denis had been preferred by the Mairie de Paris, as soon as the impracticability of building the Grand stade within Paris itself had been realised: la Plaine du Cornillon in Saint-Denis contained suitable land owned by the Mairie de Paris, and a new national stadium so close to Paris would strengthen future bids from Paris to host the Olympics.

Saint-Denis represented compromise between the rationales of *aménagement* and commercial stimulus whose confrontation had led initially to the consideration of sites as different as La Défense, former Renault factory land at Boulogne-Billancourt and Nanterre (in the West), the bois de Vincennes and new towns (in the East). Whereas in Marne-la-Vallée and Melun-Sénart, the stadium would have operated purely as a measure of *aménagement*, in Vincennes and La Défense, already well-provided for in infrastructure it would have been seen more a measure of commercial catalysis. In comparison with these sites, and with Tremblay-en-France, whose advantage was precisely its centrality to rail, air and motorways, Saint-Denis allowed the Grand stade to serve both for (re)-development through improvement of transport links and also as a spur to a stagnating local economy. Final confirmation of Saint-Denis in September 1993 by Minister of Youth and Sports Alliot-Marie led the saga of the Grand stade to its next chapter: deciding the partnership between central and local government, between private and public sectors and the choice of stadium design.

How and What?

Initially the State hoped that funding the Grand stade would come from the private sector, but the proportion of public finance of the project grew progressively, eventually reaching 47 per cent. Choosing architects and builders proved complicated, and concerns arose over the 'transparency' of the selection *concours*, and the neutrality of government in the face of the powerful Bouygues construction consortia tendering (with others) for the contract.

Debate over the split of funding between state and private sector was complicated by political manoeuvrings: in 1990, Chirac suggested that the Grand stade would require 60 per cent – 80 per cent of funding from the private sector, given the Socialist government's difficulties in limiting public spending. In an indication of party-political differences over this division of financing between State and the market, Chirac simultaneously questioned the State's readiness to consider such public-private collaboration, implicitly accusing the government of jeopardising the stadium through ideological dislike of private finance.[17]

Because of the estimated high costs (2bn francs for the stadium and up to 6bn francs for transport, parking and other facilities) and its national importance, the State was always likely to be closely involved in building and managing the new stadium, although Rocard's preferred bid from Melun-Sénart claimed to require no State funding. Given the Rocard governments' notorious attachment to budgetary rigour, many saw the choice of Melun-Sénart as financially and politically inspired, made to give the stadium to a Socialist new town, whose *aménagement* through the RER (regional rail network) and TGV would induce private investors to fund the construction of the stadium.

However, during Melun-Sénart's attempts to find private funding, it transpired that despite low costing of construction at 1.4bn francs and provision of transport and other infrastructures by the State, finding a private franchise company to manage the construction and running of the stadium was impossible.[18] Thus Bérégovoy's reconfirmation of Melun-Sénart in December 1992, despite political disagreement between department, region and town (and despite a bid from Nanterre/Hauts-de-Seine promising solely private and departmental finance), underlined Socialist attachment to the *schéma directeur*. Perhaps confirming Chirac's criticisms of 1990, the State seemingly preferred to pay more for the Grand stade in order to site it where it chose.

Once Saint-Denis was chosen, the partnership between state, private enterprise and local government which was agreed – a *société nationale d'économie mixte* (SEM) – partly answered questions about the State's involvement in the national stadium, with the novel feature for this type of company that the State was the principal partner (51 per cent), in recognition of the importance and risks of the project.[19] The State's contribution to building the stadium was initially set at 1.3bn francs, out of a final estimated total of 2.7bn francs, and although the 'SEM-Grand stade' was State-controlled, much emphasis was placed on the private sector responsibility (unique in an undertaking of this nature) for more than half the costs.[20] Created in 1994, the SEM-Grand stade is intended to have a life span of some six to ten years, first entrusting the control of the building process to another *société d'économie mixte* (la SANEM) before withdrawing in 2000–2002 to leave the exploitation of the mature stadium to its franchise holders Consortium-Grand stade SA, a three-way equal partnership between the Bouygues, Dumez and SGE companies.[21]

The natural French consensus over locating the Grand stade in or near Paris was mirrored by agreement over its necessary multifunctionality. Early in selecting the site, Jacques Chirac voiced the prevailing view that the stadium must not only seat 80,000 spectators, but would also have to be 'multi-use', suitable for a variety of sports as well as rock-concerts and other events. Choosing a multi-use stadium (more expensive to build) reflected the concern that investment in building the Grand stade should pay commercial returns after the World Cup, and was also intended to help future Parisian bids to host the Olympics.

The different designs proposed various ways of ensuring optimum utilisation of the Grand stade, ranging from straightforward inclusion of facilities for multiple sports through ranges of cultural events to the use of areas underground for storage of rainwater. More conventionally, office space in the stadium was proposed to house the Ministry of Youth and Sports or as premises for university sports training centres, and a shopping centre named 'Francilia' was suggested. Anticipating the hosting of the Olympics, plans also included accommodation for competitors in an 'Olympic village' and further housing around the stadium. Choosing the stadium design followed a two-stage competition procedure (or *concours*), which examined entries first in terms of architecture, disruption of the existing built-environment and their contribution to the local community, and secondly by cost. The first stage of selection in May 1994 retained seven submissions, plus one bid exceptionally carried forward because of its low comparative cost. The *concours* was criticised for its apparent conflation of criteria of design, cost and exploitation, thus allegedly leading to choices based less on architectural and aesthetic merit than on mere finance.[22]

Other critics saw this double selection process (described as a *'concours conception-construction'*) as a stratagem intended to settle two issues at once, namely the question of the architecture and construction of the stadium and its intended use and management. After the drawn-out wranglings over the stadium site, mixed criteria of design and exploitation supposedly enabled choices to be made more rapidly; the selection procedure was in fact completed in 'record time', as was claimed by *délégué interministériel* Kosciusco-Morizet. In total, eight bids had to be evaluated. There were four bids involving the Bouygues construction consortium (including the eventual winners Macary-Zublena-Costantini-Regembal and the 'bad-loser' Jean Nouvel-Cattani-Dragages), one bid from GTM-Entrepose (associated with the architects Pierre Chaix and Jean-Paul Morel), and three from Eiffages, including the project considered for its low costing presented by Alain Serfati.

Two projects proposed by Bouygues were selected in July 1994 (Macary-Zublena-Costantini-Regembal and Nouvel-Cattani), leading to Prime Minister Balladur's final choice of the Macary-Zublena package in October 1994. The success of Bouygues in monopolising the final play-off of bids created concern, and some competing teams of architects resented the ambiguity behind the final decision, since it was unclear whether the jury choosing the best design had had the last word, or whether ultimate choice remained with government. The losing finalist Jean Nouvel initiated legal action in protest at 'une rupture manifeste de l'égalité' (blatant inequality) in the procedure of the *concours*.[23] Nouvel eventually took his case to the European Commission, which decided in January 1997 that the French government's running of the selection procedures for designing, building and managing the stadium flouted European law on free competition in contract-tendering.[24]

The Stade de France and Sport after 1998

After its inaugural match on 28 January 1998 between France and Spain, a couple of Five Nations rugby matches, two French football cup finals, an international friendly, the opening match of the World Cup, seven other World Cup fixtures and the World Cup Final itself, the Stade de France was turned over to the Rolling Stones on 25 July; in September 1998 the Stones were followed by the French rocker Johnny Hallyday, as the Stade demonstrated its multi-use capabilities. Throughout debates over building the stadium, doubts were voiced about the future of the Stade de France, much in the way that scepticism over the real need for a giant stadium prevented one from being built between 1924 and 1998. Today, critics fear the Stade de France will be a white elephant beyond 1998, however carefully choices of design and management structures aimed to guarantee commercial profitability. Such sceptics point to the dearth of major competitions suitable to be staged in the stadium and note the surfeit of sports venues in Paris which threatens to make the Stade de France a *fin-de-siècle* folly.[25] The sports movement in general has been ambivalent about the Stade de France: the CNOSF and other sporting federations often saw their preferences of site and design ignored by government.

The government was always aware of the dangers of the Stade de France becoming a sporting *Marie Céleste* – a vast grey vessel floating abandoned on the Parisian skyline – as was the construction and management consortium. The best and perhaps the only way of ensuring continued regular use of the stadium after 12 July 1998 (apart from occasional visits by the Stones and Johnny) was always considered to be finding a top-flight football team to adopt the Stade as its home ground.[26] In its contract with the Consortium Stade de France the government rashly guaranteed that a first division football club would use the stadium throughout the period of the concession (until 2025). The search for such a club became a saga almost as long and involved as the original selection process for a site for the stadium, but for the management consortium, however, finding a resident club was not such a pressing matter, since the State is obliged to pay them an average yearly public subsidy of 70m francs as compensation for the loss of earnings from a top-flight football club. Considered by many to provide the consortium with risk-free exploitation of the stadium, this clause in the contract nevertheless allows the State the option of 'buying back' the Stade de France in 2000/2001 for 1.4bn francs.

At one stage it was envisaged that a new D1 club should be created – it was agreed that a region the size of the Ile de France should have more than Paris Saint-Germain – but such utopian visions foundered on the realities of French football. Indeed, given the structure of French football in general (relatively few professional teams) and the fact that PSG is inescapably the only D1 club in the Paris area, government pressure on PSG to move to Saint-Denis was considerable. However, the fact that PSG's home ground is the Parc des Princes and that abandoning the Parc would render it obsolete in much the same way that the Parc des Princes had killed Colombes in 1972 meant that the Ville de Paris (which contributes 33m francs annually to the PSG) was disinclined to allow the move to take place.[27] PSG-Canal Plus were apparently prepared to consider the change of ground, interested to see how the State and the Mairie de Paris would compete with each other to maintain their favours, but withdrew their candidature in April 1998, leaving only the minor clubs Red Star 93 (D2), Saint-Denis-Saint-Leu-

Sarcelles (*National*) and Racing Club de France (*National*) in the frame.[28] In June 1998 Red Star was finally chosen by the sports ministry to become the *club résident* of the Stade de France, providing that they attract enough funding to guarantee promotion to D1 in 1999/2000 (they are also required to qualify for European competitions). By the late-summer of 1998, their budget still seemed too low.

France 98 and the Role of the State in French Sport

Creating improved provincial stadium facilities illustrated the role of government in sport in the regions, where the national, republican ethos of sport as a public service applies through municipal funding of football clubs, and where sharing infrastructure costs of France 98 between State, city, department and region reflected joint responsibility for costs and profits of the World Cup. Planning and building the Stade de France revealed much about relationships between government, Mairie de Paris and local authorities, between government and sport, and between state and market. Vacillating site selection for the stadium suggested a case-study in *indécision urbaine* and *incompétence technocratique*, where rivalries between Left and Right, central and local government, Matignon and Paris combined chaotically, eventually satisfying a public wearied by endless changes of policy. The sporting community itself was systematically ignored, except when the government was obliged to withdraw its plan to avoid budget difficulties by partly funding the Grand stade from the Fonds national pour le développement du sport (FNDS), traditionally intended for mass sport rather than national monuments.[29]

Planning the Stade de France arguably fell between different rationales of construction and purpose: some maintain that post-1995, under Mitterrandian principles, 'political' (national-symbolic) criteria would have prevailed, whereas Rocardian financial constraints in the early years of planning the stadium followed by subsequent right-wing predilections for market solutions emphasised arguments of cost. Moreover, claims for the triumph of private finance in franchising the stadium are invalidated by the provisions for government compensation should its future prove unprofitable. This was precisely a complaint of the European Commission, who deemed that the French government's guarantees to Bouygues effectively ensured loss-free running of the stadium and contravened competition law.

Mayor Chirac's troublemaking for Prime Minister Rocard in 1990 showed how considering private finance in building and running the stadium highlighted residual disagreements between Left and Right over public sector and market, and problems in finding full private funding for a project of such national and public importance underlined contradictions inherent in pursuing a policy of *grand monuments* through reliance on the market. Chirac's political manoeuvring verged on the demagogic, and showed how easily the Grand stade periodically became a political football. Fraught relations between public and private sectors in France also seemed to undermine the French bid for the 2004 Olympics, which required close collaboration between State and market.[30]

European Commission disquiet over negotiations for the concession to build and run the stadium reflected a variety of problems in French politics concerning the influence of big construction companies such as Bouygues, the recurrent desire of French governments to indulge a national economic preference in prestige contracts, and the tension between creating the Stade de France as a monument for all of France, whose losses would be borne by the taxpayer but whose profits would go to the private sector. For Brussels, building the Stade de France amounted to a public-works contract subject to Commission rulings on public sector tendering, whereas the French government presented the stadium as a triumph of private sector initiative. In addition to the risk-free running of the stadium guaranteed by state compensation if a resident club could not be found, the mix between public- and private-sector finance was criticised by the European Commission, as was the clause in the concession which required 25 per cent of building work to be provided by local construction companies. Moreover, Brussels deemed the Balladur government to have significantly changed the terms of the concession tendered for by Bouygues-SGE-Dumez even while its signing was being prepared. A final criticism was that the consortium was also awarded contracts worth almost 4.5bn francs to create other infrastructures around the Stade de France without any call for competitive tenders. Notified in January 1997 of these charges, with the threat of further debate in the European Court of Justice if the anomalies were not rectified, the French government remained adamant that stadium construction would continue. Paris was confident that building the Stade de France could not be stopped and refused to renegotiate the concession. Although the European Commission eventually acknowledged defeat in April 1998, accepting the elimination of the 'local preference' for construction companies as proof that France had recognised her guilt, within France concerns were still voiced.

A confidential study by the Cour des Comptes (French National Audit Office) questioned the whole process of choosing the Bouygues-CGE-Dumez consortium to build and run the stadium. The courts in Paris agreed that Eiffage-Spie-Batignolles had been treated unfairly and awarded 25m francs in damages from the government, and a deal between the government and architect Jean Nouvel amounted to an admission of unfairness in the rejection of his design. Some commentators even saw the precipitation and favourable terms with which Balladur had given the contract to the Bouygues-led consortium as the price he paid for enjoying the support of the TF1 television channel (owned by Bouygues) during the 1995 presidential election.

Overall, building and running the Stade de France represents a complicated hybrid of public and private sector finance and motivations of *service public* and commercial profit. To use the terminology of Bourdieu and of the general debate in France over finding a new role for the state and a new *modus vivendi* between State and market, as 47 per cent 'public' and 53 per cent 'private' the national stadium reflects the gaining strength of the 'neo-liberal' ethos in French politics and society. As a hybrid, the Stade is unacceptable to Brussels, which sees no role for the State in such infrastructure development, and as the *Bosman* ruling and free-market principles in sport take effect in France, French football clubs in general will soon lose their municipal funding and force French sport ever more into the neo-liberal marketplace.

NOTES

1. See F. Chaslin, *Les Paris de François Mitterrand* (Paris, Gallimard, 1985) and S. Collard, 'Mission impossible: les chantiers du Président', *French Cultural Studies*, 2 (1992), 97–132.
2. J.-M. Faure and C. Suaud of the CNRS/Nantes University are undertaking a study of the naming of the stadium.
3. See, for example, J. Bale and O. Moen (eds.), *The Stadium and the City* (Keele, Keele University Press, 1995).
4. See 'Trop chère la Coupe du monde !', *Strasbourg Magazine*, January 1995, 20–1. and 'Strasbourg hésite devant le Mondial', *Le Monde Heures locales*, 21 June 1993, 21.
5. See 'Les villes qui accueilleront la Coupe du monde de football pressent l'Etat d'accroître sa participation', *Le Monde*, 4 November 1993, 19 and '16 millions de francs supplémentaires pour la préparation de la Coupe du monde de football de 1998', *Le Monde*, 4 March 1996, 17.
6. Trautmann had implemented a rectification of the parlous financial situation of Racing Club de Strasbourg involving further public money, followed by gradual withdrawal of municipal funding: M. Scotto, 'La ville de Strasbourg cède au privé un club de football en bonne santé', *Le Monde*, 20 February 1997, 29, and M. Scotto, 'L'Alsace et la Lorraine privées de Coupe du monde', *Le Monde*, 5 June 1998, 25.
7. C. de Chenay, 'Des "Grands stades" très consensuels', *Le Monde*, 31 October 1994, 8.
8. G. Porte, 'L'agrandissement du stade de Marseille est enfin financé', *Le Monde*, 1 March 1995, 23.
9. See P. Cherrua, 'Dérive financière pour la rénovation du parc Lescure', *Le Monde*, 22 March 1997, 23 and C. Courtois, 'Alain Juppé se remet à l'heure bordelaise', *Le Monde*, 7 July 1997, 5.
10. J.-J. Bozonnet, 'L'ombre de Paris en filigrane des candidatures de Lille et de Lyon pour les Jeux olympiques de 2004', *Le Monde*, 7 November 1995, 23.
11. See J.-R. Lore, 'Nous étions la candidature de la passion', B. Causse, 'Les Lyonnais s'interrogent sur les raisons de leur échec', *Le Monde*, 9 November 1995, 24, and 'L'ambition olympique', *Le Monde*, 8 November 1995, 14.

12. See B. Moulin, 'PSG omnisports, le club orchestre', *Sports Magazine*, 20 (March 1996), 78–85, and F. Ragot, 'Canal + tisse sa toile sur le football mondial, *Sports Magazine*, 35 (September 1997), 70–1.

13. See *Loi No. 94–1435* of 31 December 1993 (Paris, Documentation française, 1994).

14. For a stimulating recent overview of contemporary French sports policy, see P. Dine, 'Sport and the State in Contemporary France: from *la Charte des Sports* to decentralisation', *Modern & Contemporary France*, 6, 3 (August 1998), 301–11.

15. See 'Grand stade: l'illusion d'un débat urbain', *Urbanisme*, 259 (December 1992), 10–13, and M. Sutter 'Les ambitions du Grand stade', *Urbanisme et architecture*, 241 (October 1990), 11–13.

16. Glavany was much criticised by the Right, see J.-P. Lacour, 'Le Grand stade à petits pas', *Le Figaro*, 13 September 1990, and Y. Hervaux, 'Grand stade: le quarté dans le désordre', *Quotidien de Paris*, 6 November 1990, 23.

17. See F. Varenne, 'Grand stade: capitaux privés ou non ?', *Le Figaro*, 9 July 1990, 18.

18. 450m francs was to be provided by the government, thus helping to make the exploitation of the stadium profitable for private enterprise.

19. The SEM-Grand stade brings together with the state the Ville de Saint-Denis, the Caisse des dépôts et consignations, EDF-GDF, the department of Seine-Saint-Denis, the CCI de Paris and the SCET. See *Journal Officiel*, 18 August 1994, 1382.

20. Another issue settled was the contribution of the Ville de Paris, whose ownership of the stadium site was transferred to the state at the knock-down price of 150m francs.

21. See *Dossier de Presse du Stade de France* (Paris, 1998), pp.13–15.

22. S. Vincendon, 'Grand stade: contestations autour d'une règle de jeu définie par Bouygues', *Libération*, 31 July 1994, 31; and 'Alors que le maire de Saint-Denis préfère le projet Nouvel, le Grand stade "monumental" de Macary et Zublena veut célébrer le retour aux valeurs de l'olympisme', *Le Monde*, 17 September 1994, 17.

23. F. Edelmann, 'Jean Nouvel demande à M. Balladur d'annuler l'attribution du Grand stade', *Le Monde*, 12 January 1995, 28, and 'Grand stade – Eiffage et Spie-Batignolles déboutés au tribunal administratif', *Le Monde*, 5 November 1994, 19.

24. J. Quatremer, 'Carton rouge pour le grand stade', *Libération*, 24 January 1997, 17, and C. de Chenay and B. Hopquin, 'Paris refuse de renégocier la concession du Stade de France', *Le Monde*, 24 January 1997, 22.

25. The withdrawal of Canal Plus (franchiser of the PSG/Parc des Princes) and its American partner company specialised in running US sports stadiums from competition for the Grand stade franchise suggested that the project was unviable. See A. Echegut, 'Grand stade: Canal Plus n'est plus candidat à la concession' *Les Echos*, 7 July 1994, 32.

26. See, for example, 'Le financement privé du Grand stade reste lié à la présence d'un club résidant', *Le Monde*, 4 May 1995, 31.

27. G. Verdez, 'Parc des Princes: Tibéri s'accroche au PSG', *L'Equipe*, 19 February 1998, 11.

28. G. Verdez, 'Le PSG candidat', *L'Equipe*, 24 February 1998, 7, and P. Lafayette and B. Lions, 'Le PSG renonce', *L'Equipe*, 2 April 1998, 5.

29. C. de Chenay, 'Le budget de l'Etat financera le Grand stade', *Le Monde*, 7 September 1995, 20, and 'Les modalités de financement du grand stade: l'embarras du mouvement sportif', *Le Monde*, 5 October 1994, 16.

30. See K. Wheatley, 'Guests who opt to sit out the Games', *Financial Times*, 15 January 1996.

Buying and Selling the World Cup

GEOFF HARE

FIFA, Big Business, and Football Globalisation

What characterised modern sport at its outset was its autonomy as a social sphere within civil society, its ability to organise its own practices in its own terms for their own sake, and not for financial gain. This remained true for a long time in the professional era. As business practices have entered different sports at club and international level, sport has gradually been losing this autonomy. Its ludic, non-material values have been under attack from business logic. Professional football has been at the forefront of the erosion of autonomy, and its self-regulation is being broken down. The Trojan Horse of business logic, to use Bourdieu's image, is television, which has transformed football into spectacle; and the ultimate (football) televised entertainment commodity has become the World Cup. France is not alone in suffering this trend; indeed its special relationship between sport and the State has protected it better than some other countries. The different statist traditions of France and Britain, and the consequently different historical development of their broadcasting systems, have meant that the chronology and extent of the changes affecting domestic football have been different in each country. However, France too has had to adapt to the idea, especially following the *Bosman* ruling, that the market for players (football's key commodity) is no longer a national one. This may indeed have improved French players' capabilities at international level, as captain Deschamps recognised after the Final. France, like England, has been subject to the commercialisation of the international game, at the level of European club competitions and in terms of the World Cup. It is not only the market for players that is international, most other economic aspects have been globalised, especially in the case of the World Cup. The very globalisation of football meant that the commercial aspects of the 1998 World Cup were ones the host country had least control over and were the least culturally specific elements of the organisation of France 98, with one exception. This was that the geographical location of the 1998 host country created an unprecedented demand for tickets for matches. France lies of course in the centre of the densely populated, wealthy European Union, with good road and rail links with at least ten other qualifying countries in the traditional heartland of football. Two additional qualifiers were North

African nations (Tunisia and Morocco) where many French residents and citizens have close ties. Polemics over demand for tickets tended, however, to deflect attention from the fact, revealed by analysis of the economics of the tournament, that the real nature of the World Cup has become televisual.

It was the election of João Havelange in 1974 as President of football's governing body, that gave FIFA the political will to commercialise and globalise the sport that another Brazilian, Pele, had done so much to popularise as 'the beautiful game'. This essay looks therefore at the relationship between the French Organising Committee (CFO) and FIFA. It also studies some of the economic actors and processes that Bourdieu argues are obscured by the small screen's coverage of football: the links between FIFA and its preferred agent ISL, the sale of television rights, corporate interests that are expressed in official sponsorship, advertising, merchandising, ambush marketing, and corporate hospitality and ticket allocation and their effect on fans. Recurrent themes will be the pervasive influence of the televisual nature of the event, and the extent of the business and financial decisions that FIFA and its agents managed to keep outside the control of the CFO and the French authorities. Whilst the economic effects of the Adidas' World Cup sponsorship victory will be considerable on the French market for sporting and leisure goods, France will see nothing of a large proportion of the huge profits from the tournament since they belong to multinational organisations such as ISL, Sony, and indeed FIFA itself. In more general terms, the 1998 World Cup sheds light on the current state of relations between the spheres of football and economics, both of which are being globalised.

The Football Authorities and the Power of Money

The links between football and commerce are not new and pre-date the professional era. The search for gate income has even affected the laws of play. As early as 1925 the offside rule was changed to encourage more goals and make the game more exciting in order to attract back dwindling spectators.[1] Latterly the extra-time Golden Goal rule was similarly thought to increase drama and excitement for viewers. Recently the explicit issue of commercialisation of football has become more controversial because of the scale and type of changes that are now happening. Since the 1980s the entry of businessmen such as Bernard Tapie into French football set a trend, his successor as head of Adidas taking over Olympique de Marseille. Sponsorship of clubs (in most countries), of stadiums and of domestic competitions (notably in Britain) has been followed by a dozen or so English clubs becoming public companies quoted on the Stock Exchange. France has been wondering whether it should follow suit.

A recurrent theme in both countries has been conflict between the game's governing bodies and the richer professional clubs. Behind the issues they have fought over lies a continuing struggle for power. In France pressure from various clubs founded by industrial and commercial firms forced French football's governing body to accept professionalisation. In the 1950s English clubs had to pressurise a reluctant FA to allow them to enter European competitions. In France the old amateur structures of control of clubs are being eroded by companies such as Canal Plus taking over clubs like PSG. Seeing potentially greater income from television rights, clubs throughout Europe exerted pressure on UEFA, European football's governing body, to transform the European (Champions) Cup into the expanded Champions League, which includes additional clubs who are not national champions. The system of a qualifying round for lesser clubs followed by a pool system fits both the needs of the richer clubs wishing to lengthen the odds of early elimination and of major national television channels wanting a guaranteed number of matches featuring one of their country's teams (for audience and advertising income). In August 1998 UEFA was forced into agreeing to review the structure of all its European competitions after news broke of secret talks between Europe's wealthy élite of clubs who were considering forming a break-away European Super League. If this were, as proposed, a self-selecting group of the richest European clubs supported by exclusive rights to pay-per-view television, it would be another challenge to the football authorities' control of the sport and a further erosion of what little autonomy it has left.

Thus, over the years, clubs acting together have used their power to free themselves from the control of the sporting authorities, big clubs have used their muscle to free themselves of links with smaller clubs, and now a tiny élite of clubs is challenging the European football authorities – all from following rational business logic. In this context what is interesting is that the game's international governing body, FIFA, has not only been able to retain control over the administration and laws of the game, and over the most prestigious competition the World Cup, but has also been able to develop and extend its influence over non-traditional centres of interest in football in Africa and Asia. What has made this possible of course is FIFA's own adoption of a business approach in its running of football and its early initiative to commercialise its key asset, the four-yearly World Cup tournament. This begs the question of whether its two functions, of custodian of the sport's self-regulatory integrity and of agent of the game's commercialisation, are compatible. Are there tensions between the two functions, or are they synergetic? Has the development of the world game been made possible by its commercialisation, with the World Cup as the driver? Or has the game lost its soul? More importantly, in the context of this study, is how the French hosts adapted to FIFA's commercial approach.

FIFA and the Globalisation of Football

The global growth of FIFA and the World Cup has not happened accidentally. President Havelange quickly recognised the potential for growth of the world football market (now worth 250 billion dollars annually, providing a livelihood for 450 million people). Supported by representatives of newer footballing countries, Havelange and his Secretary-General Sepp Blatter (who succeeded to the Presidency just before France 98) have brought business logic to bear on the tournament and its organisation, and have pushed it to the pinnacle of the business of football as spectacle. The increase in the number of teams in the final stages from 16 to 24 in 1982 and to 32 in 1998 has allowed FIFA to offer multinational corporate sponsors extra representation from North and Central America, Africa, and Asia. FIFA has become a rich and powerful organisation in the course of the globalisation of football. It is now one of the three biggest international sporting organisations in existence, claiming 204 affiliated national associations (more than the United Nations). Profits from successive World Cups have meant Havelange has been able to leave £2.4 billion of future contracts in FIFA's coffers, with which to spread world football further in football's developing world.[2]

The mode of financial organisation adopted by Havelange and FIFA for the World Cup has been the same form of franchising as used by the International Olympic Committee (IOC). FIFA has also used the same Swiss-based marketing company, ISL Marketing Worldwide, as its exclusive marketing arm throughout Havelange's presidency. ISL (International Sport Leisure) was founded in 1983 by Horst Dassler, then head of Adidas. For successive World Cups, FIFA has sold its rights to exploit the copyrighted brands 'World Cup/Coupe du Monde' to ISL, which has additionally copyrighted a new logo specifically for each tournament. The right to use this logo in advertising has been sold to major sponsors who can associate their product or brand with the World Cup in advertising.

France 98, Television and Advertising

A few statistics on France 98 reveal the economic size of the event, and confirm that the importance of the World Cup is its televised nature. The cumulative television audience for the 64 matches was nearly 40 billion – the biggest ever audience for a single event – which was therefore 14,000 times bigger than the number of spectators in the stadiums: 2,775,400.[3] The Final was watched by 1.7 billion viewers world-wide, the biggest shared experience in human history. The spectator and viewing figures give an indication of the marketing potential of the event. Income from corporate sources amounted to over half the CFO's 2.42bn francs (£240m) turnover. Official merchandising reached 8bn francs (£800m). Whereas the broadcasting rights for the three cups from 1990 to 1998 taken together were sold for £160m, the current going-rate for European television rights is the £1.12bn price covering the two future World Cups.[4] As a point of comparison, when England hosted the World Cup in 1966, the tournament's £2m or so revenues came solely from ticket sales. A more meaningful comparison from the financial point of view is the 1996 European Nations Championship held in England, which, using similar marketing techniques to the World Cup, generated total revenues of over £150m (including ticket sales, television, sponsorship and other rights), a profit of £69m.[5] FIFA has predicted that once the final sums are done the total revenue from the 1998 tournament will be £20bn.[6]

France 98 and Television Rights

The economics of the World Cup are based on its televised nature. Financially it is only incidentally a spectacle for 'real fans' in the stadiums. The average numbers of spectators for the 32 matches in the 1966 World Cup (45,780) was higher than in 1998 (43,366) in the smaller French (all-seater) grounds. What made the difference in terms of financial size of the event was the impact of global television and consequent interest of business. The sale of world television rights to terrestrial free-to-air television companies ensured global coverage of the World Cup and assured corporate sponsors of mass exposure for their brands. Television has become the most potent mass medium for commercial advertising, and football attracts mass television audiences. The importance of international competitions like the Champions League and the World Cup is that the major commercial and industrial corporations are now operating in a cross-national (indeed a global) market and seeking global events to maximise their marketing investment.

In 1997, 13 out of 45 developed countries achieved their biggest television audience of the year when covering a sporting event, and, since the World Cup, French television is no longer the major odd one out. In Europe it is football that dominates all other sports in 13 out of 20 countries studied.[7] Football's importance to audiences induces commercial television and their public service competitors to seek broadcasting rights and evolve sports programming strategies for competitive edge, and, in the case of pay-television, to use football coverage as a marketing tool to sell subscriptions. The symbiotic relationship of football, commerce and television is now therefore firmly established in many parts of the world, particularly in Europe, but, following FIFA's efforts to spread the attraction of the game as widely as possible, also in non-traditional soccer areas.

Official Sponsors and Ambush Marketing

Not only did the French organisers have no say over television rights, which were sold even before the hosting of the World Cup was awarded to them, but they had to fight for control of part of the commercial sponsorship and its income – the smaller part. FIFA rules and franchising practices in these matters imposed constraints on the local organisers, which led to certain tensions, both with the CFO and with the French State. ISL, who bought the 1998 World Cup marketing rights as early as 1986, imposed the main (multinational) sponsors on the CFO. Twelve official sponsors – Adidas, Anheuser-Busch, Canon, Coca-Cola, Fuji, Gillette, JVC, Mastercard, McDonald's, Opel, Philips, Snickers – had paid between 150 and 200m francs for the privilege of being the sole company in its sector to enjoy official sponsorship rights. This exclusivity is taken to extreme lengths: for example, hotels accommodating FIFA members could not sell Pepsi, since Coke was the official sponsor, and the brands of television sets in stadiums had to be taped over if they were not Philips.[8]

However, competitor companies used ambush marketing to associate their brand name with the World Cup. The most prominent example was Nike, competing with official sponsor Adidas in the sport and leisurewear market (see below), who used television advertising images of World Cup stars Ronaldo and friends fooling around with a football on a beach and in an airport, while scrupulously avoiding using the words World Cup or shots of stadiums. Kodak (competing with Fuji) had street photographers outside the stadiums, dressed as in their colour-snatcher ads. Panasonic (competing with JVC) covered an office block next to the Stade de France with a huge picture of a football breaking its windows. Canon almost took the CFO to court for signing a local sponsorship agreement with Hewlett-Packard over supply of computing hardware.

What each official sponsor got for its money was exclusive rights to pitch-side billboards and the right to use the World Cup logos in their own advertising and promotional events before and during the tournament, on which they spent at least as much again. Mastercard admitted that their total spending on marketing at the 1998 World Cup could reach three or four times the value of the original rights fee. Their aim, like other sponsors, was to swamp France and the wider global television audience with images of their brands. A company such as Mastercard with no direct or obvious links to sport as part of its ordinary business activities, has recognised the force of television and football to reach young men especially, with whom they have been keen, as official sponsors of Euro 96 and France 98, to raise brand awareness and establish brand loyalty. Mastercard regards the perimeter

5. CFO official sponsor Danone makes a noise before the Final.

6. Ambush marketing near the Stade de France.

7.   Brazilian star Ronaldo in a television advertisement for Nike.

8.   In Nike Football Park – another form of ambush marketing.

9. Young businessman enjoy corporate hospitality.

10. Fans, flags and replica shirts at the Stade de France.

board exposure alone – equivalent to seven minutes per match on television – as far exceeding the sponsorship spend.[9]

While the French Organising Committee could not deal directly with official FIFA sponsors and received less than a third of FIFA's income from this source (some in the form of services or equipment), the CFO needed to raise income from corporate interests to balance its books, and in the end other commercial sponsorship brought in half of its total budget, namely 897m francs (about £90m). For the first time the local Organising Committee dealt directly with second-tier sponsors (*partenaires officiels*) rather than handing all marketing over to an outside agency. Whereas FIFA's traditional sponsors are multinationals, the CFO did not express an exclusively national preference in its contacts with second-, third-, and fourth-tier sponsors. However, most were French companies. The Crédit agricole bank provided the infrastructure for selling match tickets; France Telecom was its official telecommunications operator (beating off a bid from Philips to equip the stadiums with 15,000 telephone lines); Hewlett-Packard, however, beat the French firm Honeywell-Bull in the bid to provide computing hardware. The other five second-tier suppliers were: EDS (supplier of IT services), Sybase (software), Manpower (organiser of volunteer labour), La Poste (official mail carrier), and Danone (supplier of dairy products). ISL was unhappy that Danone, which has beverage interests, had been signed up, since it could be in competition with Coke.[10] These eight *fournisseurs officiels* (official suppliers) brought the CFO 600m francs. Additionally, the CFO jointly with ISL signed up nine further suppliers of 'official products and services' at a cost of 160m francs, half of which went to ISL. Finally, 16 official *prestataires agréés* (equipment or service providers), brought in 90m francs to the CFO.[11] The list of the two lower-tier sponsors is almost exclusively French: Air France, SNCF, Total, Michelin, Accor (hotels), Yves Saint Laurent, and others. Unlike the 12 key official sponsors, the CFO's 'partners' had no rights to pitch-side advertising, except for one billboard per match for the second-tier, but all could use the France 98 logo and most employed the Footix mascot in their advertising and promotions.[12]

French Values Challenged by International Capital

An example of tensions between the World Cup organisation and the French State over sponsorship was another round in the continuing battle between commercial interests in sport and the anti-smoking and anti-drinking health lobby. The issue concerned whether or not pressure from FIFA, the organisers, and a multinational company could persuade the French government to amend the 1991 Evin Law (named after a Socialist Minister of Health) banning advertisements for alcohol and tobacco at sports events, or more precisely, since an amendment of 1994, the banning of television coverage in France of events in stadiums where there are such advertisements. The issue shows tensions between the world of international sport and governments, but also between Right and Left in France, and between different ministries (Ministry for Youth and Sport and Ministry of Health). In more general terms it can be seen as part of a continuing struggle between a French State wedded to notions of public service and collectivism and the neo-liberal ideology of European institutions. Anheuser-Busch, the world's biggest brewer and producer of Budweiser beer, a FIFA sponsor since 1986, had spent £10m to become one of the main sponsors of the World Cup, and lobbied the European Commission in an attempt to find a way round the law. Under existing legislation the CFO could not feature Budweiser in its posters or official communications, and ISL confirmed there could be no Budweiser advertising in the stadiums or adverts on French television, although there had been an agreement about French television broadcasting tobacco-sponsored Formula 1 motor racing, and over certain events from abroad. The European Commission ruled the law infringed European legislation on free movement of services (advertising) and threatened to take France to the European Court of Justice. Reports suggested the right-wing Juppé government would extend the Formula 1 exception to the World Cup allowing Budweiser to advertise in the national stadium, ironically by declaring it extra-territorial. However, after the surprise spring elections of 1997, the new left-wing government and Communist Sports Minister Mme Buffet refused to reinterpret the Evin Law to accommodate Budweiser. Budweiser finally contented itself with a 17m franc advertising campaign around France, without mentioning the World Cup, and sold its pitch-side advertising to Casio.[13]

The Merchandising of France 98

An undisputed victor of France 98 was Adidas, a firm that, although founded in Germany, has come to be seen, following the Tapie era, to be as much French as German. Louis-Dreyfus's sports equipment and sports-wear company invested millions in three different aspects of the commercialisation of the World Cup. Adidas was again an official sponsor of the event, and Adidas France was an official sponsor of the French national team and a holder of a licence to manufacture official merchandise, in particular shirts, sports bags, and balls. Adidas's key products are sports related, but more importantly its fashion-sensitive market is very dependent on brand image. As official sponsor of the event it could associate its brand with a major sporting event (and in France with the national team) and advertise itself and its existing products. In buying a licence to manufacture merchandise it could also produce new products specifically for the period around the tournament.

The merchandising of a big sports event looks very like the marketing of a club's franchised and official products to supporters. Most British professional football clubs now use club shops and sports outlets to sell not only replica shirts, scarves and videos about the club, but also other club-branded products less obviously connected to football: from baby clothes to club credit cards. Merchandising constitutes a highly significant secondary revenue stream for clubs like Manchester United. Their annual turnover from merchandising is £29m.[14] French clubs have lagged far behind English ones. Paris Saint-Germain opened its first prime-site shop on the Champs-Elysées in May 1998. Its merchandising income for the 1997–98 season was estimated at only 20m francs (£2m).[15]

Sony's World Cup: Footix and Official Merchandise

Official merchandising was a further commercial aspect of the World Cup (the 'jackpot') that was controlled by FIFA and its franchisees, and not by the French organisers, although a lump sum payment went to the CFO in respect of the merchandising agreement. The exclusive World Cup merchandising rights were bought from ISL by Sony World Cup Paris (SWC), a company set up specifically for the France 98 operation, and jointly owned by the Western and Eastern merchandising subsidiaries of the Sony Corporation. SWC was created with a limited life-span: October 1995 to December 1998. Its contract with ISL was based on an undisclosed percentage of its turnover going to ISL. Similarly SWC took a royalty (12 per cent) of the pre-tax turnover of all sales of licensed products. It signed about 230 licences for products world wide covering about 1,500 separate product lines. One hundred and twenty of the licences covered Europe. The licences allowed the use of the World Cup France 98 logo, the emblem of the World Cup trophy, and/or the Footix mascot on merchandise.

The buyers of licences ranged from Adidas, manufacturing sports clothing and the official match balls, to Zippo refillable lighters. Other products ranged from plastic castanets made in Lyon and frisbees made in Hong Kong, to champagne and the famous all-purpose Opinel folding knives from Savoy, that just about every French family possesses, and which were the subject of some controversy in the British media, which immediately assumed they would encourage football violence. Holders of licences were responsible for manufacture and distribution of the goods, except that SWC, in addition to running a major outlet for official merchandise on the Champs-Elysées (Espace Officiel France 98 – 6,000 visitors per day, unofficial annual turnover 40m francs), sold exclusive ranges of official products from stalls inside every World Cup stadium. This latter facility was the subject of a court-case against the CFO by a small French company, Coquelicot: contesting the right of ISL to award the concession, the CFO had expected to be able to use Coquelicot to sell official merchandise in and around the stadiums.[16] Official products were also available over the counter world-wide, or by mail-order from a Trois Suisses catalogue, and through a web site (expected to sell 100,000 items). The final sales of official merchandise (about 40 per cent of sales were in France) were of the order of the predicted world-wide pre-tax turnover, viz. 8 billion francs, twice as much as the 1994 total.[17]

The merchandising sales pattern in France reveals the same attitudes to the French team as Patrick Mignon discusses elsewhere in this volume. Fans' support of the team was not unconditional or pre-existing, but grew with success. French distributors foresaw this: at the end of 1997 they were not rushing to stock the products. Relatively poor sales of merchandise during the Atlanta Olympics in 1996 and lack of confidence about the French team progressing beyond the First Round were blamed. There were also fears about the French public rejecting the World Cup because of media over-kill and over-commercialisation. However increasing public interest in the progress of *les Bleus* towards the Final had an enormous effect on sales. Sales of the official Adidas Tricolore ball, not cheap at 490 francs, took off after the victory over Paraguay taking France into the quarter-final, and increased thereafter match on match, until they sold out. The Hexagone chain sold out of the official (adult size) French replica shirt (250,000 sold at 349 francs), and could not get any more from suppliers Adidas, who also seem to have underestimated support or the success of the team. In the first half of the tournament Brazil shirts were reportedly selling well, then after the victory over Italy in the quarter-final the trend was reversed, with the number 10 Zidane shirt proving most popular. On the day before the final, the big Décathlon sportswear store in central Paris sold a whole consignment of 600 French shirts.[18]

In addition to their use by the licensees, the France 98 logo and Footix mascot could also be used by the official FIFA sponsors and the CFO's official commercial partners. The French Post Office was one such CFO sponsor. Their World Cup stamp sold 120m copies in the course of a few months, 15 times the usual sale of a special collection stamp. Outside of official or obviously football-related merchandise, manufacturers of the French national flag were also rubbing their hands. They had never known such demand since the death of General de Gaulle.[19]

Adidas versus Nike: The Other World Cup?

In view of the buoyancy of the sports- and leisure-wear sector, and the importance of the fashion sales side of it, especially in France (where household spending on sports goods in 1995 was the highest in Europe at 1,170 francs),[20] the two fastest growing manufacturers Adidas and Nike could not afford to neglect the *Coupe du monde* band-wagon as a marketing opportunity. Adidas dominates the European market, especially in football, Nike's strength is in America, in athletics and basketball. Adidas seeks to expand into the American market (where it has only a six per cent market share); and if Nike is to expand in Europe, it needs to conquer the football-related products market (it has ten per cent of market share of a £3bn world market for brands). Press and television saw good copy in what they portrayed as the 'other World Cup', the duel between Nike and Adidas, which suited the duopolistic ambitions of both, to the detriment of Reebok, Puma, Umbro, Kappa and other competitors.[21] The meeting of Brazil and France in the Final, sponsored respectively by Nike and Adidas, did nothing to undermine the idea of the close association of national teams and commercial sponsors, which nonetheless raised ethical issues about the links between sport and money.

First of all, the circumstances of Brazil's defeat in the Final cast a shadow over an otherwise lively Nike advertising campaign featuring Ronaldo as their central figure. Nike would no doubt have been disappointed if he had not played in the Final, and had to field awkward press questions about possible pressure from the company or the Nike-sponsored Brazilian Federation to force an unfit star onto the pitch in the final. Despite denials on all sides, this certainly constituted bad publicity.[22] A whiff of scandal for one, as *Le Monde* put it, apotheosis for the other, as the Adidas slogan 'La victoire est en nous' was projected onto the Arc de Triomphe on victory night and the victorious team paraded the Cup the next day wearing Adidas tee-shirts. Nike's December 1996 contract paying the Brazilian Football Federation $200m over ten years and associating Nike with 50 friendly matches by the national team, had previously been criticised as taking too much control out of the hands of the Brazilian soccer authorities. FIFA was sufficiently concerned that in May 1998 they set up a working party to look into the 'growing interference of sportswear manufacturers in the organisation of international friendly matches'.[23]

Buying and selling 'les Bleus'

National Federations and players do not compete simply for the honour of representing the nation. Their participation makes them a lot of money. The winning Federation received a cheque for 35m francs. FIFA paid each qualifying team 3m francs for preparation expenses, and 4m francs for each match played (therefore 28m francs for reaching the Final). Players and staff received 1,200 francs 'expenses' per day. Player power is becoming greater in modern football following the *Bosman* ruling, and players are important commercial actors. A World Cup is both a showcase for a player's value and an opportunity to bring in sponsorship money to individuals and to the national squad. The French squad made full use of this.

Quite apart from their annual club salary, the players made money from three sources in connection with representing the national team: their kit sponsor Adidas offered 30,000 francs per international match for wearing their boots and kit (although an indicator of increasing economic individualism is that, following the World Cup, individual players in international matches will be free to wear boots from individual sponsors irrespective of team sponsor). Their winning bonus from the FFF was negotiated as a scale rising from nothing for elimination before the quarter-finals, to one million francs each for winning the trophy. However, their main income came from commercial sponsorship of the national team, organised by a company, Football France Promotion, set up at the initiative of the Players' Union (UNFP). Income from sponsors is divided between company, Federation, League, UNFP, and international players (who receive more than half). Jacquet bread (not linked to the manager's family, but how could they resist the wink in his direction), Bresse-Bleu cheese, Vittel mineral water, Candia milk, Club Med holiday villages and 25 others brought in about two million francs per player. All this adds up to over £300,000 per player.[24] Their club transfer and salary value inevitably went up, although those who changed clubs, like Desailly and Pires, had completed the negotiations before the tournament. Does this, as with French fans, indicate lack of confidence in the outcome?

Public Relations and Corporate Hospitality: Towns and Tickets

The World Cup ticketing issue was one of the most fraught for the CFO, and the way it was initially organised illustrates the priorities and values of the football authorities as stakeholders, and the different pressures that constrained the CFO's room for manœuvre. The allocation finally reflected the balance of power between various stakeholders: French and foreign fans, the French football authorities, the French State, FIFA and big business. The eventual large share of tickets obtained by the latter is a reflection of the way money and corporate interests now dominate football. The disgruntlement of foreign fans over ticket allocation had an impact on the host towns, both in terms of security problems and selling the image of the towns for purposes of inward investment or tourism.

CFO and French Stakeholders

The interests of domestic football in France were always going to carry weight with the CFO in the allocation of tickets. One of the main aims of the French Federation and League, parent bodies of the CFO, was to use the World Cup to promote French football (a) to benefit from the building of a new national stadium for hosting future international matches and major competitions; (b) to use the State's and local authorities' interest in the success of the overall event to gain public funds to improve general facilities at the nine existing stadiums; and (c) to increase the future supporter base of the game by building on interest generated during the month-long unprecedented media coverage of the sport. Lack of spectators and income has been a recurrent structural weakness in French football. This historical fact informed the main concerns of the CFO and the French football authorities. However, ease of access to France and rising public interest in football among the young middle class used to going abroad indicated neighbouring fans would travel. Michel Platini admitted in July that the CFO had underestimated demand for tickets, but the CFO was concerned how best to ensure full stadiums for 'unattractive' first round matches like South Africa v. Saudi Arabia.[25]

Since the CFO had no public subsidies and relied on two (roughly equal) sources of revenue – commercial sponsorship and ticket sales, 'its absolute imperative' in ticketing policy was to fill the stadiums and to generate income from tickets in order to balance the books at the end of the event.[26] Secondly, the CFO's constitution and its ethos were non-profit-making and 'republican', in the sense that the backgrounds of its governing body were in the amateur *associatif* world of football officials and the public service. They were happy to allocate large numbers of tickets to the home market and to keep prices down, in a democratic spirit. They professed the aim of making France 98 accessible to the largest possible number of people by maximising the number of matches played at weekends, and by a 'user-friendly ticketing policy': pricing was intended to be as democratic as possible: half a million tickets cost less than 150 francs, and one ticket in two cost less than 250 francs.

Sixty per cent of total tickets were sold either to the general public resident in France, or to the French footballing community (players, club members at league and district level), who got first pick. For the 55 first round games (with the exception of the Opening Match) tickets were on sale as part of the France 98 Pass package (giving entry to all first round games in one city). They sold out by May 1997, before the draw for matches, so people were buying them irrespective of which teams they might see. The nine big matches (the opening match, plus the quarter-finals onwards) saw the general public's share (227,000 tickets) allocated by lottery, after they had been over-subscribed threefold in September–October 1997. Ticket purchases were limited to four purchases per customer. The CFO regarded this system as fair, transparent, easy to use and accessible. Remaining individual tickets for the games preceding the quarter-finals went on sale in March 1998.

The CFO sold about 135,000 tickets at high prices to 17 authorised Travel Agents across the world who put these together into expensive packages. One report showed Wagonlit Sports selling tickets for the opening match at 6,250 francs (face value 850 francs). Another company had tickets for the Final at 15,570 francs. Minister Buffet called these prices scandalous.[27] This category of tickets brought significant income to the CFO. However, if this was one way of keeping other ticket prices down for 'real' French fans, it will be seen, when taken in conjunction with sales to big business, that it implies a tension (not to say a contradiction) with the Republican spirit proclaimed regarding the sale of the 60 per cent of 'ordinary' tickets.

'Real Fans' or Corporate Hospitality?

FIFA also had its own interests to promote in imposing its allocation rules on the host country. About 20 per cent of tickets (half-a-million) were reserved by FIFA for the affiliated national Football Associations / Federations (compared to 15 per cent in USA 1994, where stadiums were bigger). Each Federation had equal rights to numbers of tickets, with no special arrangements for near neighbours of France. The allocation of tickets to national federations in early 1998, which caused all the polemics, was done according to FIFA rules. This meant that for an England game, initial allocations saw eight per cent of stadium capacity go to each competing nation, and four per cent between the other affiliated FAs. Some confusion was caused by the CFO's underestimate of available seats, since numbers needed for the media and final stadium capacities following renovation work on seating and decisions about fencing were not known precisely until late. Pressure from the European Commission and neighbouring countries where demand was greatest led to the CFO finding more seats, sold over a ticket hot-line. Controversy again flared when it was revealed that proportionately more lines were available for callers from within France than outside. European law on non-discrimination between member states seemed to have been flouted. Some British MPs got very hot under the collar. The European Commissioner for Competition policy made official enquiries.[28]

Other ticketing issues included scare stories in Britain about non-segregation of fans that might lead to trouble – they proved generally groundless, since the violence was practically all outside stadiums, with some minor exceptions in the England–Argentina game. More problematic for fans were the broken promises of some travel firms offering tickets in

TABLE 1

DESTINATIONS OF TICKETS

Direct sale by CFO	37.6 per cent	General public	22.3 per cent
–		'French football family'	14.2 per cent
–		Handicaped	1.1 per cent
Sale abroad	28.4 per cent	FIFA and Federations	23 per cent
–		CFO Authorised Travel Agents	5.4 per cent
Sponsors French and foreign	17 per cent	Private companies	14.2 per cent
–		Public companies and local authorities	2.8 per cent
Executive boxes and Prestige seats	8.4 per cent		
Various operations	4.3 per cent		
Remaining to be sold to general public in May	4.3 per cent	–	

Source: CFO figures May 1998.[29]

the expectation of getting them from unofficial sources. A British company was wound up after failing to deliver 25,000 tickets; directors of the Paris office of a US company were investigated after claiming tickets had been stolen. Alleged corruption led to prosecution of executives of ISL France, for failing to deliver 14,500 tickets Japanese fans had paid for. More disturbing was the selling on of many tickets from at least one national federation (Cameroon) – unsold tickets should be returned to FIFA by federations, but they seemed to be sold on at profit to travel agents. Black market tickets were available especially at later matches. The ticketing affair certainly produced bad publicity, and incoming FIFA President Blatter felt in hindsight that it should be done better next time.[30]

An important issue was that the equity sought by the CFO in distributing the tickets seemed to break down under pressure to satisfy vested interests and sponsors. The World Cup followed the pattern of major sports events where the 'real fan' is being ousted in favour of VIPs or corporate guests. However, there seemed to be two distinct phases in terms of who got tickets: the matches before the quarter-finals were left to the general French public, plus contingents of foreign fans, and the later rounds were watched by football's VIPs and the beneficiaries of corporate hospitality, plus relatively small numbers of 'real fans' of whatever nationality. FIFA's arrangements with its 12 Official Sponsors also involved guaranteeing 180,000 tickets for promotional and hospitality purposes. Over 14 per cent of tickets (about 350,000) went to the CFO's French and multinational commercial sponsors as part of the sponsorship deals, to be used for promotional purposes and for corporate hospitality. In addition there were a number of Executive Boxes and Prestige Seats sold directly by the CFO to companies and local authorities for corporate hospitality (8.4 per cent of tickets were Prestige or Box tickets – 201,000). The Parc des Princes has boxes for 400 guests, and the Stade de France has 2,900 such seats in its 152 boxes, including 12 luxury hospitality boxes. These seats and boxes were so much in demand by companies that they brought in 759m francs to the CFO, more than total 'ordinary' ticket sales. Alcatel, for example, bought five boxes (two in the Stade de France), plus 2,000 ordinary seats for its clients. Mastercard invited 600 VIPs to the semi-final and final matches for a week of exclusive luxury. The organisation of contemporary football exerted such financial pressures on the hosts that they could not ignore corporate interests, which increasingly, as the tournament progressed, excluded 'real fans'. French players' complaints about the numbers of dark suits and the lack of noisy support in the Stade de France in the semi-final seemed to bear out this interpretation.[31]

Host Towns, Inward Investment and Public Relations

Another view on who the real audience was might come from the state and local authorities arguing that the World Cup was also about selling 'le produit France' to the half-a-million foreign supporters among whom were a good proportion of VIPs invited by sponsors, as well as a thousand foreign journalists, and many 'deciders' from French companies. The key public relations operation was organised by the host towns in collaboration with the DATAR, the regional Development Agency. The host towns invited 120 foreign company directors, in a highly targeted fashion. Thirty American industrialists in biotechnology were invited to Lyon; Belgian food industrialists to Bordeaux; British aeronautics and aerospace interests were present in Toulouse, and so on.[32]

Host towns and regions saw themselves as important economic stakeholders. Inward investment into local economies, image building, as well as local political communication were at stake. One of the important issues for the ten host towns was to do with public relations, and creating distinctive market positions and corporate images to endow the town with a recognisable personality. The aim was to encourage inward investment, often to promote tourism (France is after all the world leader as a tourist destination), as well as to engage local citizens in a common purpose.[33] Municipal public relations is often built around annual events organised by the town or with which the town is associated through sponsorship or participation. Some events have achieved international notoriety and are powerful vectors of image: the Montpellier Classical Music Festival and the Avignon Theatre Festival. Being a *ville d'étape* in the Tour de France is highly sought after (and costly). The World Cup was seen by host towns as a once-only opportunity. Bordeaux has a tradition of municipal support for and use of the local football team for promoting the city and region. Investment in activities around the World Cup matches in Bordeaux was an extension of this activity. The city 'put on a show' for the duration of the World Cup, under the slogan 'Bienvenue au monde', with a 'Welcome to the World' village, showcasing wine, local culinary specialities, crafts and cultural highlights.

Other cities organised more extravagant entertainments and 'animations' (events). Paris had a 50-strong World Cup working group based in the Hôtel de Ville, with a budget of 20m francs. It organised the street parade on the eve of the opening match and the Three Tenors concert. Montpellier, at the centre of the smallest host conurbation (248,000) among the host cities, and one of the farthest advanced in its planning at an early stage, used the World Cup to fit into its longer-term communications strategy, based on music and culture; not an easy task. It organised a musical competition where two orchestras 'played against each other', not simultaneously, while images of famous World Cup matches of the past were projected onto a giant screen behind the orchestras in the city centre. In Lens, the smallest host town (35,280 inhabitants), but part of the major conurbation centred on Lille, ambitions were more parochial, but none the less important for the future of the town and its stadium that will henceforth hold 41,275 seated fans for its European Champions League campaign. Racing Club de Lens targeted 30 surrounding *communes* with a transportable mini-football pitch during the World Cup in an attempt to interest new young supporters in the club as the regional standard-bearer. The general gain for the host towns was in becoming better known abroad (brand awareness). As one mayor said: 'In the collective memory, Montpellier will be one of the ten best known French cities in the first quarter of the 21st century.'[34]

Conclusion: Commercial Values and Sporting Values

How many different stakeholders had something to buy and sell in France 98? And how many different ways are there of selling football? FIFA through ISL sold sponsorship rights to allow companies to associate themselves with the event, and also sold rights to television channels to broadcast matches; official sponsors bought the goodwill of clients through corporate hospitality hoping thereby to sell them their goods or services in the future; catering firm Lenôtre sold their services to providers of corporate hospitality; television channels sold either subscriptions to viewers or advertising space around broadcast matches to any company who could pay for it; television manufacturers sold more new wide-screen sets and video-recorders; FIFA through SWC sold rights to manufacturers to sell official merchandise associated with the event; the CFO sold tickets to spectators to watch matches in stadiums, and also to travel agents, who sold expensive packages; building firms sold their expertise to build or renovate stadiums; the CFO sold executive boxes and VIP seats to companies, and sold rights to suppliers to associate themselves with the event; the FFF sold sponsorship rights to allow companies to associate themselves with the French team; players sold their skills; agents sold players to new clubs; Adidas sold a lot of replica shirts and balls made in the Third World; some ticket-holders sold tickets on to touts, who sold them at grossly inflated prices to 'real fans' ... It is hard to escape the view that the World Cup was about buying and selling. And most people thought they were getting their money's worth. But sporting values were originally intrinsic, about playing for enjoyment, for expressing skills, for the satisfaction of achievement and participation, for trying to win, but in a spirit of fair play. Sporting competitions were organised for their own sake, not in order to make money. And yet of course they have always needed resources to organise them. Today élite sport as a professional career and sport as an entertainment spectacle imply an inescapable commercial dimension.

The World Cup was therefore inescapably a massive commercial event, even when organised in France, a country where Republican and public service values have held back the growth of a fully commercial dimension in sport, and helped retain some of its autonomy. Decisions about the 1998 World Cup illustrated the way participatory and spectator sport has been seen in France as a legitimate concern of the public authorities and as a public service, 'une mission de service public'. The whole of the financing of 1994 World Cup in America had been private, and public investment in Euro 96 in England (admittedly smaller than the World Cup) was limited to £100,000. However the French State, local authorities and public sector companies subsidised France 98 by the equivalent of £525m.[35] In Britain, sport, like many other social practices, has remained independent from the State, the price of which has been increasing dependence on private enterprise and commerce. For France 98, the public sector financed the necessary infrastructure, the CFO the strictly sporting side. The French

Republican State justifies high levels of intervention in terms of the need to 'ensure the general interest of sport prevails over the multitude of private interests that traverse it'.[36] In the case of the World Cup, France's image was also at stake, and, in the context of the State's use of symbolic capital to assert its place in the international order, that is regarded as priceless.

The economics of France 98 reveals a tension between FIFA's approach and the dominant French view of the relation of sport and the State – a tension that produced a sometimes uneasy compromise. The size of the World Cup and FIFA's *modus operandi* is a function of a philosophy that gives much weight to commercial considerations and puts great faith in business logic to make an event work. The compromise of France 98 worked in so far as there were no significant financial or organisational disasters. Critics, however, have regarded the sharing of responsibility between public and private sectors as a 'nationalisation of losses, and privatisation of profits'.[37] A number of private firms, among them multinationals like ISL and Sony, and FIFA itself, will have made a lot of money out of the World Cup. Sponsors like Adidas in particular will have succeeded beyond their expectations in their communication strategy, and in selling sports merchandise. Their shareholders can expect higher dividends. A lot of jobs in Third World shirt factories will have been guaranteed for a while longer. French terrestrial television companies will have sold advertising more profitably than they might have thought, but harder times are ahead. French and foreign recipients of corporate hospitality from firms buying their piece of the World Cup will feel indebted to their hosts. Those fans lucky enough to have bought tickets for France's key matches will be satisfied at not having sold them on the black market at a large profit.

If Pele and Havelange represent two opposite approaches to the development of world football as the beautiful game and the money game – the two clashed bitterly in 1997 over the reform of Brazilian soccer,[38] then a compromise between their two philosophies about how to run a World Cup could only have been personified by a Chairman of the French Organising Committee like Michel Platini – as the epitome of French champagne football who has become a millionaire sports businessman.[39] It will be interesting to see how Platini, with his ambitions to play an important future role in world football's governing body – he was a key supporter in Blatter's election as FIFA's new president – manages to influence the evolution of football in the struggle between its traditional values and commercialism.

NOTES

1. M. Polley, *Moving the Goalposts: A History of Sport and Society since 1945* (London/New York, Routledge, 1998), p.67.
2. P. Smolar, 'Les milliards de l'entreprise FIFA', *Le Monde supplément Le Mondial*, 10 June 1998, vii; A. Constant, 'La "der" victorieuse du président Havelange', *Le Mondial*, 9 June 1998, 4. See also A. Tomlinson, 'FIFA and the World Cup: The Expanding Football Family', in J. Sugden and A. Tomlinson (eds.), *Hosts and Champions: Soccer Cultures, National Identities and the USA World Cup* (Aldershot, Arena, 1994), pp.13–33.
3. See Ministère de la Jeunesse et des Sports and FIFA web sites.
4. B. Hopquin, 'Les bons comptes du Comité d'organisation', *Le Mondial*, 4 December 1997, VI; J. Cordelier, 'Les milliards de la Coupe', *Le Point*, 1320 (3 January 1998), 65; P. Smolar, 'Les milliards de l'entreprise FIFA', *Le Mondial*, 10 June 1998, vii.
5. D. Thorpe, 'Golden goals', *Leisure Management* (November 1996), cited in Leicester University Centre for Research into Sport and Society web site.
6. S. Millar, 'Advertisers drain the Cup dry', *Guardian*, 10 July 1998, 3.
7. *1997: une année de sport dans le monde*, Eurodata TV-Médiamétrie, 1998, see G.R., 'Le monde entier est dingue de sport', *Le Journal du dimanche*, 31 May 1998, 15.
8. G. Le Solleu, 'Mondial, une marque qui protège ses partenaires', *La Tribune des Marchés*, 10 June 1998, xxxii.
9. P. Harverson, 'Sponsors give 110 per cent to achieve the right result', *Financial Times*, 31 May 1998.
10. W. Echikson *et al.*, 'The Real Match', *Business Week*, 8 June 1998, 16–18.
11. J. Cordelier, 'Les milliards de la Coupe', *Le Point*, 1320 (3 January 1998), 65.
12. For a discussion of Footix, see D. Hand, 'Footix: The History behind a Modern Mascot', *French Cultural Studies*, IX (1998), 239–47.
13. H. Réquillart, 'La loi Evin mise en bière', *Impact Médecin Hebdo*, 333, 13 September 1996, 24–5; J.-Y. Nau, 'Le gouvernement prépare un dispositif pour contourner la loi Evin', *Le Monde*, 19 April 1997, 10; P.G., 'Nouvelle entorse à la loi Evin, *Le Figaro*, 3 May 1997; M. Dalloni and C. de Chenay, 'Mme Buffet remet en cause les projets de son prédécesseur', *Le Monde*, 27 June 1997, 26; B. Danet, 'La face cachée du Mondial', *Sport's Magazine* (April 1998), 22–3; G. Meignan, 'La Bud est restée sur sa soif', *La Tribune*, 17 June 1998.
14. R. Cowe, 'Deal highlights poor relations of football', *Guardian*, 5 August 1998, 17.
15. A. Zennou, 'PSG: un football à but lucratif', *Le Figaro*, 16 March 1998.
16. J.-J. Chiquelin, 'Un business sans concession, *Nouvel Observateur*, 27 November 1997, 96–8; 'Une PME française attaque le CFO', *La Croix*, 7 January 1998, 11.
17. Information from interviews with G.-L. Epstein (Administrative Director) and J.-G. Welgryn (Marketing and Communication Director) of SWC in June 1997 and August 1998; Y. Puget, 'Le Mondial à l'assaut des rayons, *LSA*, 18 December 1997, 86–7.
18. V. Hacot and O. Baccuzat, 'Ventes record pour les objets du Mondial', *Le Parisien*, 14 July 1998, 15.
19. P. Goujon, 'La Poste a vendu 120 millions de timbres ronds', *Le Parisien*, 14 July 1998, 15; J. Frasnetti, 'Ruée sur les drapeaux', *Le Parisien*, 14 July 1998, 15.
20. S. Seguin, 'Le commerce du sport, un secteur en forme', *INSEE Première*, 597 (July 1998), 1–4.
21. For example the following headlines in quality papers: 'Le match entre Nike et Adidas se durcit sur le terrain du football espagnol', *La Tribune*, 26 November 1997; 'Equipements: Adidas et Nike se livrent un match sans merci', *Les Echos*, 17 June 1998; 'Adidas-Nike, l'autre match', *France-Soir*, 10 July 1998, 10; 'Adidas-Nike: l'autre finale du Mondial', *Le Figaro Supplément économie*, 11–12 July 1998, i; 'Nike et Adidas se livrent un duel sans merci', *Le Monde*, 17 July 1998, 20. See also *Financial Times* exposure index throughout the Finals, e.g. 13 June 1998, and 11–12 July 1998, 5.
22. See, for example, V. de Montclos, 'Ronaldo aurait-il joué sans les pressions de Nike?, *Marianne*, 20–26 July 1998, 21.
23. F. Amalou, 'Nike et Adidas se livrent un duel sans merci', *Le Monde*, 17 July 1998, 20; S. Fatsis, 'Nike aims to tackle soccer on its Tour de France', *International Herald Tribune*, 8 July 1998.

24. 'Les chiffres de la Coupe du Monde', *Sport's Magazine* (April 1998), 23; G. Sitruk, 'Jackpot pour les Bleus', *France Football*, 2722 bis, 12 June 1998, 44–5; E. Moati, 'Ces Bleus qui valent de l'or', *Stratégies*, 1059, 5 June 1998, 10–11.
25. D. Courdier, 'Platini: "Allez la France"', *France Football*, 2725 bis, 3 July 1998, 37.
26. B. Hopquin, 'Les bons comptes du Comité d'organisation', *Le Monde supplément*, 4 December 1997, VI.
27. M. Deger *et al.*, 'Les tour-opérateurs jouent la Coupe du monde aux plus hauts prix', *La Tribune*, 25 May 1998.
28. Interview with K. Van Miert, 'Le sport professionnel ne doit pas être au-dessus des lois communautaires', *La Tribune*, 6 July 1998.
29. *La Tribune*, 25 May 1998.
30. See *Dispatches*, Channel 4, 28 May 1998; *Le Monde supplément*, 27 June 1998, iv; A. Smith, 'Ticket fiasco will never happen again vows FIFA boss', *Daily Telegraph*, 20 June 1998; *Le Monde*, 18 June 1998, *supplément*, vi, and 20 June 1998, i.
31. B. Hopquin, 'L'envahissante présence des «invités» dans les tribunes du Mondial 1998', *Le Monde*, 16 January 1998, 25; P. Galinier, 'Escroqueries, cambriolage, marché noir: le feuilleton des billets, *Le Monde supplément*, 20 June 1998, p.VI; G. Renault, 'Festin avec vue sur le match', *Libération*, 28 June 1998, 27; F. Amalou, 'Mastercard chouchoute les banquiers', *Le Mondial*, 24 June 1998, iv.
32. A. Echégut, 'Mondial 1998: une facture de 9,4 milliards', *Les Echos*, 4 December 1997, 54–5; and 'La France a montré son savoir faire', *Les Echos*, 13 July 1998, 39.
33. See G. Hare, 'Communications Strategy, Cultural Tourism and the Vitality of the Small Rural *commune*: The Case of Fontvieille (Bouches-du-Rhône)', *Francophonie*, 12 (Dec. 1995), 28–33.
34. A. Echegut, 'La France a montré son savoir faire', *Les Echos*, 13 July 1998, 39.
35. See B. Hopquin, 'Les bons comptes du Comité d'organisation', *Le Monde supplément*, 4 June 1998, vi: State 3.1bn francs, local authorities 1.62bn, RATP and SNCF 528m francs.
36. C. Miège, *Les Institutions sportives* (Paris, PUF-Que sais-je?, 1993), p.68
37. R. Perrot, 'Les bénéfices ont été privatisés … et les pertes nationalisées', *Evénement du jeudi*, 9–15 July 1998, 12.
38. *Panorama*, BBC1, 8 June 1998.
39. See J.-F. Bourg, *Football Business* (Paris, Olivier Orban, 1986), pp.13–21.

Policing and Security:
Terrorists and Hooligans

CLAUDE JOURNÈS
(Translated by John Roach)

The soccer World Cup staged by France in June and July 1998 was both a sporting event and a societal phenomenon charged with emotion. It was a kind of 'party' whose climax was reached when France won in the Final. The World Cup crystallised some collective beliefs and ways of behaving in France, and also showed something of the workings of the State, especially the security forces – the national police and the *Gendarmerie*.

Policing a Unique Event

The World Cup was perceived as potentially the occasion for three threats to security: terrorism, hooliganism and common criminality. Faced by these threats the public authorities working with the organisers of the World Cup set up a series of measures, which on the whole worked well. These measures were based on technical structures, legal provisions, professional expertise and risk analysis. Together they produced the desired results to a large extent, though not completely. The aim of this essay is to explain the relative success of the measures taken, using a theoretical model based on the idea of the indetermination of public policy developed by the French political scientists Bruno Jobert and Pierre Muller.[1] The World Cup lends itself particularly well to this approach because in many ways it is a unique event. France has already staged international events like the 1992 Albertville Winter Olympics or the World Youth Days organised around the visit of the Pope in the summer of 1997 and has derived important technical expertise about their organisation and policing. But compared with these events – which were relatively limited in time and space – the World Cup is on another scale altogether by virtue of its duration of five weeks, the participation of 32 countries (compared with 24 in USA 94), the playing of 64 matches located in ten sites spread all over France, and the attendance of over 2.5 million spectators and 10,000 journalists.

The Indetermination of Public Policy

Political and administrative decision-makers are faced with random, complex and heterogeneous data. Thus, for example, there was the possibility of a terrorist act during the World Cup with no possibility of determining in advance where or when it would occur or its scale. However, acts of terrorism could come from a great number of sources and though hooligans were better identified the authorities had underestimated the emergence of new individuals, not previously known to the police forces, in this modern expression of collective violence, as well as the significance of the copy-cat factor, as in, for example, the behaviour of German hooligans determined to outdo their English counterparts. The organisers sometimes took decisions arising from the need to reconcile security with the spirit of the festival of football. Nor could they be sure in advance what the consequences of their decisions might be, thus, for example, a strong police presence can act to reassure or on the contrary can provoke a hostile reaction from the crowd. The authorities thus endeavoured to minimise uncertainty. This reduction of uncertainty was particularly difficult to achieve when formulating the security policy of the World Cup. Due to factors already mentioned, the security forces were faced by threats of an international nature. Though a number of forms of international police co-operation were established, they were confronted by the weak Europeanisation of policing policies. Policing remains a national matter and the European dimension remains extremely uneven.[2]

In order to establish how the police forces operated, I have drawn on the bibliographical sources indicated in the footnotes, interviews with senior personnel in the police in Lyon with particular expertise in public order (who wished to remain anonymous) and written documentation which they provided. The use of press sources, especially the regional press, creates a special problem in that although it can provide original material there is a tendency to highlight the spectacular events. Journalistic approaches and sociological analyses are based on very different intellectual principles. I shall concentrate on developing a sociological analysis.

Security at Sporting Events in France

To understand the measures taken in relation to the World Cup, one needs to note that the law of 21 January 1995 in relation to security under Article 23 requires that, under certain circumstances, the organisers of profit-making sporting events should provide the security. When the number of police and gendarmes present exceeds what is basically required by law, the organisers must pay for the supplementary presence. This is why it was decided in May 1997 that there would be a sharing of the costs between the French Organising Committee and the French State authorities. Under that agreement the organiser would be responsible for security within the stadiums and the state authorities for the security outside the stadiums. It was agreed that the police and the gendarmes could intervene, if needed, inside the stadiums, when asked to do so by the private operator or in circumstances when they judged it necessary. Within the stadiums video surveillance and other technical measures were to be supported by stewards, a human resource developed in England, who have a dual function, as guides and security agents. One third of them were recruited from professional security services and the rest were volunteers.

In many circumstances the forces of law and order treated security issues in a holistic way, so that intelligence, the safety of players and referees as well as VIPs and the searches on the turnstiles were all directed at hooligans as much as at terrorists. Initially, some forms of criminality were probably underestimated; for example, ticketing was essentially designed to control hooliganism. In the event, the real problem was fraud, since tickets which had been paid for were not delivered and the French Organising Committee had to go to the courts. I shall only deal with the major risks and the measures taken with regard to them, not according to their frequency but rather in decreasing order, according to the level of danger they represented: terrorism, hooliganism and criminality.

Terrorism

A few days before the World Cup, Captain Paul Barril, who had been responsible for the safety of President François Mitterrand, gave an interview in which he stressed the seriousness of the terrorist threat to this event.[3] Indeed, there were numerous groups for whom the World Cup could be a major publicity opportunity, given its vast media coverage. First and foremost were the Algerian fundamentalists, who could draw on a pool of young persons from the peripheral city estates, as had happened a few years previously, in particular in the Lyon conurbation. France is host to between 3.5 and 4 million foreigners, of whom almost half are from the Maghreb (essentially Algerians); European immigrants are mainly Portuguese, Italian and Spanish. Then there were the members of the Corsican separatist movement recently responsible for the murder of the prefect of Corsica, M. Erignac. Finally, there were the supporters of the 300 terrorists of all hues held in French jails. Terrorism is less responsible than everyday antisocial behaviour for the climate of insecurity born in France in the 1960s and 1970s. Exacerbated by the disorder of mass demonstrations, this climate gave rise to the adoption of the so-called Peyrefitte law in February 1981 dealing with 'Security and Freedom', which constrained the right to demonstrate by introducing a collective legal responsibility on the part of demonstrators for damages caused. The law was rescinded by the new left-wing government later in 1981.

Terrorism is a sociological phenomenon, but it is also a breach of the law as defined in 1996 following terrorist acts committed in Paris against various forms of public transport. Under article 421-1 of the new penal code, terrorism requires that two conditions be met.[4] First, certain breaches of the law such as attempts on a person's life, sequestration or the destruction of property. Among other offences defined under the law one can highlight those relating to combat (that is, armed and organised) groups, as well as the act of importing, obtaining, making, possessing or illegally transporting explosives. The second condition requires a certain minimum planning, since there is no terrorism without strategy. The new penal code defines the above breaches of the law as acts of terrorism, if they have been committed 'intentionally with an individual or collective purpose with the aim of causing serious disruption to public order through intimidation or terror'.

Terrorism is punishable by a prison sentence, with a maximum of life, and other sanctions such as the withdrawal of civic rights, disbarment from professional activities and, for foreign nationals, exclusion from French soil. There is also the possibility of reduced sentences for those who may have committed or abetted a terrorist act but who warned the authorities in time and possibly enabled the guilty to be identified.

'Vigipirate' and Preventive Measures for France 98

In concrete terms, the French authorities introduced a series of measures for the World Cup. Firstly they strengthened the *Vigipirate* plan so as to protect the most vulnerable areas such as transport (airports, rail stations, the underground), telecommunications and energy distribution. There was a heightened visible presence of police and military personnel in such areas, as well as covert surveillance. *Vigipirate* is the codename of a government plan to co-ordinate all the anti-terrorist services. It was introduced in the summer of 1995 following an attack on a Jewish school in the Lyon area. It was scaled down in 1996 but reactivated in December of that year following an attack in a station of the Parisian regional rail network (RER).

The RAID (special police unit: Recherche-Assistance-Intervention et Dissuasion) whose specific task is the fight against terrorism and international crime, was brought into action, as were the special intervention units of the police and the gendarmes. The French police was responsible for the security of all the foreign teams and their entourage, as well as for all VIPs, from the moment they landed in France. A range of preventive measures were taken, such as searches of all the official hotels and reception venues by the bomb squad, changes of itinerary, permanent guards and checks for delegations such as those from the United States and Iran, which were the focus of special precautionary measures.

Furthermore, before the start of the tournament, on 26 May 1998, the police forces of a number of European states, France, Germany, Italy, Belgium and Switzerland, undertook some 100 preventive arrests of Algerian fundamentalists with known links to the GIA (Groupe islamique armé – Armed Islamic Group). A few days previously Britain had carried out a number of arrests, thus breaking with the previous minimalisation of the Islamic threat and more broadly of terrorism following the ceasefire in Northern Ireland. It appears that the persons arrested were seeking to set up logistical networks, but it was not clear whether their target was the World Cup.

Security Weaknesses

In spite of all the measures taken the security structure seemed to have certain weaknesses. The first of them being the plurality of, not to say the competition between the various branches of the French security forces, that is, the police and the gendarmes to which one might add, at times, foreign police. It should be noted that unlike in the United Kingdom, for example, the police forces in France are highly centralised and characterised by a dual system which dates back to the *ancien régime*. Thus in 1995 France was policed by 134,000 officers of the Police nationale, responsible for urban areas and, as civil servants therefore civilian, controlled by the Ministry of the Interior; alongside these *policiers* were 92,000 *gendarmes* under the authority of the Defence Ministry, and therefore part of the military, responsible for security in rural areas. In practice, some duties such as riot control are shared between units of the Compagnies républicaines de sécurité (CRS) and other police intervention groups on the one hand, and the *gendarmerie mobile* on the other.

The second weakness of security was due to the fact that it was not possible to check everyone at the gates of the stadiums, especially those participating in the organisation of the World Cup or responsible for surveillance. In truth, explosives can be miniaturised and taken in by various persons or even already be located in the stadium. This was the reason why the police sometime checked the content of sandwiches, since a baguette or half-baguette could easily conceal a flare or a detonator. Furthermore, an explosion could be the result of a booby trap car or a package left in some crowded spot close to the ground, as was the case in Atlanta in 1996. In Lyon the proximity of an oil storage depot to the ground meant that there was an increased risk factor, which in turn required special security measures. It would also have been possible to launch a terrorist attack on a stadium via model aircraft crammed with explosives, let alone the use of other terrorist tactics such as poisoning the water supply. However, the risk of a terrorist attack was judged to be lower than at the time of the G-7 summit in 1996, due to fact that few heads of state were present. In Lyon in 1998, six mobile units (around 500 officers) were established: two years before there had been 45 such units. In fact, the World Cup was disrupted by no terrorist incidents, and the real danger was to public order and came from hooliganism.

Hooliganism

Hooliganism defines the violence perpetrated in or around the ground by supporters of the teams playing there. In England, the footballing public has since the end of the nineteenth century been more closely linked to working-class culture than in France, and hooligan behaviour as a reaction against trends in society and sport developed there much earlier, in much closer relation to the working classes, and in a more violent manner. The extent and the mediatisation of this phenomenon have provoked numerous and varied interpretations which are considered discretely or in combination. Michel Comeron, a researcher at the University of Liège in Belgium, has established a classification of these interpretations, which I shall draw on freely in developing my own analysis.[5]

11. Security and police outside the Stade de France before the Final.

Approaches to Football Violence

At the level of the individual one can analyse football violence as the conjunction of an aggressive personality and a propitious environment. At a group level one can establish the extent to which the rivalry between teams intensifies supporters' partisanship and encourages the denigration of the opposition through the symbolic violence of insults. As an example, one can cite the veritable anthology of slogans chanted in April 1998 by fans of Marseille during a game against Paris Saint-Germain: 'Paris-Paris you're going to get stuffed', 'Parisian we're going to f*** your mother, we're going to kill you', 'Parisian poofters must die'. Supporters do not constitute a homogeneous group but are made up of numerous sub-groups, each having its own territory in the ground which they will at times fight to protect. Thus, to use the example of Marseille fans, '"The Winner's" [*sic*] are very different to the "Ultras", the "MTP" (Marseille Trop Puissant), the "Yankie's" [*sic*], the "Fanatic's" etc...'[6] It is also possible to explain hooliganism in terms of the notion of a crowd whose component parts lose their autonomy or who conform all the more readily to the behaviour of the largest number as the idea of individual responsibility vanishes.

Finally, the analysis of hooliganism may be formulated in social terms. This form of analysis has been advanced by sociologists at Leicester University inspired by Norbert Elias. According to this approach, the invention of sport corresponds to an historical process of social pacification which requires both the State monopoly of violence and self-control on the part of individuals. However, this process of civilisation, originating in courtly society and progressively diffused into the bourgeoisie and then the working class, is neither absolute nor homogeneous. It hardly reaches the lower segments of the proletariat and as a consequence gives rise to the association of sport and hooliganism.[7] In many ways it represents an affirmation of identity within certain sections of the working class through values such as virility or physical strength.[8]

The French State and Violence at Sporting Events: France 98

As regards the societal or State approach to hooliganism, the English experience undoubtedly provides a precedent and France is arguably lagging behind, with the World Cup acting as a catalyst.[9] However, in 1986 France ratified the European convention on violence and excesses by spectators at sporting events, introduced the previous year following the Heysel disaster in Brussels. This convention established the introduction of repressive measures, the deployment of sufficient security forces and the co-ordination between states in the movement of supporters. The convention also established the separation of rival groups of supporters in the stadium, the control of ticket allocations, the sale of alcoholic drinks and even the control of fireworks.

The 1993 law on security at sporting events established a fine of 50,000 francs for being drunk in a stadium or for carrying drink into a stadium. The fine is doubled and coupled with a one-year prison sentence for anyone who, inside a stadium, is responsible for acts of violence which lead to an injury which prevents work, or who has incited violence, or has manifested symbols of a racist or xenophobic nature. Carrying flares, fireworks or a weapon into a stadium carries a three-year jail sentence. Among the more specific sanctions one can point to the decree of 13 March 1998 preventing the manufacture, importation and sale of laser pointers such as those used for medical purposes but which can be dangerous when used aggressively against opposition players or supporters.

More recently a range of preventive measures was introduced with the World Cup in mind. The first related to the training of police officers. It was felt necessary to teach officers about crowd behaviour driven by emotion rather than by reason and about the intensification of these factors under the influence of alcohol. This theoretical approach was complemented by case studies using videos and photographs. The goal of such training was to facilitate the control of situations and to promote a measured response to possible violence so as to avoid provoking an aggressive response from the crowd. The second set of measures concerned liaison with foreign countries. It related to the introduction of a ban on alcoholic drinks on all coaches and trains carrying foreign supporters and the scheduling of their arrival as close to kick-off as possible and their departure as soon after the final whistle as possible. Attaining this level of co-operation with foreign police forces was indispensable. The third element covered the distribution of tickets so as to avoid fraud or access to tickets by undesirable elements.

The issue of fencing between the stands and the pitch was finalised rather late. These wire fences were initially intended to contain the spectators and to prevent them from running onto the pitch, but threatened under certain circumstances, such as a sudden surge in the crowd, to constitute a death-trap. Having learned from the English experience of this problem that treating spectators like animals encourages them to behave as such, French sporting officialdom and much later the French Interior Ministry realised that it was preferable to provide stewards and a calmer environment at the matches by taking away the fences and replacing them with moats or other features. The presence of stewards (*stadiers*) to interface with the fans was considered essential.

Controlling Foreign Supporters

With regard to the stay and travel of foreign supporters, a permanent shadowing of potential troublemakers was established by the police together with the creation of a centralised system of information. There were also to be searches at the point of departure in the country of origin, searches by customs, road checks, compulsory itineraries for coaches, the presence of uniformed police in certain trains, while foreign police officers could also accompany coaches. There would be police forces on standby to intervene on the obligatory itineraries should the need arise. In the city where a match was to take place, as well as surveillance in and around the stadium, it was also decided to segregate the areas where potential groups of troublemakers were staying and to allow for the use of patrols, as well as the creation of accommodation centres for young people arriving without tickets and with little or no money.

Around the grounds there were to be patrols to detect ticket touts. A security perimeter patrolled by police would enable them to direct ticket holders to the appropriate gate, as well as conduct searches for any dangerous objects and alcoholic drinks and to refuse entry to persons who were drunk. Opening up the grounds two or three hours before kick-off was also designed to minimise the consumption of alcohol. In the stadium, as previously indicated, police would carry out searches for explosives and uniformed police would monitor spectators throughout the game while plain clothes officers would mingle with groups of potential troublemakers. The aim was to identify the ringleaders and to eject them without causing problems for law-abiding spectators. There would also be a system designed to prevent spectators from invading the pitch and ensure protection for players and VIPs. Competing groups of supporters were separated in the stands by fencing which prevented any contact between them, and generally, their movement in and out of the grounds was kept separate. Furthermore, mobile intervention forces would be there to pursue troublemakers while, in the event of serious trouble, a reserve force, out of sight of the spectators, would be called into action.

At each World Cup venue all this police network was placed under a central command equipped with state-of-the-art video surveillance equipment and working closely with the stewards and the people responsible for security for the teams and host grounds. The video surveillance was intended to identify troublemakers; its use is much less widespread in France than in the United Kingdom and is subject to considerably more regulation. The presence at each venue of a magistrate authorised to issue warrants, guaranteed a rapid and appropriate judicial response. This was obviously an exceptional measure decided jointly by the Ministries of Justice and the Interior. Finally, at the end of the match the use of the police network outside the ground would enable the security services to control the crowd and achieve a swift and safe dispersal of supporters.

In reality the problem of hooliganism manifested itself much more outside the grounds than inside. The perpetrators were frequently different to those who had been anticipated at the outset and the frequent confrontations between foreign supporters and French youths of North African descent clearly aggravated the hooligan aspect: it was as if pre-existing urban conflicts had mutated into football hooliganism. These urban conflicts are somewhat similar to the disturbances involving black youths from the inner-cities in the United Kingdom; in France the most underprivileged urban areas are usually the suburbs peripheral to the major conurbations, where, as in the United Kingdom, it is the least well-integrated youngsters (in France those of Maghreb immigrant origin – *les Beurs* – 'Arabe' in backslang) who participate in urban disorder. There was, in consequence, a partial restructuring of the public order strategy which aimed to build on the lessons learned from the first incidents and to make the best use of the available co-operation with foreign police forces.

One should remember that as early as March 1998 the British Home Secretary, Jack Straw, had warned hooligans of what they could expect, pointing out that the French police were not known for their restrained approach and that they had powers of identity checks unknown in England, and he went on to urge supporters not to go to games if they did not have tickets. A number of English officers came to France to visit the various grounds and the deputy Chief Constable of the South Yorkshire Police Force was given a special role in this.

The Incidence of Hooliganism and Crowd Violence

The incidents that arose often resulted from confrontations between foreign supporters from European countries and *Beurs* identifying themselves with a Maghreb country or with France. The divide between the groups of fans was thus both socio-economic and cultural.

Marseille

It was on Saturday 13 June that incidents of hooliganism began in Marseille, two days before the scheduled England–Tunisia game on the afternoon of 15 June. The troubles escalated on the Sunday afternoon following clashes in the Vieux Port district, between rival supporters hurling beer cans at each other and at the police. Some English fans burned the Tunisian flag, which was felt to be a highly charged symbolic act of violence, that of a major state against a smaller one. The action provoked a violent response from their opponents and in particular from the young Marseillais of North African origin. During the evening and into the night these young men, originating from the estates in the north of the city and armed with clubs and iron bars, engaged in a veritable hunt for English fans.

In the late morning of the day of the game there was a renewed upsurge of violence with further throwing of cans and street fights. During the game, on the Prado beach where a giant screen had been installed, there was a serious outburst of violence following the first English goal. Shortly after, at the ground at the end of the game, youths from Marseille clashed with the police (perhaps because of a perceived passivity of the security forces towards the English fans), breaking car windscreens and smashing shop windows. The local daily, *La Provence*, spoke of urban guerrilla warfare as the police chased small groups of violent youths throughout the city.[10] Even though 80 arrests were made the police came under criticism for not having intervened more quickly when the initial troubles broke out and the English police was blamed for not having identified the English hooligans thereby helping the French officers control them. This inability to identify the potential trouble-makers was partly explained by the fact that the English supporters arrested for violent behaviour did not correspond to the 'high-risk' (category 'C') supporters expected by the police. Those who caused trouble in France were generally not previously known for hooligan behaviour, but were people who had started to behave – while abroad and under the influence of drink – in ways untypical of themselves at home.

The prefect of police in Marseille and then the regional prefect responded to this criticism by pointing out the relatively minor nature of the damage done, one million francs for the damaged shops, and went on to point out that instead of the expected known and classified hooligans, elements unknown to the English police had arrived.[11] Furthermore, they argued, that if the police had shown restraint at the outset this was because in a democratic state there is a need to refrain from the use of disproportionate measures infringing civil liberties. It was not possible to arrest the English simply because they had shaven heads and were drinking cans of beer. However, it is a fact that due to their equipment and organisation, the CRS remained relatively static and seemed to be less well prepared than the rapid intervention groups such as the anti-crime brigades. It should be remembered that the CRS are relatively large units of police whose deployment and action in situations of civil disturbance are governed by strict rules of hierarchy and discipline which leave very little room for initiative on the part of their members (and which also provide some guarantee of predictability of their behaviour for normal citizens).

In order to avoid a repetition of the incidents in Marseille, and in anticipation of the Holland–North Korea game, Saturday 20 June, the regional prefect banned the sale of alcohol from Friday 2 p.m. to midnight on Sunday 21 June; he also banned the drinking and even carrying of alcoholic drinks in public places. Furthermore, the prefect banned the sale of alcoholic drinks in all bars and restaurants after midnight on the Friday and Saturday.

The security forces relied on the use of the anti-crime brigades, the intervention groups with special expertise in the maintenance of public order, and of CRS deployed in groups of ten maximum to enable them to be more mobile. It was also decided to keep greater numbers of CRS in reserve as well as members of the *gendarmerie mobile*. Finally, adopting a tactic used by the Dutch police, French and Dutch officers would break up large groups of fans all wearing the national orange football shirts.[12]

Lens

On the heels of the English hooligans the German hooligans descended on Lens on Sunday 21 June for the Germany–Yugoslavia game, and in the violence after the game they seriously wounded a *gendarme*. Unlike the incidents in Marseille, initially the violence was not between supporters but between certain groups of supporters and the police. Nor was the violence prolonged as in Marseille. However, just as in Marseille alcohol played a large part since the person assumed to have attacked the gendarme was drunk. The events in Lens provoked considerable media interest. In the United Kingdom a feeling of relief at the behaviour of the German fans was evident, as it allowed a new perspective to be taken on the activities of the English supporters, as well as focusing the attention of the French on memories of the German occupation during the War. Contrastingly, in Germany there appeared a feeling of guilt linked to the country's Nazi past, since some German football hooligans, especially those linked with anti-Turkish-immigrant movements, shared neo-Nazi ideologies. The German police had warned the French authorities of the hooligans' arrival, resulting in increased numbers of security forces, but the most violent supporters had not been previously identified. After the incidents at Lens the German police instituted frontier-post identity checks on out-going fans in order to help the French police arrest those fans known to be violent. Lastly, the German Federal Interior Minister decided to prevent known violent supporters from travelling abroad to competitions.

Other Venues

There were further incidents elsewhere, as in Toulouse around the England–Romania game (22 June) with three wounded and 30 arrests, even though measures had been implemented to restrict the consumption of alcohol. At Châteaurenard, in the Bouches du Rhône department, following Morocco's failure to qualify for the next round despite their victory against Scotland, French North African youths attacked and damaged the town hall, the police station and the church. These incidents seemed to have been premeditated, and provoked originally by a feeling of rejection and frustration amongst the youth of a town whose council was accused of having recently refused to build a mosque and a youth centre.

In subsequent days the police tactics became more proactive. Thus at Montpellier on 25 June for the match Germany–Iran, 1,500 police officers were deployed and systematically checked all youths who bore any resemblance to a hooligan. At the same time the sale of alcoholic drinks was restricted. For the England–Columbia game in Lens on 26 June, the prefect for the Pas-de-Calais department banned the sale of alcohol not only in Lens but also in Lille and Calais. These measures were not entirely effective since, for commercial reasons, the ferry companies chose not to close their bars or their duty-free shops. Some fans arriving by car stocked up before leaving home or bought drinks in Belgium.

Given its proximity to England, the game in Lens was considered by the English police to be potentially much more dangerous than that in Marseille. In the event, 50,000 English supporters made the trip and there were clashes between the CRS and certain groups of fans in Lens, while there was also violence between fans and police and fights with French North African youths in Lille. Following the English win there were some 450 arrests and exclusions from French soil.[13] There were also arrests at Ostend in Belgium.

On 30 June in Saint-Etienne for the England–Argentina game (a game highly charged with symbolism due to the memory of the Falklands War) there were also measures taken to isolate English supporters to prevent clashes with the police and with French North African youths. Echoing events in Marseille, a British flag was burned, following which two North African youths were sentenced to jail. Further preventive measures were taken such as the decision by the prefect of the Rhône to ban the sale of alcohol in railway stations or their proximity. In Saint-Etienne there were 1,500 police and gendarmes stationed at all the possible flash points who could, if necessary, deploy specially designed anti-riot vehicles equipped with water canons. Overall, these measures proved to be fairly effective, so that the games between Germany and Croatia in Lyon (4 July) and, indeed, the France–Brazil final on 12 July, gave rise to no serious public order disturbances, other than cases of drunkenness and, in Lyon, an assault on a German police officer.

Controversial Measures

Among the wide range of measures used by the Interior Minister, Jean-Pierre Chevènement, two in particular gave rise to a certain amount of controversy. First was the matter of immediate expulsion. An initial judgment taken in Marseille against five English supporters and one

Tunisian was in the end revoked. On the other hand, six Germans arrested in Lens and four English arrested in Toulon were deported because, according to the minister, their attitude represented a threat to public order, that is, before they had committed any offence. This created some concern in Britain and among civil rights activists in France. The second controversial aspect was the decision by the Interior Minister to activate a safety clause in the Schengen agreement to enable him to reintroduce border checks. As we know, Schengen abolishes border controls between the signatory states, among which Britain does not figure. The French Prime Minister Lionel Jospin, much more pro-European than his Interior Minister, refused to sanction his proposal, nevertheless the Germans did carry out border checks in order to prevent the travel of hooligans.

It can consequently be seen that there is a divergence between the symbolism of European integration requiring the free circulation of citizens, including the free movement of delinquents, and the need for each state to ensure law and order. The solution reached during the World Cup apparently consisted in the replacement of the border controls which could have been done by the French authorities by checks made by the German police in Germany. This implied joint action between states relating to offences of an 'international' nature. Time alone will tell whether this kind of joint action is the best solution.

Alongside hooliganism there was the problem of common criminality, to which we now briefly turn.

Common Criminality

Throughout the World Cup there were numerous acts of common criminality. Some supporters fell victim to taxi drivers or unscrupulous chamber maids. However, the major problem was pickpocketing, largely attributable to gangs from South America and Eastern Europe. Such thieves operated mainly at airports, rail stations, in the big hotels and among the crowd before or after the games. In particular, Japanese tourists carrying large sums of money were easy targets for Peruvians who bear a certain physical similarity to them. In the Paris region the specialised anti-theft brigade headed by François Abjean, known as 'Boxer' due to the broken nose he sustained during an arrest, and the special railway police service for the Paris region, arrested some 40 thieves, many of them well known to the police.[14] In Lyon, two Croats who had attacked two English fans in an attempt to steal their tickets were summarily tried.[15]

Conclusion

All in all the World Cup was relatively successful from the security point of view. However, there was a degree of anxiety right to the end, as evidenced by the fact that when, on 8 July, during a meeting of the French Council of Ministers, President Jacques Chirac congratulated the Minister of the Interior Jean-Pierre Chevènement on the smooth running of the World Cup, Chevènement reminded him that there were still four days to go before the Final.[16] To sum up, if the experience gained in the prevention of terrorism and the protection of public order has been invaluable, there can be no guarantee of success in any similar circumstances in the future.

Overall, the original hypothesis of the indetermination of public policy seems to be confirmed, even though it is certainly possible to reduce the uncertainty. For the World Cup, the various technical measures implemented in grounds were successful, but the aim of identifying hooligans was not achieved completely. On the other hand, the innovations put into practice to control hooligan behaviour – such as the restrictions on alcohol and the arrest of certain 'high-risk' supporters – appeared to be more successful. The virtue of international police co-operation still remains a matter of debate. In total during the World Cup 1,000 people were arrested, 1,500 were refused entry into France, and 167 were prosecuted (including 76 French, 40 English, 2 Scots, 13 German, 6 Dutch, 5 Argentine, 5 Croat, 5 Tunisian), leading to several sentences of short terms in prison accompanied by bans on attending matches or entering France.[17]

It is clear that for financial reasons above all, but also due to the limited capacity of the stadiums, the 'spectacle' took place as much outside the grounds as inside. It was outside that there was the most lively atmosphere and it was outside that the problems of maintaining public order were the most acute. The management of the immense crowds gathering after the victory went off with no great problems except for the unforseeable one of cars being driven recklessly and causing injuries and a fatality.

Finally, symbolism and in particular the symbol of the national flag played a major role. At a time when the creation of Europe raises the issue of national sovereignty, football remains one of the pillars of national identity. Furthermore, the major contribution to France's victory made by Zinedine Zidane, a player of Algerian parentage, who grew up in a deprived area of Marseille, and the mobilisation of young French North Africans (the *Beurs*) gave football a power of integration which had hitherto been the responsibility of the French school system.

NOTES

1. B. Jobert and P. Muller, *L'État en action. politiques publiques et corporatismes* (Paris, PUF, 1987) pp.40, 49.
2. C. Journès, 'Politiques de sécurité et syndicalisme policier en France et en Grande Bretagne', *Les Cahiers de la sécurité intérieure*, 31, 239–57.
3 P. Barril, *Lyon Mag*, 71 (June 1998), 38–41.
4. Y. Mayaud, *Le terrorisme* (Paris, PUF, 1997), pp.7, 41.
5. M. Comeron, 'Hooliganisme : la délinquance des stades de football', *Déviance et société*, 21, 1 (1997), 97–113.
6. *Charlie Hebdo*, supplément du n°308 (1998), 'L'horreur footballistique', 6–8.
7. N. Elias and E. Dunning, *Quest for Excitement, Sport and Leisure in the Civilizing Process* (Oxford, Blackwell, 1986).
8. E. Dunning, P. Murphy and J. Williams, *The Roots of Football Hooliganism: An Historical and Sociological Study* (London, Routledge, 1988).
9. P. Mignon, 'La lutte contre le hooliganisme, comparaisons européennes', *Les Cahiers de la sécurité intérieure*, 26 (1996), 92–107.
10. *La Provence*, 16 June 1998, 30.
11. *La Provence*, 17 June 1998, 28; *Le Monde*, 20 June 1998, supplément 'Le Mondial', viii.
12. *La Provence*, 18 June 1998, 26.
13. *The Times*, 27 June 1998, 1.
14. *La Provence*, 19 June 1998, 11; *Le Figaro*, 24 June 1998, 36 and 10 July 1998, 24.
15. *Lyon Figaro*, 6 July 1998, 13.
16. A. Chemin and N. Herzberg, 'L'influent ministre citoyen', *Le Monde*, 11 July 1998, 10.
17. *Le Figaro*, 17 July 1998, 8.

Reporting the World Cup:
Old and New Media

LUCY McKEEVER

The 1998 World Cup was billed as the biggest media event of the twentieth century, and perhaps nowhere was its media impact more noteworthy than in the host country itself. Long-established French television viewing and newspaper sales records were shattered. New radio stations and television channels were created especially for the tournament. The *savoir-faire* of France's media professionals was on show to the world, and, with 40,000 press pass requests received for the tournament's media nerve centre in Paris, the world's media was on show to France.

The 1998 World Cup provides therefore an opportunity to explore the French media in three main contexts. Firstly, the media as a mirror of French society, portraying a nation on a collective voyage from proud hosts to delirious victors. Secondly, the media as a powerful agent in its own right, influencing and being influenced by the society it portrays, possessing functions far beyond that of passive communications mechanism. Thirdly, the media as an industry, with 1998 providing a particularly apposite time for analysis since it finds France's media industry on the threshold of immense technological, financial and political upheaval.

It is on these three pegs that our analysis will hang, as impacts *of* and *on* the French media during the tournament are explored for each media category in turn, beginning with its oldest established sector, the press.

The French Press and the World Cup: A Chance for Recovery?

The 1998 World Cup marked an opportunity for the French press to arrest a decline which was gathering momentum as competition from newer media such as the Internet and cable television exacerbated the damage already done by the impact of television. Although the French press overall seems healthily diverse, with over 3,000 titles reflecting the nation's geographical, social and cultural heterogeneity, daily newspapers have long had less impact for the French than for their European counterparts; only one in five French people read a daily newspaper, compared to just over one in two Britons, and the impressive total of 80 Parisian daily newspapers in 1914 has fallen to just 11 today.[1] Could the 1998 World Cup, perhaps the most significant national event in the lifetime of most French adults, re-establish the authority of the French press as the nation's leading commentators? Certainly, it was an unprecedented opportunity, but first the French press would have to surmount one small matter: its profound lack of interest in football.

The Generalist Press and the 1998 World Cup

One of the most significant impacts of the World Cup on the French generalist press was the universal decision to break with long-standing tradition and carry extensive daily football coverage. Throughout the tournament, every major daily newspaper produced a football supplement of an average eight pages every day, in striking contrast to the average single page per week devoted to all sports. Readers accustomed to minimal sports coverage were greeted with pages of statistics, reports, interviews and analysis as the tournament progressed; even the austere *Le Monde* assigned 40 journalists to its daily pull-out supplement, although it still devoted its main editorial to the Japanese general election on the day after the Final. Coverage was not limited to separate supplements either; as the tournament wore on, football news became headline news, with all other stories pushed to the inside pages.

The victory of the French team on 12 July was greeted with euphoric press coverage, as newspapers portrayed a country transformed by delight. Most editors sought to place it in context by comparing the impact on the nation with that of other pivotal events in recent French history, such as the Libération (*L'Equipe* and *Libération*), the 1789 Revolution (*Le Parisien*) or the May '68 student uprising (*France-Soir* and *Le Figaro*). Headlines ranged from the breathless, 'Incredible, crazy, unimaginable, fabulous, fantastic' (*Aujourd'hui*); the graphic, 'A tricolour orgasm' (*France-Soir*); the patriotic, 'It's ours!' (*Le Parisien*); and the poetic, 'La vie en bleu' (*Libération*). Elsewhere, the words 'fabulous', '*triomphe*' and 'thank you' were omnipresent.

Journalists also sought to deconstruct the wider significance of the event, analysing the harmonising impact of victory on a nation which had not always been at ease with itself in recent years. Analysis included the introspective ruminations of *Libération*'s editor Serge July: 'Victory in the World Cup final does not change social reality, but it can change the image the French have of themselves',[2] and the presaging tone of *Le Monde*: 'the dominating theme behind the euphoria which has overtaken the country is the idea that something has changed in the collective conscience'.[3] The outpouring of joy even led to an unprecedented show of unity between the right-wing *Le Figaro* and the Communist *L'Humanité,* with both viewing the victory as a triumph for France's multiracial society. It is hard to conceive the following eulogy to multiracial France appearing in *Le Figaro* before or since: 'What would we be without our ethnic communities? Thank you to our overseas territories, thank you Africa, and thank you Kabylia.' France's four principal weekly news magazines were also gripped by the tournament, devoting several pages of coverage to the victory.[4] Only *France-Soir* managed to introduce a discordant tone, that of writer Bernard Clavel, protesting against the chauvinism and excessive riches of the tournament.

For those regions of France containing host cities, the World Cup was a major news event as well as a sporting one, and throughout the tournament, the major regional papers such as *La Dépêche du midi*, *Le Progrès*, *Sud-Ouest*, *Nord-France*, and *Midi-Libre*, produced daily World Cup supplements, as well as substantial coverage in the main part of the paper, dominated by photographs of (usually) smiling foreign fans mixing with proud locals. France's vibrant regional press, which accounts for 70 per cent of the total French newspaper market, flourishes primarily because of the country's strong sense of regional identity, and regional papers have also traditionally tended to take a closer interest in sports coverage than their national counterparts, given their greater geographical and emotional proximity to local teams, coupled with the commercial imperative: 'For the regional press, good results for local teams are a powerful sales boost.'[5] However, high-profile scandals at provincial football clubs in recent years have led some commentators to question the objectivity of regional football reporting, since the papers are themselves often under the patronage of the very local politicians and club presidents embroiled in the scandals. Nonetheless, the World Cup banished all talk of scandal, as every region united behind the French team.

Of the less mainstream papers, the satirical *Charlie Hebdo* declared itself *Le journal de l'anti-Mondial*, producing its own spoof supplement *L'horreur footballistique*, while the leading satirical weekly, *Le Canard enchaîné*, provided typically caustic coverage, deconstructing the sometimes murky business of football, and lampooning everything from *nouveaux* football supporters to inane television commentators.

Yet while France's newspapers were agreed that the World Cup would have a lasting impact on the nation, France 98's impact on the press itself appears to have been more transient. *Le Figaro* has not entered into any more ideological pacts with *L'Humanité*, and football coverage has reverted to its status of little more than a *fait divers*; a mere four weeks after the victory, *Le Monde* devoted just one page of coverage to the start of the French domestic football season in an entire week.

The French Sports Press and the World Cup

Like its counterparts in the generalist press, France's specialist sporting press is characterised by a lack of pluralism and dynamism, with *L'Equipe*, the most widely read daily newspaper in France, exercising a monopolistic stranglehold which can be attributed as much to the conspicuous lack of sports coverage elsewhere in the French press, as to the quality of its writing, which has made it one of the world's leading sports papers. Twelve years ago, a short-lived rival magazine, *Sport*, was founded by a group of rebel journalists from *L'Equipe*, but it soon folded, thereby suffering the same fate as other putative rival publications such as *Le Miroir des Sports* and *Sport Mondial* in the 1960s, and one of the rebels, Jérôme Bureau, is now safely installed as *L'Equipe*'s current editor.

Specialist football publications are similarly thin on the ground. Other than glossy magazines aimed at adolescents, such as *Onze* and *Planète Foot*, the twice-weekly *France Football* is the only magazine to offer serious treatment of the sport. Owned, like *L'Equipe*, by the Amaury group, *France Football* focuses on French football at club and international level in prolific depth, and is a major success story of the French specialist press, having achieved record sales in 1996, with an average circulation of 230,000. Yet despite the clear demand for specialist football publications in France, there is little sign of any competition to challenge the Amaury hegemony, other than plans of a former *France-Soir* journalist, Robert Ichah, to launch a new football weekly called *Carton Foot*, which promises to be the *Canard Enchaîné* of football, in other words, satirical and irreverent. Indeed, far from encouraging an opportunistic flurry of new football titles, the World Cup seemed to mark a tightening of Amaury's stranglehold on sports coverage, as firstly both *France Football* and *L'Equipe*, anticipating a World Cup-led surge in readership, increased their publication frequency, with *France Football* also upping its number of journalists by 50 per cent, and secondly, in October 1997, *L'Equipe* launched plans for a sports news channel with the digital television company, CanalSatellite. This latter move was the latest evidence of a growing trend towards cross-media ownership by companies such as Amaury, Hachette and Havas, which dominate the increasingly concentrated proprietorship of today's French press.

L'Equipe *and the Mondial: l'affaire Jacquet*

For *L'Equipe*, the World Cup promised potentially its finest hour, but almost proved to be its nadir. Jubilation at victory on 12 July was tempered with embarrassment at the fallout from its long-standing campaign against Aimé Jacquet and his tactics, expressed by polemical headlines such as 'What sort of match is that?' and 'Mourir d'Aimé' ('Dying of Aimé [love]'). Just before the tournament, the deputy editor had summed up the team's prospects scathingly: 'It's no longer the national French team. It's a corner shop,' an approach which seemed far removed from *L'Equipe's* loyalty during the 1982 World Cup, when it famously awarded a plaque to the French team after their heroic defeat in Seville.[6]

Although *L'Equipe* did throw its weight wholeheartedly behind the team as the tournament progressed, exhorting the players with banner headlines such as 'You can do it,' and 'It's your destiny,' Jacquet felt the paper had greatly overstepped the boundary between reporting and distorting. He trenchantly refused to forgive his critics, arraigning them as 'hooligans, dishonest and imbeciles', which in turn drew a stinging riposte from *L'Equipe's* editor, Jérôme Bureau; 'Nothing legitimises the extreme violence of the words you have used. What a sad creed it is which advocates the lynching of those who did not think in the same way as you.'[7] Bureau did, however, admit he had been proved wrong, an admission which Michel Chemin, commenting in *Libération*, attributed to the realities of commercial life and the compelling weight of a nation's opinion.[8] None the less, the spat did not appear to have any deleterious effect on the newspaper's relationship with its readers, since sales rose by 30 per cent during the tournament, including a record 1.7 million copies the day after France's victory, beating all post-war records for a single edition of a newspaper. It also sold a third of a million of its experimental Sunday edition, enough to convince it to continue after the World Cup.

Yet the longer lasting legacy could prove more damaging, particularly as divisions on the editorial staff caused by *l'affaire Jacquet* were so swiftly followed by the catastrophic drug-ridden Tour de France, an event heavily sponsored by *L'Equipe*. Since the reporting of news is now news itself, French newspapers were quick to offer their verdict on *l'affaire Jacquet*. *Le Figaro* called for lessons to be learned; 'It's not a case of laying into *L'Equipe* … but we need to acknowledge that the media world's belief in its own infallibility leads to arrogance and injustice,'[9] while *Libération* attributed it to *L'Equipe's* lack of competitors: '*L'Equipe*, monopolising the market, has constantly to make itself distinct without any competitors … And make events happen … nurture them, report them, even create them.'[10]

France Football avoided the controversy excited by its stable-mate, having long maintained a loyal stance towards Jacquet (interviewed on 12 July on 98 Radio France, one of the magazine's journalists called Jacquet 'a formidable tactician and an exceptional human being'). The magazine's rather dense content of World Cup reports and results was balanced out by more quirky features, such as *enfant de la balle*, in which stars such as Sacha Distel discussed their love of football, a fantasy football league and colour photographs of every single goal scored in the tournament. It delighted in France's victory.[11]

For the specialist press, therefore, the World Cup provided record sales, wonderful copy, and a final result they could hardly have dared dream of, though there is some disquiet that Amaury's lack of competitors has led to a complacent slackening of standards in its two leading sports publications. Jacques-Marie Bourget, a former professional footballer now working as a journalist for *Paris Match*, feels for example that while today's *journalistes diplômés* at *L'Equipe* know the height and width of a goal and can cite reams of statistics on request, their style is far removed from the *beauté poétique* of the era of former editor Antoine Blondin, and the blandness of content is further exacerbated by fear of reprisals from club presidents, which prevents them from engaging in any investigative journalism worthy of the name.[12] Such concerns have also permeated into sports journalism on French television, the medium to which we now turn.

French TV and the World Cup: The Success Story Continues?

If the World Cup presented a chance for the French press to arrest a steady decline, it offered French television the prospect of consolidating its position as the country's richest and most influential mass media. Furthermore, it also promised to mark the apogee of the relationship between football and television in France, which, having for so long been characterised by suspicion and hostility, has since the 1980s been transformed into one of mutual opulence. For television, football's blend of stardom and live action makes it an irresistible televisual prospect. For football, the riches now pouring into the game from television rights have metamorphosed it beyond the dreams of any club president: in 1997, television channelled 1.2m francs into French football, almost half the value of the entire budget for the Ministry of Youth and Sports that year.

Football on French Television: Affluence and Attrition

The blanket television coverage of the 1998 World Cup contrasted sharply with that of the 1962 World Cup Final between Brazil and Czechoslovakia in Chile, which did not even manage an appearance on French screens until 48 hours after the match, and even by 1973, with French football in the doldrums at national and club level for many years, only ten hours of football were broadcast on French television during the entire year. However, the emergence of the Saint-Etienne team towards the mid-1970s led to a concomitant upsurge in televised football, as *Les Verts*' European matches were broadcast and captured the nation's hearts. In the 1980s a series of developments in French television sowed the seeds for the stratospheric rise in the importance of televised football which dominates today's television landscape.[13]

Firstly, the arrival of Canal Plus in 1984, France's first subscription channel, which now has subscribers in 4.3 million homes, and is the most profitable channel on French television. Canal Plus recognised the enormous potential of the demand for televised sports coverage, and football in particular. Shaking up the market for televised football by aggressively buying up rights and introducing innovative stylistic techniques to its match coverage, it rapidly left other French channels trailing in its wake, so that by 1995 Canal Plus accounted for 32 per cent of sport broadcast on French television, and between 43 and 61 per cent of total football coverage.[14]

Secondly, towards the end of the 1980s, the increasing commercialisation of French television, which culminated in the privatisation of the leading channel, TF1, in 1987, intensified the competition to secure sports coverage rights, and gave TF1 the financial power to outbid its competitors. The result was that the ten hours of football broadcast in 1973 had grown to 257 by 1988, almost doubling again by 1995. Although this was part of a general increase in sports coverage, which grew fourfold from 1982 to 1992, it was football which easily accounted for the greatest proportion of sports broadcast. Yet still demand outstrips supply: in 1995 football accounted for 47.5 per cent of sport watched, but only 22 per cent of sports broadcast, and it occupied 18 out of the 21 most watched televised sporting events in Europe in 1996. This phenomenal demand, bringing clear attractions for advertisers, has led football to be virtually the only sporting event now shown at peak viewing time on French television.

Inter-channel feuding for football rights has now become a permanent feature of the French broadcasting landscape, dominated by the attempts of the smaller channels to fight the monopoly of TF1 and Canal Plus, who have long operated a UEFA-endorsed cartel for the broadcasting of French clubs' exploits in European competitions. Recent years are littered with anecdotes of petty rivalry, such as TF1 attempting to prevent personnel from other television channels entering stadiums at which it was covering matches, or announcers on rival channels subverting the statutory requirement to acknowledge use of TF1 football footage by using sarcastic voice-overs, deliberately covering up the on-screen TF1 logo, or simply refusing to comply. The hostility towards TF1 stems largely from its aggressive approach in the marketplace for football rights, as a rival recently stated: 'TF1 buys up the rights to football coverage ... just to ensure that the other channels can't have them.'[15] So absurd did the situation become that the Commission Sport et Télévision, founded in 1991, introduced a sports broadcasting *code of conduct* in 1992, which was signed by representatives from all channels and led to an uneasy truce.

Yet as the World Cup dawned, evidence suggested that television's love affair with football was beginning to cool. It seemed football was beginning to price itself out of the market: French football league television rights soared to an average 5m francs in 1996, compared to 0.2m in the mid-1980s, while Champions League rights rose by an astonishing 60m francs from 1996 to 1998. At the same time, viewing figures were plummeting, a crisis to which TF1 responded by paring down its football coverage, whereas Canal Plus, sensing a sea-change in the future of televised football, responded more bullishly by launching its pay-per-view football channel in September 1996. The project immediately became a new source of dispute, drawing strong criticism from the clubs which felt the rights had been sold for a ludicrously low fee (50m francs per year, compared to 300m in Italy, and 720m in the United Kingdom) and from rival television channels which felt Canal Plus had been given scandalously preferential treatment by the league, with decisions taken after minimal consultation and explanation. None the less, the first two seasons of pay-per-view suggest it has already secured a firm foothold in France, boosted particularly by the fact that supporters tend to live further away from clubs than in Britain or Italy, which are still resisting its introduction.

French Television and the 1998 World Cup: TVRS 98

Thus, as the global reputation of French television was put on trial by its coverage of the 1998 World Cup, it was clear that strong efforts would be required by all channels to dispel the climate of feuding and disillusionment which was threatening to engulf French television's relationship with football.

Preparation for the 1998 World Cup began in earnest in 1993, when TF1, France Télévision, Canal Plus and Radio France formed a joint production and broadcasting company, the Groupement des radiodiffuseurs français (GRF), which in turn gave rise to the project TVRS 98 (Télévision radio services 98). Six producers, three from Canal Plus, two from TF1, and one from France Télévision, were charged with producing all 64 matches. Although the initial consensus among French television channels had been against taking sole responsibility for broadcasting to the world, the tradition of the host country providing all the broadcasting services in this fashion is a long-standing one, and it was felt that France could not countenance breaking it.[16] Thus, even before the first pictures were broadcast, the World Cup had had a huge impact on French television, marking the first and probably the last occasion on which all public and private sector channels had collaborated in such a major way. The tournament marked another significant technological innovation, since it was the first time a major international sporting event had been filmed entirely in digital format, bringing sharper quality for viewers and greater flexibility for producers. This continued a tradition of the World Cup as a forum for introducing new televisual techniques, following the introduction of action replays in 1966, colour in 1970, and reverse angle shots in 1986.

If the conception of TVRS 98 was marked by reticence, the finished product was impressively grandiose, manifested physically by the joint broadcasting and press centre, the CIRTV, built at the Parc des Expositions in Paris at a cost of 100 million francs. A cursory glance at the statistics demonstrates the immense logistical scale of the project; 1,500 people worked for TVRS 98, producing 16,500 hours of television coverage, or 318 hours per match, and spending a budget of over 150m francs.

The strategic imperatives driving TVRS 98 caused some controversy. As the company would be responsible for the broadcast of sound and vision to almost 200 countries, its aims were made clear from the outset; the priority was to ensure that transmission was reliable and standardised. It was not the time for experiments, reinforced by the company's mantras: 'The World Cup is not a laboratory' and 'Airbus rather than Concorde.' However prudent this conservative approach may have been, it did frustrate some members of one of France's most innovative broadcasting sectors, with one producer talking of 'a return to the television of our fathers' generation, flying in the face of the formidable innovations introduced by Canal Plus since 1984 ... no attempts to portray emotion or aestheticism'.[17] Stylistic freedom was further frustrated by FIFA restrictions, which stipulate, among other matters, equality of coverage to both teams and limited use of slow motion replays. Thus, every match was filmed according to a strict set of guidelines, with 17 cameras deployed for each match in the same positions, together with eight slow motion and four super-slow motion systems, although more important matches were reinforced by additional portable cameras.

In the end, the caution appeared justified – opinion on the performance of TVRS 98 was generally positive, and there were none of the technical lapses which had bedevilled opening matches of USA 94. Indeed, the only cause for concern was raised by one of TVRS 98's few stylistic innovations – the super-slow motion replays, 'especially when they are shown as a goal is almost being scored or another incident is taking place elsewhere'.[18] For the individual channels, however, critical reaction was less unified.

Canal Plus – Vive la différence!

For Canal Plus, the 1998 World Cup presented two stern challenges. Frustrated by the TVRS 98 restrictions, it had to find other, subtler ways of

12. The French press reports victory.

demonstrating the superiority of its coverage, which had set it apart from rival channels for so long, using techniques popularised in Britain, including slow motion, varied camera angles, expert analysts, and touchline interviews. Secondly, it also marked the first occasion on which Canal faced direct competition from other channels broadcasting the same match simultaneously.

Canal responded confidently, opting for blanket coverage, with all 64 matches broadcast live at a total cost of 100m francs, 30 million more than its closest rival, TF1. Attempting to set itself apart from the other channels with the slogan 'a different viewpoint, a different emotion', it circumvented many of the production restrictions, deploying six extra cameras of its own in each stadium, showing 40 matches in widescreen format, adding its own reverse angle shots, slow motions, and the famous split-screen replays of reactions on the bench to action on the pitch, which provided some of the tournament's most memorable images. Commentating was led by its experienced duo, Charles Biétry and Thierry Gilardi, and complemented by expert summarisers such as Basile Boli, Luis Fernandez and Arsène Wenger.

The tone of Canal's output was quirky and humorous; matches were interrupted by quickly drawn cartoons, while the nightly prime-time *Journal de François Pêcheux* provided a slick and witty round-up of the day's events, glamorous guests and a roving reporter flying to a different competing country every day. They even managed a nonchalant post-modern reference to the nature of viewing, with François Pêcheux reflected in a mirror interviewing a reporter who was in turn filming Pêcheux with a hand held camera. Canal's stylistic embellishments such as these invariably end up being emulated by rival channels, a process described by a BBC cameraman covering the World Cup as the cyclical transformation from pretentious to artistic to standardised to clichéd.[19] There is more to Canal's coverage than clever gimmicks, though: for example, its level of analysis of play was far more advanced than rival channels, primarily because its viewers tend to be more knowledgeable, a fact acknowledged by Michel Platini, himself one of Canal's pundits.[20]

Canal's gamble to opt for saturation coverage appeared to pay off – it received excellent reviews, 'Canal have really shown their savoir-faire in the production and broadcasting of major events',[21] and perhaps unsurprisingly it was a Canal Plus producer, Jean-Jacques Amsellem, who was awarded the contract to produce the Final. Audience approval was high too – 90 per cent of Canal Plus subscribers watched at least one match, and total subscriptions rose by more than 50 per cent. It also made some scoops, being the first channel to secure an interview with one of the team (Barthez) as the final whistle blew on 12 July, and the only one to capture Jacquet's tears after the Croatia match. Canal Plus' status as one of the sponsors of the French team also allowed them privileged access to the team's Clairefontaine headquarters to make a fly-on-the-wall documentary broadcast shortly after the tournament,[22] and all in all, the tournament confirmed Canal's position as 'the true partner of French football'.[23] However, Canal's favoured status does not come without its critics. There are those who feel the channel is wide open to possible collusions of interest, as it not only sponsors the French national team but Paris Saint-Germain as well, leading Guy Roux, trainer of rivals Auxerre and TF1 pundit, to comment dryly on more than one occasion, 'In the game of Monopoly, the banker is not supposed to be one of the players as well.'

TF1 – 'Tous en finale avec TF1'

For TF1, France's leading commercial channel in terms of viewing figures, the World Cup arrived just as it was beginning to scale down its coverage of football in general, for the ostensible reason that 'too much football kills football', although most observers believed the decision was related more to a slump in viewing figures: TF1's French championship audiences had fallen by almost two million in five years, and it had recently given up contracts to cover the UEFA and Cup Winners Cup, fearing similar slumps. Nonetheless, with football still representing 65 per cent of its sports programmes, TF1 approached the World Cup positively, covering 26 matches live in alternation with the state network, France Télévision, and securing big-name pundits such as David Ginola. Like Canal Plus, TF1 tried to innovate around the TVRS 98 restrictions, for example, introducing 'Virtual Replay', which fades video action into 3-D graphical representations, enabling viewers to see a key incident from any angle.

In recent years TF1 has been criticised for sacrificing quality in the rush for audiences, and critical opinion on its World Cup coverage reflected this. It got off to a bad start with a stamina-testing six-hour broadcast of the opening ceremony, widely derided for its torpor. The other main source of reproach was TF1's infamous commentating duo, Thierry Roland and Jean-Michel Larqué. The former is something of a legend in France, having covered ten Olympic Games, nine World Cups, and achieved national irritant status to such an extent that L'Evénement du Jeudi headlined its World Cup supplement 'Football without Thierry Roland – it is possible', illustrated with a picture of him gagged. He is known for his outspoken comments, earning a ban for calling a referee a 'bastard' on-air in 1978, and more recently venturing opinions on a variety of matters including his sympathy for the death penalty, the extreme-right Algerian war terrorists the OAS, and National Front leader Jean Marie Le Pen.[24] His commentating skills do not appear to compensate for his unpalatable views, either.

Websites cataloguing his commentating inanities flourished during the World Cup, and one observer recently drew this stinging portrait of him: 'Thierry has cultivated the most exasperating linguistic tics ... small-minded observations, bigoted ramblings, boorish in every way.'[25]

The criticism of TF1's coverage was not unexpected. The apparent decline in the integrity and insight of its sports journalism has been seen as a by-product of its over-enthusiastic embracing of the football rights circus, which has made it loath to risk offending football club presidents. Hence, the 20-year longevity of TF1's blandly uncritical programme *Téléfoot* contrasts sharply with the fate suffered by its investigative sports programme *Va y avoir du sport*, which ruffled so many feathers that it lasted only one year, although at least long enough to secure the amazing on-screen admission from Bordeaux club president, Claude Bez, that he had bribed match referees with prostitutes.

None the less, while not achieving critical acclaim, the World Cup demonstrated TF1's immutability in the audience ratings war, which saw it score 92 out of the top 100 best audiences in 1997. Fortunate enough to have secured coverage of France's final and semi-final in the allocation of matches with France Télévision, TF1 was rewarded with its highest viewing figures of all time, and its team was unable to resist gloating at its loathed rivals at Canal Plus on the night of the Final, with TF1's summariser Guy Roux reminding viewers of the merciless lampooning of Zidane before the tournament on Canal's satirical puppet show *Les Guignols*.

France Télévision – 'France 2, Ennui 0'

If the World Cup found TF1 scaling down its football coverage, the reverse was the case at France Télévision, the country's public service network, comprising France 2 and France 3. Having been completely football-free since 1994, France Télévision had recently taken over League Cup coverage from TF1, and was therefore looking to re-establish itself as a leading football broadcaster. It rose to the challenge, warming up for the tournament by producing a series of football-related programmes including *Un monde foot* and *My Canal is British* [*sic*], featuring French players in England. Boasting the perky slogan *France 2, Ennui 0* (France 2, Boredom 0) it shared the broadcast of 38 matches between France 2 and France 3, using six pairs of commentators and consultants including Chris Waddle, Roger Milla, and its jewel in the crown, Pele.

Although the luck of the draw with TF1 meant France Télévision was unfortunate enough to miss out both on France's semi-final and final appearance, it received very positive reviews, even of its mammoth seven-hour coverage of the opening match.[26] Although its two main commentators, Pierre Sled (journalist) and Paul Le Guen (former player), mirror the journalist/ex-player format of TF1's Roland-Larqué, the likeable duo are always able to exploit the indubitable fact that they are *not* Roland and Larqué. Unable to compete financially with Canal Plus and TF1, France Télévision steered clear of gimmicks.[27]

Away from match coverage, France 3 broadcast the nightly hour-long *Le Club du Mondial,* hosted by the experienced sports broadcaster Gérard Holtz, which averaged a million viewers, or 20 per cent of the audience, receiving good reviews for its mixture of features, guests and resident experts. After the Final, the programme was broadcast until 6 a.m., complete with dancers from the Moulin Rouge, and secured the scoop of Zidane's first post-match interview.

One of the more interesting effects of the World Cup on French television was the choice of programme when football was on the other channel, and while most channels chose this slot to broadcast their cheapest programmes, France Télévision chose a deliberate policy of *contre programmation*, showing more offbeat programmes, thus reflecting State television's responsibility to provide public service broadcasting to all.[28]

M6, La Cinquième and Arte: 'Absolutely no foot'

The three minority channels did not show any live matches, but were unable to avoid the pervasive impact of the World Cup, broadcasting football-related programmes including La Cinquième's series *La planète ronde,* and the football theme night by the cultural channel, Arte.

M6, the low-budget commercial channel, which targets a younger audience with its heavy diet of pop music and American imports, was the only one of the three smaller channels to attempt to challenge their rivals' live football monopoly, going to court in December 1997 in an effort to overturn the refusal of the European Broadcasting Union to allow M6 to join and thereby secure eligibility for rights to broadcast World Cup matches. The campaign did not succeed, but, undaunted, M6 determined to make a virtue of its lack of football, promoting itself as it had done in Euro 96 as the channel providing a refuge from football, with the slogan '0 per cent foot – 100 per cent M6'. Its policy seemed to work – audience figures remained as normal, suggesting it had succeeded in its aim of reaching the 37 per cent of households with two or more televisions. The '0 per cent foot' campaign was sponsored by the food mixer company, Moulinex, in anticipation of popularity with female viewers, and promoted *grands séducteurs* evenings of films starring heart-throb actors, although the next section reveals a possible flaw in this marketing strategy. Arte also launched an 'absolutely no foot' campaign, led by its flagship comedy import from the United Kingdom *Absolutely Fabulous.*

French Television and the World Cup: General Implications

The impact of the World Cup on French television was seen most clearly in the tournament's viewing figures, the most significant of which are highlighted in the following table. All channels broadcasting live matches smashed audience ratings records, with France 2 scoring its highest audience of the year, and TF1 and France 3 securing their highest audiences of all time. Indeed, the figures listed below do not reflect the magnitude of the event as a televisual phenomenon, as the calculations of *Audimat* (the national broadcasting survey) only allow for a maximum of eight people per household and thus did not take into account the thousands watching in bars and on giant screens across France. Conversely, the night of the final saw France 2 scoring its lowest ever viewing figures with just 1.2 million watching its film *Tess*, while Arte's film choice *Jamon! Jamon!* attracted a lamentable 366,000. However, if TF1 won on quantity, Canal Plus triumphed on quality – Canal Plus viewers awarded the channel 8.4/10 satisfaction ratings, compared to 6.6 for France 3, 6.4 for France 2 and 6.2 for TF1. One of the most commented-upon viewing statistics was the unprecedented popularity of the tournament with women – almost 1 in 2 viewers of the Final was female, which led television advertising companies to adjust their input accordingly as the tournament reached the closing stages.

TABLE 1

WORLD CUP AUDIENCE RATINGS – FRANCE 98

Top Ten audience ratings for matches broadcast on French television

France v Brazil (final)	TF1	20, 577,480
France v Croatia (semi-final)	TF1	17,697,680
France v South Africa (first round)	France 3	13,508,880
Brazil v Holland (semi-final)	France 2	13,037,640
France v Italy (quarter-final)	France 3	12,200,000
France v Saudi Arabia (first round)	TF1	12,190,880
France v Paraguay (second round)	TF1	10,054,120
England v Argentina (second round)	TF1	9,424,800
Brazil v Morocco (quarter-final)	France 2	9,163,000
Brazil v Denmark (quarter-final)	France 2	8,534,000

That the World Cup had a major impact on French television is indisputable. Never before had so much football been shown on French television – away from the matches themselves, the week before the first match saw no fewer than 12 football-related documentaries on all channels. Never before had so much television been watched – the year leading up to the World Cup saw a 144 per cent increase in television sales in France and a 236 per cent increase in widescreen television sales. Never before had television earned so much from advertising revenue – TF1 made 50m francs from advertising during the Final alone, which compares favourably with its outlay of 40m francs to secure rights for the entire tournament.[29] Add to that the unique inter-channel collaboration, the birth of digital and the unprecedented focus of the world on French broadcasting, and it is clear the World Cup could mark a turning point in French television history. Jean Réveillon, head of sport at France Télévision, urged channels to seize the strategic initiative brought by the tournament, while others want to use the experience as a springboard for future innovation, with one Canal Plus producer speculating on possibilities such as installing microphones in players' shirts or in the ball.[30]

It was also the first World Cup in which the influence of cable and satellite television in France was really evident. Eurosport, the satellite channel owned principally by TF1 and Canal Plus, and watched by 77 million households in Europe, showed all matches live, even providing commentaries in Breton to selected regions, the brainchild of Eurosport's two Breton presidents, Canal Plus' Charles Biétry, and TF1's Patrick Le Lay. The popularity of its coverage came as a relief to Eurosport, which had recently been prevented by an internecine dispute between TF1 and Canal Plus from broadcasting French Division Two matches, forcing it to show instead the somewhat less marketable sports of darts and tug-of-war.

In competition against Eurosport, France Télévision used the World Cup to launch its channel, Superfoot 98 , freely available to subscribers to the digital satellite network TPS. A daring venture for the less financially dynamic public network, Superfoot 98 invested 70 France Télévision employees and 19m francs in broadcasting all matches, including 44 in widescreen, totalling a staggering 16 hours of programmes a day, and even managed to be the only channel with female presenters. The project attracted the wrath of Canal Plus, particularly as France Télévision offered matches free of charge to cable channels, on condition that they promoted Superfoot 98. Nevertheless, Superfoot 98 was considered a success, gaining an audience satisfaction rating of 85 per cent, attracting two out of three TPS subscribers to at least one match, and more than covering its costs with advertising revenue.[31]

Radio and the World Cup: New Horizons, New Challenges

The recent history of French radio, like television, is characterised by turbulent reform and growing commercialisation.[32] Although a less pervasive medium in France than the press or television, radio still reaches almost 80 per cent of the population every day. The World Cup therefore presented opportunities for established stations to diversify, for new stations to develop, and for the medium as a whole to take advantage of growing disquiet about the visual pollution of on-screen advertising during French football coverage, which led the television magazine *Télérama* to comment recently: 'Our eyes now have to slalom in and out of the advertising logos to spot the players.'[33]

98 Radio France

The World Cup marked a brave departure for Radio France, the national public service network, which comprises different channels such as France Inter (general), France Culture (arts), France Musique (classical music) and France Info (news), together with a regional network of stations. It decided to create an entirely new channel, 98 Radio France, which took over France Inter's long wave frequency for the duration of the tournament. Experience during the preceding Olympics and World Cup had led Radio France executives to conclude that only a dedicated channel would suffice for sports events of such magnitude, and that the only other feasible alternative, to use France-Info, would involve too much disruption to France-Info's successful 'repetitive' news format.

All 64 matches were commentated live, with reporters seconded from all Radio France channels, together with expert summarisers such as Patrick Battiston, Alain Giresse, Yannick Noah, and others whom they shared via an innovative bi-medial and public-private sector agreement with Canal Plus. The station also provided regular news updates in major languages, weather, travel and accommodation information, together with broadcasts from regional Radio France studios.

The station's aim was twofold: to bring the atmosphere and excitement of the tournament into listeners' living rooms: 'a channel which will take you behind the scenes of the stadiums, which will take you onto the pitch, take you around the world',[34] and to capitalise on the cultural riches of perhaps the greatest international event in recent French history. Thus, a live broadcast from a packed Brazilian bar in Paris at half-time might be followed by a laid-back discussion on the artistry of football between poets from competing nations. The commentary on the Final itself will surely become one of the most heavily repeated excerpts from French radio – the sheer astonishment of the commentators screaming 'Buuuut! Zizou Zizou Zizou!' were more reminiscent of an ecstatic fan than a broadcaster from the country's public network, as the commentator himself admitted, 'We're allowed to be selfish, we're allowed to be partisan.' The excitement of matches was enhanced by amplified crowd volume, and commentators taking over from each other in quick succession as the other appeared to lose his voice or become overwhelmed with excitement. The only yellow card awarded to Radio France was the discovery that France-Info had been faking commentaries, with its 'commentator' cosily installed in a studio watching the match on television.

The experiment was felt to be a success and one which Radio France's manager Gilbert Denoyan promised to repeat for future sporting events of such magnitude. It also installed the Internet as a key strand in the future of radio broadcasting – listeners were able to pick up 98 Radio France all over the world via its Internet site, which gained 100,000 hits per day during the tournament, compared to 8,000 normally.

Commercial Networks and the World Cup

Of the main commercial networks, the generalist RTL, still France's most popular station, declared itself keen not to disrupt its predominantly middle-aged audience by opting for the 'Radio-Foot' of 98 Radio France, although they still provided extensive coverage, including live commentary of all French matches and other major games with star summarisers such as Gérard Houllier and Luis Fernandez. On the day of the Final, the station promised all its staff would be covering the day's events, deploying correspondents in 'all corners of France and the world' including Rio, New York and Aimé Jacquet's home village of Sail-sous-Couzan. As with 98 Radio France, their approach became steadily more patriotic as the tournament wore on, with the host introducing the Final with the following plea to listeners: 'Put your blue football shirts on, don't hesitate to chant and scream: the players want you to and need you to.'

Other generalist commercial stations such as Europe 1 and RMC also went against saturation coverage, though they did provide live commentary on all French matches and other important games, with Europe 1 using TF1's Guy Roux and David Ginola as summarisers, and launching a nightly chat show with various celebrities talking about football. Europe 1 has well-established credentials as a football broadcaster, boasting one of the nation's best-known commentators, Eugène Saccamano, and one of the most popular sports programmes on French radio, *Europe Sport*, which attracts 600,000 listeners.

FM Stations

An enormous variety of nationally networked and regional independent stations dominate the FM band, particularly in Paris, and few of these were able to avoid the World Cup. Surfing the FM band during a match delivered a cornucopia of commentaries of all languages and styles to the listener. Among the most notable examples was Latina (99 FM), a station aimed at Spanish, Italians, Portuguese and South Americans, which obtained two extra frequencies during the tournament to provide live coverage for the 400,000 South Americans in France during the tournament. Reporters were seconded from Latin American stations to broadcast on Latina as well as their own countries' networks, and its huge success saw it become one of the most popular stations in France, obtaining more listeners than Radio France's France Culture.

Alternative Football Coverage: From Fanzines to the Internet

While the 1998 World Cup enabled the established mass media to provide saturation coverage, it also marked the chance for new and alternative forms of football reporting to gain a hearing. In France, however, the tournament reinforced the fact that football reporting is still very much a mainstream activity, with alternative football reporting still in its infancy. For example, the spread of football fanzines, one of the most notable developments among British football supporters over the past ten years, has completely failed to take off in France. In Britain today there are now 1,000 football fanzines in existence, selling 100,000 copies a month, and over a million annually, with content varying from the humorous to the irreverent to the downright abusive, and more recently, football fanzines have begun to emerge in other countries such as Germany, Spain, Sweden and Italy, often with English names such as 'Terrace Talk'. Yet the notable exception is France. Although fanzines are prevalent in France in other spheres such as cinema, art and politics, the only known football fanzine indigenous to France was a national bulletin for supporters' groups, *Supmag*, which sold 25,000 copies a month during its peak between 1992 and 1995. Today, there is just one solitary French football fanzine, *Aux armes*, which is actually edited and produced by an Englishman, James Eastham, and sells about 150 copies per issue.[35] Indeed, so amused were the French by what was seen as a peculiarly British labour of love that he was granted an interview in *L'Equipe* in 1994.[36]

The lack of appetite on the part of the French for football fanzines has been attributed to the general absence of fervour from French football fans (analysed elsewhere in this volume), together with a deficiency of the kind of off-beat humour which provides the creative impulses for most football and music fanzines, as a recent article about French pop music culture intimated: 'The French rock magazine, *Les Inrockuptibles*, is a joke-free publication in which the musicians' pearls of wisdom are gently collected and carefully burnished.'[37]

The World Cup on the Internet

If the football fanzine phenomenon appears to have bypassed France, it seems that the do-it-yourself publishing ethos which lies behind football fanzines may instead have made the evolutionary leap straight onto the Internet, which, with its widespread accessibility and lack of hierarchy, offers an ideal medium for the flourishing of alternative football reporting.

Although club-related World Wide Web sites have been slow to take off in France, the World Cup saw an explosion of football-related sites, many based in France. Indeed, the range of unofficial Web sites was so diverse that *Libération* and *Le Monde* devoted daily columns to World Cup Web sites, with particularly close attention paid to the site created by the French reserve goalkeeper, Bernard Lama.[38] Lama's site promised to include behind-the-scenes pictures of the French team, together with Lama's views on football, literature and cinema, but its ambitions were soon scaled down by Aimé Jacquet's alarm at the prospect of lurid revelations. The most technologically advanced sites included add-ons such as Real Audio for match interviews and vide-printer systems which flashed up key developments on the user's desktop, proving particularly popular with office workers. Fans with opinions to express were not disappointed either, as live chat and fans' forums abounded, and anti-World Cup groups were also able to get their message across, including *La Coupe est pleine* and the *nofoot* site.[39]

Yet the Internet is far from being simply an underground publishing forum, it is now a major instrument of corporate communication, and 1998 was the first proper chance to witness the significant commercial impact of the Internet on the World Cup. However, the Internet's influence was emasculated by a marketing anomaly, since media rights for the World Cup were negotiated in 1987, long before the World Wide Web was prevalent in everyday life, which meant that not one of the thousands of World Cup websites was allowed to show live football action. FIFA defended its decision by declaring that it was too late to renegotiate rights and that it had reservations about the quality of Web broadcasts, but it seems inconceivable that Internet broadcasting rights will be omitted for the 2002 tournament. None the less, the corporate presence of the World Cup on the World Wide Web was established long before kick-off on 10 June, with the official site being launched in May 1997, and had already received a billion hits midway through the tournament, including a record 73 million hits on one day alone.[40] The site allowed users to send messages of support to their team, join in an on-line chat system, view action photos, and of course keep up to date with the games. The Internet was also a pivotal communication tool for the world's media in France; a specially created Intranet, *Info-France-98*, staffed largely by volunteers, linked stadiums with the CIRTV in Paris to provide the latest news to the 13,000 press, aiming to improve on the IBM glitches of the 1996 Atlanta Olympics which led to the broadcasting of incorrect results and timings.

Conclusion: Whose Reality?

The 1998 World Cup will be seen as a landmark event in French media history. From the private-public sector collaboration between Radio France and Canal Plus, to the left-right alliance between L'Humanité and Le Figaro; from the suave dinner jacket-attired Canal Plus commentators on the night of the Final to the cacophony of screams from the FM stations – it is safe to predict that its like will not be seen in France again. The global magnitude of the tournament, and the French decision to act as sole broadcaster meant that the eyes of the world were on the nation's media as never before. France did not disappoint the world, with its technically flawless production boosting its image as a high-tech nation, while at the same time retaining a national flavour to its coverage, evidence of the national identity which has helped the French media resist the globalising and homogenising impact of Rupert Murdoch.

We have seen how the media reported and sought to analyse and interpret the impact of the tournament and the eventual victory. The tournament reinforced the notion that the reporting of news is news itself, as the public was subjected to intertextual bombardment such as the press reviewing the radio and radio broadcasting press reviews. Conflicting themes abounded in the flurry of analysis. While L'Equipe was accused of stirring up controversy due to a lack of competitors, too much competition was blamed for the absence of probing and probity in television's football coverage, which has led public service journalists such as Alain Vernon to claim that television sports journalism in France is now dead.[41]

For the media as an industry, the World Cup laid bare the competing energies which drive and distort it, including advertising, ownership, technology, finance, society and government policy. It brought winners and losers, and change and continuity, in equal measures to the French media. L'Equipe and TF1 confirmed their unassailability in their respective ratings wars, though both suffered widespread opprobrium. Previously disputatious television channels collaborated seamlessly on TVRS 98, but the carping continued off-stage. Older media such as radio and press embraced the new by broadcasting and publishing on the Internet. All in all, the experience confirmed the media as a product of the nation to which it belongs, with the French media a microcosm of many of the tensions which characterise French society: Paris versus the regions; public service versus commerce; Left versus Right; and national identity versus globalisation.

The World Cup reinforced the importance of football for radio and television, if not for the press, and with the majority of the French population watching the Final on television, it is television coverage which has dominated this analysis. None the less, despite the record-breaking figures, the innovation, and the world-wide critical acclaim, the principal consequence of the 1998 World Cup could be that it will be the last ever to be broadcast on French terrestrial television. A postscript to the tournament was provided by the news that the pay-television company Kirch, which has bought television rights from FIFA, plans to charge as much as 500m francs for French television coverage of the 2002 World Cup, a huge leap from the 50m francs of 1998. Furthermore, given that advertising revenue will fall sharply as matches are broadcast live early in the morning, public channels are likely to be priced out of the market, and pay-per-view may be seen as the only profitable option for the remaining channels. The gravity of the situation led Jean Réveillon of France Télévision to evoke memories of May 1968 in pleading, 'money should not determine the law ... In May 68 people demanded the return of football to the footballers, today we must remember that football cannot survive without television viewers.'[42] However, whatever the means by which football is viewed in the future, it is clear the product to be viewed will be elevated to new heights. The World Cup demonstrated the desire of television producers to transform sports events into something better than ordinary reality, with Canal Plus' Charles Biétry declaring with vaulting ambition: 'We are still in the Middle Ages as far as television coverage of football is concerned ... Only 30 per cent of the possibilities have been explored. As long as the viewer is better off in the stadium than in his living room to watch a match, we will not have succeeded.'[43] The consumers of France's highly mediatised sports coverage could be forgiven in the future for wondering if they are watching a real event or a media-created virtual reality.

NOTES

1. For a brief history of the French press, see R. Davison, 'The Press', in J.E. Flower, *France Today*, 8th ed. (London, Hodder and Stoughton, 1998), pp.189–217. For a comprehensive history of French media in general, see R. Kuhn, *The Media in France* (London, Routledge, 1995).
2. S. July, 'Un rêve français', *Libération*, 14 July 1998, 3.
3. *Le Monde*, 14 July 1998.
4. Based on the format of *Time Magazine*, France's other three news weeklies are *L'Express*, *L'Evénement du Jeudi* and *Le Point*.
5. P. Mignon, *La passion du football* (Paris, Editions Odile Jacob, 1998), p.183.
6. For a summary of *L'Equipe*'s campaign against Jacquet see A. Salles, 'L'Equipe bat des records de vente dans un climat de malaise', *Le Monde*, 21 July 1998, 14.
7. J. Bureau, 'A Aimé Jacquet', *L'Equipe*, 14 July 1998, 2.
8. *Libération*, 14 July 1998, 14.
9. *Le Figaro*, 14 July 1998.
10. M. Chemin, 'L'Equipe à l'heure de l'autocritique', *Libération*, 14 July 1998, 9.
11. G. Ernault, 'Les conquérants de l'impossible', *France Football*, 14 July 1998, 5.
12. Interviewed in Paris, 27 June 1998.
13. See E. Maitrot in *Sport et Télé, les liaisons secrètes* (Paris, Flammarion, 1995). For an

overview of French broadcasting history read G.E. Hare, 'The Broadcasting Media', in J.E. Flower, *France Today*, pp.218–45.

14. TF1 provides an average of 40 per cent of football coverage, France 2 and 3, 13 per cent, and La Cinq, 0.3 per cent. Source: *Sport et télévision, 1991–1996. bilan de dix années de régulation* (Paris, Conseil Supérieur de l'Audiovisuel, 1997).

15. France Télévision's Pierre Salviac, quoted in H. Haget, 'Télé: l'indigestion de foot', *L'Express*, 26 December 1996, 36.

16. See 'TVRS 98: L'airbus plutot que le concorde', *Dossiers de l'audiovisuel*, No.77 (Jan.–Feb. 1998), 23.

17. B. Poiseul, 'L'été sera show', *France Football*, 9 June 1998, 72.

18. R. Kempson, 'It's slo-mo progress for French TV', *The Times*, 20 June 1998.

19. Interview with Stuart Nimmo, Paris, June 26 1998.

20. Michel Platini interviewed by D. Psenny, 'L'argent du football rallume la guerre des chaînes', *Le Monde*, 14–15 April 1996.

21. D. Psenny, 'Canal Plus cultive sa différence', *France Football*, 30 June 1998, 56.

22. S. Meunier, *Les Yeux dans les bleus*, broadcast on Canal Plus, 7 August 1998.

23. F. de Montvalon, 'Canal Plus feinte TF1 et marque', *Le nouvel économiste*, 31 October 1996, 104.

24. See, for example, A. Giraudo, 'Thierry Roland persiste dans "Présente"', *Le Monde*, 17 January 1997, 22.

25. *L'Evénement du Jeudi*, 4–10 June 1998.

26. D. Psenny, 'Les chaînes vont droit au but', *France Football*, 12 June 1998, 46.

27. *L'Equipe*, 23 June 1998.

28. E. Demumieux, *Le Monde*, 7–8 June 1998, 3.

29. M.S., 'Les Bleus ont fait exploser le petit écran', *Le Parisien*, 12 July 1998, 12.

30. D. Psenny, 'Le mondial de tous les records', *Le Monde Télévision Radio Multimedia supplement*, 19–20 July 1998, 2.

31. D. Psenny, 'Le succès du Superfoot', *Le Monde Télévision Radio Multimédia* supplement, 19–20 July 1998, 3.

32. For an overview of French radio, see G.E. Hare, 'The Broadcasting Media'.

33. *Télérama*, 27 May 1998, 155.

34. Radio-France's magazine, *La Semaine*, 6–12 June 1998, 3

35. Available from J. Eastham., 4 South End, Preston, Lancashire, PR1 8HA.

36. 'Quand le football français s'écrit en anglais', *L'Equipe*, 8 November 1994.

37. R. Yates, 'Sacre bleu! French pop is how you say, not bad', *Guardian*, 10 January 1998, 5.

38. http://www.bernardlama.com/

39. http://www.mygale.org/00/nofoot/

40. http://www.france98.com/

41. B. Poiseul, 'La doyenne des émissions sur le foot a 20 ans', *Libération*, 15 September 1997, 4.

42. D. Psenny, 'Le mondial de tous les records'.

43. Charles Biétry, interviewed in 'L'argent du football rallume la guerre des chaînes', *Le Monde*, 14–15 April 1996, 4.

'33 jours de fête': A Diary of France 98

HUGH DAUNCEY and GEOFF HARE

The month-long period of the Finals had always been evoked by the organisers as an intended 33 days of festivities, with spectacular football in the grounds and non-stop sporting and cultural activities throughout France. As the success of the French national team gradually grew, leading France to their first Final and then victory, *la fête* – the term chosen to describe the competition – eventually became reality, when hundreds of thousands of French people celebrated on the Champs-Elysées. The following narrative chronology of the month of France 98 sets out the salient features of France's experience of the World Cup; it intermingles discussion of football, security, culture, media, fandom and infrastructures, and aims to provide an easily readable panorama of events, starting with the final selection of the French squad by manager Aimé Jacquet.

Preliminaries

During 11–16 May French players under consideration for a place in the squad underwent team-building in the Alps in the form of a 'stage de récupération et oxygénation' at Tignes. It was an opportunity for players in clubs abroad to meet those still playing in France. After the Alps, 28 players were taken to Clairefontaine, the French football national coaching centre in the Paris region, for a week's training (18–24 May), and on 24 May Jacquet selected his final squad of 22. Over the following week (25–30 May), France played friendly matches in the *Tournoi Hassan II* at Casablanca against Belgium and Morocco, before returning to Clairefontaine on 2 June, their base for the duration of the World Cup. During 4–8 June, as the new FIFA President Sepp Blatter (with running-mate Michel Platini of the CFO) was elected, the squad spent a long weekend in Finland for another friendly. Their first match in the Finals was to be on Friday 12 June against South Africa, in Marseille.

First Round: Parades, Goals and Red Cards

France 98 was intended to be an entertaining World Cup on the pitch, and its first round was a festival of goals: in the 48 first round matches 126 goals were scored (2.62 per match, marginally more than in 1994 when 93 goals were scored in 36 matches). It was the highest average since 1962 with the exception of 1982 (2.77). France was top scorer at this stage. Every team scored at least one goal. Thirteen penalties were awarded, all converted. Sixteen red cards were issued (against eight in 1994 and 1990). *France Football* explained the extra goals by the increasing importance of dead-ball set-pieces (33 goals) and the gain in real playing time by such reforms as banning the pass-back to the goalkeeper, forcing him to release the ball within six seconds, quicker throw-ins and goal-kicks by the use of more ball-boys and girls and extra balls, and by the fall in the number of free-kicks.[1]

Opening ceremony: the festival of football in Paris

On Tuesday 9 June the promised '33 jours de fête' got under way as the slow, the bad and the ugly opened the Festival of Football in Paris. In the tradition of Paris street parades for the 14 July or the Bicentenary of the Revolution, the World Cup was inaugurated by a parade of giants representing the 'four primary colours of humanity' and of the football world. Seventy feet high, each weighing 38 tonnes, with a specially modified fork-lift truck in each foot, the latex-covered steel skeletons moved very slowly (one mile per hour), making very poor television. Accompanied by 4,500 dancers, musicians, contortionists, jugglers and acrobats, the giants set off from four different sites in central Paris at 6 p.m. A stereotypically yellow Ho was Asia, starting from le pont Neuf, a blue Romeo represented Europe, starting from the Opéra Garnier, Pablo in orange was the Amerindian, starting at the Arc de Triomphe, and the ebony Moussa stood for Africa, starting from the Champ-de-Mars. During a year and a half of planning, theatre director Jean-Pascal Lévy-Trumet devised the event as an allegory symbolising the 'meeting and playful confrontation of people and cultures, the universality of football and its World Cup'. Moussa was meant to 'wake up near the Eiffel Tower and discover civilisation and its rules', Romeo the European was to 'encounter Olympia, the Urban Woman and enjoy voluptuous pleasure'. Along the 15 miles of routes, the Paris City Council had demolished four traffic islands, removed 78 traffic lights and pruned thousands of trees. Three and a half hours after setting off the parade finally reached the obelisk of the place de la Concorde, specially decorated as an 80 foot replica of the World Cup.[2]

French win in Marseille but France 98 loses Sastre

On Friday 12 June France opened their account in Marseille. The main plus point of the hosts' first victory over South Africa was the goal and return to form of substitute striker Dugarry, whose poor ball-control, general clumsiness and tendency to miss open goals had earned him ridicule from the French media following his return from Barcelona to Marseille in mid-season. His celebration on scoring the first of France's three goals showed his relief at being transformed from villain to hero, and the Marseille crowd, the noisiest in France, showed their appreciation. Rumours circulated that Dugarry was only in the team because he was Zidane's best friend.

After the match French coach Aimé Jacquet criticised the referees for being too liberal with yellow cards and not strict enough on violent fouls. Prior to the Finals, World Cup referee Michel Vautrot had been to Clairefontaine to give the French squad a seminar on the new interpretations, especially on the tackle from behind. Defender Marcel Desailly claimed the referees were being over-zealous to please their superiors. Prophetically, Le Monde's Elie Barth was already worried about the *gestes d'énervement* (ill-tempered actions) for which Zidane was becoming noted.[3]

On Saturday 13 June the co-organiser of the Finals, Fernand Sastre, died after a struggle against cancer. Michel Platini paid tribute to his CFO colleague; Sastre had been most responsible for the World Cup being hosted in France and ultimately for France's strong participation.[4]

More refereeing controversies

Tuesday 16 June witnessed new controversy over refereeing, as newly elected President of FIFA Sepp Blatter and Michel Platini complained publicly that referees had forgotten about tackles from behind, and about goalkeepers holding on to the ball for up to six seconds only. Concerned perhaps that a Moroccan had not been punished for leaving his stud marks on the upper thigh of the tournament's brightest star, Ronaldo, they encouraged officials to be stricter. 'Players have to be protected.' 'If a referee doesn't show a red card because he doesn't feel he can take the pressure, then he shouldn't be at the World Cup.' Platini was equally critical of referees ignoring tackles from behind, and threatened them with being sent home. He also complained that some, while applying the rules, did not have a feeling for the game, and suggested one solution was professionalisation and the use of former players as referees. Blatter had made the elimination of the tackle from behind part of his campaign for the FIFA presidency. As a partisan of the beautiful game, he had wanted the tackle from behind to be automatically sanctioned by a red card. David Will, the Scottish chairman of the FIFA referees' committee, managed to persuade the International Board, overseer of the rules of the game, to amend Blatter's proposal to make it that only tackles endangering the physical integrity of the opponent should receive the red card. Blatter had, according to Le Monde, found this defeat difficult to swallow, even more so since Will had tacitly supported Lennart Johansson for the presidency. This might explain Blatter's anger on seeing the referees acting as if the new guideline did not exist.[5]

Red card for Zidane; green light for France

Matches following this disagreement were much affected by it, as Thursday 18 June became Red Thursday. Whereas the first 20 matches had produced four red cards, the day's two games produced five. France's key player, Zinedine Zidane, seemed incredulous that his petulant if not dangerous stamp on a Saudi opponent should provoke a sending-off from the Mexican official. At least it was deliberate. A less violent Saudi challenge on Lizarazu, mistimed and from the side rather than from behind, had earlier produced a dismissal for Al-Khilaiwi. Earlier in the day, a Colombian referee had sent off two Danes and one South African, only one of whom had committed a tackle from behind.[6] The match had not been particularly dirty.

In the furore of debate that followed Zidane's sending off, France's victory and guaranteed qualification for the second round were almost overlooked. Dugarry's serious injury looked like depriving the hosts of their only real target man for two weeks at least. He joined striker Guivarc'h in the infirmary, leaving France with ever more of a striking problem, partly off-set by the form of Monaco's young Thierry Henry. Another even more serious problem was the loss of playmaker Zidane through suspension for two matches.

On Wednesday 24 June French squad players eased ahead of Denmark. As imperious captain for the day, Desailly, marshalled his reserve defence around him, conceding a penalty, after Djorkaeff had opened the scoring also from a penalty. Petit scored the winner on a hot afternoon in Lyon. An enthusiastic President Chirac was interviewed live on television by France 2 after the match from his seat in the stands next to former Prime Minister and ex-Mayor of Lyon Raymond Barre. Meanwhile, on the following day, France's traditional footballing nemesis Germany also qualified for the next round.

Security fails for England and Germany, but works for Iran–USA

England's first match at Marseille against Tunisia on Monday 15 June led to considerable difficulties over the weekend and on match-day, in maintaining order in the city centre, as large numbers of England fans drinking in bars sparked fighting with local people, many of whom were French citizens of Tunisian or other Maghreb descent. Of the 31 people held by police after the pitched battles on the Prado beach, in the city centre or elsewhere, 15 were British and 16 from Marseille itself, emphasising the view taken of events by many that provocation had come from both sides.

Although drunken aggression from some English fans had led to incidents such as the burning of a Tunisian flag and retaliatory violence from their opponents, it was generally accepted that the presence of English 'hooligans' and the disturbances caused by them had been exploited by youths of immigrant origin from underprivileged areas in the north of Marseille. As well as premeditated violence against English fans, these disaffected youngsters attacked shops and indulged in looting and vandalism, representing an extension of traditional French problems of sometimes fragile law and order in sensitive immigrant areas.

On Sunday 21 June the match between Iran and the United States was a major test for security. The two teams posed for a joint pre-match photograph to underline the diplomatic *rapprochement* that the game symbolised. Football in Iran, as seen in the celebrations both following the qualification for the finals and following their victory against the United States, was taken over as an opportunity for progressives, and particularly for women, to break out of the Ayatollahs' cultural and social straitjacket. The French authorities and the television coverage did their best to prevent the game from becoming a propaganda event for opponents of the Iranian regime. None the less, a large contingent of Iranians managed to enter the stadium wearing anti-regime tee-shirts. In deference perhaps to the watching millions in Iran, the television cameras also refrained for once from showing close-ups of scantily dressed young women supporters comporting themselves in ways not officially approved of under the Islamic regime.

England fans outdone by Germans

After Marseille, as the English fans moved across country to Toulouse for the England–Romania match on Monday 22 June, the authorities in both Marseille and Toulouse took action to limit any problems which might recur. Toulouse was concerned to avoid the violence which had characterised England's weekend in Marseille, and Marseille was anxious to prepare for Holland–South Korea and also for the possible return of England for a semi-final match. The giant television screens were taken down in Toulouse, and extended opening hours (until 3 a.m.) for bars and cafés were rescinded, with a closing time of 11 p.m. being imposed until English fans had left town. The music festival planned for Sunday 21 June was postponed, and extra police officers and gendarmes were drafted in to the city. Although one English supporter was knifed and arrests were made, most of these were of local adolescents, some of whom were armed with baseball bats. In Marseille, the perceived threat of the Dutch supporters produced a ban on alcohol sales and early closing-hours for bars.

Elsewhere, however, different security and policing problems arose as rioting German fans left a gendarme for dead in Lens on Sunday 21 June. A hundred German fans running away from police outside the Germany–Yugoslavia match in Lens sprinted into a narrow street where three policemen were guarding police vehicles. Two fled, and a third, Daniel Nivel, was set upon by a group of about 20 and was kicked, beaten, and hit repeatedly on the head with his own tear-gas launcher. He was taken to hospital in a deep coma with suspected irreversible brain damage and not given a strong chance of survival.[7] Concern was widespread that German fans were now outdoing the excesses of British hooligans, and the French press discussed at length the supposed links between German football hooliganism and the extreme Right. Chancellor Helmut Kohl spoke of the 'shame' of his country, but Sepp Blatter took some comfort from the belief that what had happened in Lens was an incident more connected with professional trouble-makers of the German extreme-right than with football itself.

Refereeing again: red cards and national bias?

Having called for get-tough policy, Sepp Blatter supported the referees who had shown five red and 11 yellow cards by 18 June. However Platini thought it was going too far. He was supported by a FIFA official spokesman, Keith Cooper, who said the theme of a meeting between a FIFA deputation and referees was to seek the right balance between leniency and punishment. England team manager Glenn Hoddle, while supporting the attempt to eliminate the tackle from behind, was worried that over-zealous referees over-reacting to other types of offence would ruin the World Cup as a spectacle.

More refereeing controversy arose on Wednesday 24 June as FIFA President Blatter called in David Will, Chair of FIFA's Referees Committee, following two controversial decisions which resulted in the elimination from the competition of Cameroon and Morocco. A Hungarian referee had disallowed two 'goals' by Cameroon; the second one would have qualified Cameroon for the Second Round. No foul was visible on television replays. The decision had provoked riots in Yaoundé, including attacks on foreigners. The most contested decision was the award of a late penalty by an American referee to Norway against Brazil that resulted in a goal and unexpected victory that eliminated Morocco. The controversies, coming on the same day and eliminating two African nations in favour of teams from Europe and South America, fuelled debates about the use of television or other technological aids to help referees and the use of professional referees or of former professional players as referees, or the setting up of an élite corps of referees for big competitions, rather than selection on geographical criteria. Shots provided later by Norwegian television showed conclusively that a foul had been committed.

Second Round, Quarter-Finals and Semi-Finals

The Second round involved Brazil, Italy, France, Nigeria, Holland, Germany, Romania and Argentina as group-winners, and qualifiers in second place in the respective groups Norway, Chile, Denmark, Paraguay, Mexico, Yugoslavia, England and Croatia. After the plethora of matches in the first round and the almost constant coverage of matches on television, the knock-out matches of the rest of the competition allowed fans and the French overall to focus on the greater stakes of each match, and to become progressively more enthralled by the evolving fate of *les Bleus*.

Blanc and Owen score Golden Goals

Sunday 28 June saw France win at Lens against Paraguay. The suspense of one-way traffic, but France unable to score, heightened the drama as a nation of viewers hardly dared look. After 90 minutes of regulation time and 23 minutes of extra-time had elapsed without a goal, the first 'golden goal' in World Cup history was scored by defender Laurent Blanc against the 'revisionist' (*International Herald Tribune*) man-to-man marking system marshalled from the back by goalkeeper captain Chilavert, one of the characters of the competition.

Last tango in Saint-Etienne as England, reduced to ten men against Argentina (after Beckham is sent off), lose on penalties after extra-time produces no goals. Did Beckham deserve a red card for his petulant flick from a prone position? No, said manager Hoddle. It is a matter of opinion: 'Nous sommes tous des arbitres de foot,' said media personality and football nut Bernard Pivot.[8] A consolation for England was that their young star player from Liverpool scored an outstanding individual strike – a golden goal except that it happened in normal play – which for many commentators was the goal of the tournament.

Nigeria crashed out in Saint-Denis after FIFA had rejected their protest at the choice of a European referee (a Spaniard) for their game with Denmark, who surprised the Super Eagles with their scoring potential, winning 4–1, and on Monday 29 June other old enemies of France, Germany and Holland, squeezed through into the quarter-finals.

Sigh of relief as England fans go home

Arguably, the final high-risk match for hooliganism was the England–Argentina game in Saint-Etienne on Tuesday 30 June. Various incidents of fighting between English fans and *stéphanois* youths occurred, shop windows were broken in the city centre, photographers and cameramen were jostled, and groups of England supporters tried to provoke the police by name-calling and bottle-throwing. Once again, only a small number of arrests were made, and the consensus seemed to be that policing had been successful, despite local irritation at the way the perceived threat from the English fans had 'spoiled the party' through cancellation of the local music festival and by causing bars to close early. After the elimination of England, it was noted that the tournament suffered no more hooliganism, and memories of Michael Owen's goal did much to outweigh the negative impressions left by some English fans, whose behaviour was always compared very negatively with the humour and friendliness of Scotland's Tartan Army.

France reach the semis again but the Germans don't: schadenfreude

In the quarter-finals on Friday 3 July France won a local derby against Italy, as the nation held its breath. With seven of the French squad playing their club football in Italy, the two teams knew each other's game too well for there to be a lot of open play. Aimé Jacquet surprised the Italians, however, by playing a 4-3-3 formation, bringing in a third ball-winner, Karembeu, to help midfielders Deschamps and Petit, and to release his wing-backs. In the penalty shoot-out, France came out ahead, and bars that had been full and hushed suddenly erupted in an orgasmic 'Ouiiiii!' only to empty just as quickly; a much longer and louder cheer rocked the foundations of the Hôtel de Ville in Paris, where thousands of people had invested every vantage point from window bars to lamp-posts, for the whole game in front of the big screen. Suddenly cars with tricolour flags waving from open sun-roofs were hurtling along the riverside dual-carriageway, on every road horns were honking to the tune of 'On a gag-né, on a gag-né', and within half an hour 40,000 people were stopping traffic on the Champs-Elysées. Jacques Chirac, in the players' dressing room after the game, revealed that his wife could talk of no one else but Emmanuel Petit. Who said the French did not care about their football? But was beating their *frères ennemis* and reaching a semi-final of the World Cup really the height of their ambitions?

Brazil qualified for the semi-final against Denmark (3–2) and then on Saturday 4 July the Germans lost in Lyon. 'Frankly, who's complaining?' chortled a French headline at the Croatians' unexpected victory, or rather at the Germans' defeat. Certainly not the French watching the match in the Brasserie Saint-Malo at Montparnasse, where the cool Croatians' second and third goals were greeted with enormous cheers of glee and not a little relief that *la revanche* (revenge) for 1982 and 1986 (not to mention 1870 and 1940) had been accomplished vicariously. The Germans blamed the referee for his fortieth minute sending off of defender Wörns, due to play next season for PSG.

Historic victory at last puts France in Final

The competition moved on to the semi-finals on Wednesday 8 July with a victory for France over Croatia that was His-to-ri-que! France 2 Croatia 1. Joy was unconfined when France emerged victorious over Croatia in the semi-final, thus reaching for the first time in their history the Final of the World Cup. France became the ninth host country to reach the Final. After a close first half, Croatia took the lead, but immediately afterwards Thuram equalised after a one-two with Djorkaeff. Thuram had never scored in any of his other 37 matches for the national team, but then scored a second winning goal. France had to play the last 15 minutes with ten men as Laurent Blanc was controversially sent-off after play-acting by Slaven Bilic. Zidane was so exhausted at the end that he vomited on the pitch. The French press unanimously commented that Blanc was the player who least deserved to miss the Final. President Chirac's first words for the television cameras were to salute the performance of Thuram. Prime Minister Jospin left the stadium with Karembeu's shirt.[9]

As the whole country celebrated, the usually taciturn inhabitants of France's second city let their hair down. An estimated 15,000 massed in front of the big screen in the Croix-Rousse suburb overlooking the centre of Lyon, having started to arrive with flags, scarves and red-white-and-blue painted faces as early as two-and-a-half hours before the kick-off. Teenage girls, with tricolour flags painted on both cheeks, and older women and men, with the now common red-white-and-blue wigs, and young men and small boys with replica shirts, and face and hair completely painted in the national colours, chanted their support for the nation as much as for its footballers. So hard was it for late-comers to see that they invested trees, railings, bus-shelter roofs and even the roof of the nearby post-office, from which the CRS had to move them for fear of a collapse. At half-time many dashed for the metro to find a bar or home for a better view. After the final whistle the festivities were transferred to the centre of Lyon, place Bellecour and beside the Saône. One newspaper estimated the number of celebrants at 30,000 people, chanting 'Thuram, Thuram' and 'On est en finale'. The sound of car horns saluting the victory on the quays and city centre streets could be heard well into the night.[10] In Marseille on the Vieux-Port, the violence of the earlier rounds was forgotten. In Paris, even without any particularly obvious alcoholic assistance, and with no damage reported, 300,000 Parisians took over the Champs-Elysées, brandishing flags and chanting 'Allez la France!' and 'On a gagné' until 3 or 4 o'clock in the morning.[11]

French team ask for more support; 'Allons, enfants de la patrie ...'

The following day Thursday 9 July saw coach Jacquet's bitterness at long-term criticism of his management by *L'Equipe* newspaper spill out in a radio interview after that morning's editorial had expressed belated congratulations. 'We have expressed our mistrust of him quite enough not to now feel obliged to pay homage to him. We had doubted his ability to take this great team to the very highest level, but nevertheless he has done it, after his fashion.' Editor Jérôme Bureau could not however bring himself to make a full apology, adding: 'We still do not share his ideas on how to play.' Jacquet, who hitherto had not publicly responded to L'Equipe's two years of attacks, replied that since the daily was in a monopoly position it could say what it liked without taking any risks: 'It's really shameful, shameless and faithless.' The readers, who have no real choice, have continued to buy L'Equipe in increasing numbers: sales are 30 per cent up since the beginning of the World Cup and beat the previous record (the Marseilles–Milan European Cup Final of 1993) on 9 July, the day following France's semi-final victory.[12]

Just as Jacquet wanted more support from L'Equipe, on Friday 10 July French players called for more support in the stadium. Goalkeeper Fabien Barthez said collar and tie should be banned from the Stade de France as inappropriate dress for a football match: 'They should come in jeans and trainers.' He did not think it was right that the players should have to warm up the crowd. 'It's a football match not a classical music concert.' Captain Didier Deschamps was surprised to see whole stands full of men in dark suits as if at a funeral. He called for more noise from the French supporters saying he did not want to hear Brazilian sambas throughout the final. Coach Jacquet described the public as following the team rather than pushing them along. There were calls for President Chirac to wear a replica shirt as a sign of support. The allocation of tickets mainly to official guests, VIPs and corporate hospitality for the later stages, to the exclusion of real fans, was implicitly criticised as the major reason for there being a lack of atmosphere in the stadium for the semi-final. In the street, in bars and in front of the big screens was where the real supporters were. The squad were feeling cut off from this support in their sylvan hide-away at Clairefontaine.[13]

But some say all of France is behind the team: 'La vie en bleu' ...

The atmosphere in the national stadium was all the more disappointing to the players since the whole country seemed behind the team, young and old, men and women, 'black-blanc-beur', from poor suburbs to rich suburbs, such that all the news stations from France-Info, to Europe 1 seem to be devoting half their coverage to the World Cup, and Le Monde claimed that the World Cup had shattered France's traditional psycho-socio-cultural blocks. A huge tricolour banner supporting the national team was unfurled outside the National Assembly, 'Allez la France!'. Prime Minister Jospin saw in the national team the best possible example of national unity in diversity: Frenchmen all, whether first, second, or fiftieth generation, with Basque, West Indian, Armenian, Guyanan, Breton, Argentine, Marseillais, Italian, New Caledonian, Portuguese, etc. origins. As a socialist *député* put it, with reference to recent polemics about the reform of the law on French nationality, now not automatic for those born in France of foreign parents and requiring an application for nationality at age 18, 'In my area there was an enthusiasm on the part of young people – some of whom were younger than 18 – who visibly didn't have to apply for French nationality to feel truly French.' Whereas up to the quarter-finals Brazilian colours had been the choice of many youths from the poor suburbs near the Stade de France, *Libération* reported that after the semi-final victory, everyone was looking for French shirts with Thuram on the back. However there were still those who did not assume things were going to change overnight in terms of integration: 'Children of foreigners who help France win are accepted as French, but when they go to prison, it's always mentioned that they are of immigrant origin.'[14]

Music and fireworks: The Three Tenors and Jean-Michel Jarre

On Friday 10 July the Three Tenors followed their traditional World Cup mass concert after their original 1990 Baths of Caracalla (Rome) and 1994 Dodgers' Stadium (Los Angeles) concerts with a performance in front of the Eiffel Tower and over the Champ-de-Mars. Accompanied by the Orchestre de Paris, Carreras, Domingo and Pavarotti were heard by an estimated 150,000 people – far more at least than in the other World Cup venues. Not all the paying seats (10,000 varying in price from 810 to 6,700 francs) had been sold by the time the police had cut off the whole surrounding area leaving only a few entrances to the Champ-de-Mars. Those watching for free, although filling the 600 x 300 metres of the mainly grassy park, were less densely packed than expected.[15] A number of big screens and a clear if slightly under-powered sound system transmitted the concert to the multitudes, who were still arriving as the second half started and as others were already drifting away. After criticism of the muted reaction of the football crowds, the watching thousands were not likely to raise the roof of the Eiffel Tower, and it was concluded that the Three Tenors had been rather a damp squib.

Again in the spirit of festivities, before the traditional Fireworks display to celebrate Bastille Day on 14 July, Jean-Michel Jarre gave a rare experimental music, synthetic image and laser concert on the Champs-de-Mars in front of a rather bigger audience than the three tenors had attracted. Some of the audience were audibly less than satisfied with what they saw and heard, although the 20 minutes of fireworks around midnight sent most of the crowd home happy. The 208 sprains and twisted ankles that the emergency services had to deal with gives an idea of the crush. The mayor of Paris had initially felt the pyrotechnics of the Jarre concert would allow him to dispense with the traditional fireworks display but had relented. Lacroix, the number one European fireworks display company, was again responsible for the 'splendid' end to a mixed evening.[16]

Le Tour 98 = Dirty; France 98 = Clean?

The Tour de France began with two stages in Ireland, rather later than usual because the organisers (including its founders, *L'Equipe* newspaper) knew the World Cup would push it off the front pages. This was just as well perhaps since what looked like the most serious drugs scandal for some years blew up whereas there had been no positive results in the random testing of footballers at the World Cup.[17] A Festina team trainer was arrested at the Belgian frontier with large amounts of banned substances. Festina was regarded as the top team in the Tour and included team leader and French favourite Richard Virenque, who was quoted as being *effondré*. The Sports Minister commented that justice should take its course.

   L'Equipe quoted a 'well-informed source' implying that the trainer might not be supplying the cycling world but some other market. In smaller type, Jean-Michel Rouet wrote that it was time to ask the real questions, and that one wrong would perhaps make a right, if it allowed cycling to return to what it was in the days of Anquetil, Merckx and Hinault, the implication being that it has been mostly drug free. He criticised inefficient testing and recalled that 56 other sports had suffered drug-related incidents. One might argue that *L'Equipe*'s interests would not be served by suggesting that drug-taking was inherent in cycling. Commercial pressures from sponsors and television were also blamed for adding indirect pressure on riders to go higher and faster; in fact, the 1998 Tour had one fewer hard climbing days, that have recently provided the kind of duels that guarantee high television audiences, and some commentators had seen this as a result of new blood-testing processes. *Le Monde* claimed that the Festina affair showed this was not so, and the Sports Minister Mme Buffet recalled the responsibilities of sports organisers and managers: 'The obligation of results at any price is an incitement to doping. The increasing number and increasing frequency of competitions pose a problem.' The Festina case suggests the authorities are now attempting to reveal the systematic use of drugs in the sport, and thereby to re-establish fair and equal competition.[18]

The Final: 'le jour de gloire est arrivé'

On Sunday 12 July, to take a line from the Marseillaise, the day of Glory had arrived, and the result of the Final match meant that France's *Fête nationale* was brought forward two days.[19] The CFO had originally wanted to stage the final on Bastille Day, but the needs of the global television audience had prevailed. The Final was preceded at 7.30 p.m. by a parade of 300 of the most beautiful mannequins in the world (including Adriana, partner of Christian Karembeu) dressed by Yves Saint Laurent, to celebrate the company's 40 years of *haute couture* and to promote France's major luxury goods industries.

Stade de France and Equipe de France

The Stade de France was soon to earn its name as by 2.30 p.m. many gaudily clad supporters with or without tickets gathered around the inviting promenades of the national stadium, some in the yellow and green of Brazil, many in red-white-and-blue. What struck the visitor was the noise. Apart from the cars passing on the nearby dual-carriageway, many sporting flags out of windows or sun-roofs, and most honking their horns, there were air-hooters, shrill whistles being blown in rhythm, a number of small bands, and the continual uproar of shouts, chants and songs. 'Allez la France, Allez la France, Allez.' Increasingly significant numbers of yellow shirted Brazilian supporters arrived as the afternoon wore on, but they were always in a minority as more and more blue-shirted French fans spilled out of the RER trains and waved their flags. A lot of corporate hospitality ticket-holders there might have been, but they were far less noticeable than in previous matches from their suits and ties. The new national stadium's name that had been criticised as being anodyne in the extreme suddenly took on its real dimension, and once inside with the game in progress, the patriotic crowd made up for earlier muted support. As *Le Monde* wrote, the Stade de France had found its *Equipe de France*.[20] Canal Plus television coverage of the build-up to kick-off showed celebrities such as Johnny Hallyday and Jean-Paul Belmondo wearing French kit with their names on the back of their shirts.

Une France qui gagne ...

Journalists were shocked to discover that Ronaldo was not to play, then at the last minute Coach Zagallo sent a hand-written latter to the press apologising for the wrong information. Ronaldo had indeed been ill, but would play. Speculation was rife that the Brazilian sponsor Nike had pressed to have their star on the pitch. Jacquet started with the same line-up that had won the semi-final, with the exception of the ineligible Blanc, replaced by Chelsea's Franck Lebœuf in the centre of the defence, although Blanc still kissed the bald head of Barthez in a pre-match good-luck ritual. France dominated possession in the first 20 minutes, although Rivaldo forced Barthez into a fine save in the 24th minute. However, Zidane scored a rare headed goal from an in-swinging corner taken by Petit. Scoring with his head is not Zidane's strong point, but Jacquet had told him he could go to the near post during corners, since he had noticed that the Brazilian marking at corners was not as tight as it should be.[21] Guivarc'h saw a good chance saved towards the end of the half, before, in the last minute of the first half, Zidane scored with another header from another corner.

The Brazilians pressed hard in the second half and Barthez brought the crowd to their feet with a remarkable save from Ronaldo six yards out. Desailly kicked off the line. France looked to be holding off the Brazilian attacks with Zidane becoming more dominant, when fate once again seemed to threaten to overcome their hopes: Desailly, the star of their defence throughout the tournament, was sent off in the 68th minute for a second yellow card. While the ten players conceded possession and ground to Brazil, Thuram and Petit especially distinguished themselves in robust defence. With ten minutes to go crowds in front of the Saint-Denis big screen began to chant 'On a gagné', and indeed in the last minutes the French controlled possession, before a fine move involving Zidane, Dugarry and Vieira allowed an indefatigable Petit to move into space beyond the Brazilian defence and score France's third in the match and France's one thousandth international goal since the first in 1904. After 684 minutes of play in the Finals, France were champions.

Having conceded only two goals in the tournament and scored more than any other team, France became the seventh nation to win the World Cup in its sixteenth edition. Right-wing President Chirac unveiled his number 23 team shirt, and he was joined in the players' dressing room by his left-wing Prime Minister Jospin to join in the singing with the players. Some saw in this a symbol of national unity that the victory was irretrievably coming to represent.

Une France qui regarde ... celebrates victory

The match broke all records for television audiences: 20,577,480 viewers (75.6 per cent of audience share) watched on TF1 and a further 3 million on the pay-television channel Canal Plus. Many others watched on big screens or in bars. 50,000 people watched on a big screen in the Charléty Stadium in the south of Paris. Taking into account that 9 per cent of people were away on holiday and could not be polled, Médiamétrie estimated that about half the population watched in one way or another.

One non-football fan reported that during the match not a single car was to be seen moving as he walked down the Boulevard Saint-Michel, cafés were packed, and suddenly when the first and second goals were scored fans surged out of packed cafés and ran around in circles shouting their joy, before piling back in again to see the television replay. On the final whistle, there were suddenly cars on all the streets, horns blaring, people hanging out of passenger windows waving flags and chanting: 'On est les champions! On est les champions!'. A veritable tidal wave of people spilled out onto the streets and swept into the city centres from the suburbs throughout the country. Forty thousand in the centre of Bordeaux and Lyon, and 60,000 in the centre of Marseille, chanting the name of local boy Zidane. It could have been the night of Mitterrand's victory in 1981, but then only half the country was celebrating. Now the whole country could share the joy, and it was far noisier and more euphoric. Three thousand people waited at the training camp at Clairefontaine in the forest of Rambouillet to welcome back the team bus, which took half-an-hour to complete the last 300 metres home.[22]

Tout le monde aux Champs ...

In Paris more people took to the streets than in the May 1968 demonstrations and counter-demonstrations, and journalists compared the sight and the atmosphere to that of the Liberation. Some reports said a million and a half people took to the streets of Paris. The aptly named Arc de Triomphe was the target for many, a pilgrimage even. Illuminated letters spelled out 'Champions du monde' across its stone work.[23] Sporting the national flag, painted faces, or red-white-and-blue scarves, shirts or hats, they chanted, and danced and sung well into the night. Car horns blared, and drums, trumpets and air-hooters and whistles beat out the rhythm of the chants.

There was little or no violence during the celebrations. However, the night was spoiled by two or three accidents involving cars and pedestrians: either people falling off car boots, or more seriously, cars in city centres running into celebrating groups of fans. An accident in Grenoble, in which a number of people were injured, nearly ended in the lynching of the driver. The two most serious incidents were in Paris. First an Alfa Romeo driven by a 33-year-old London lawyer wearing a French team shirt injured ten people. He was driving over the limit in terms of blood alcohol level. He was imprisoned. The more serious accident involved a black Volkswagen Golf driven by a 44-year-old a primary school teacher. She had lost her way in the crowds and panicked as her car was surrounded. At around 3 a.m. she appeared to accelerate into the crowd of revellers on the Champs-Elysées injuring 80 people, 10 seriously, one of whom died from his injuries two days later. She managed to escape the crowd, spent the night on the pavements of Paris and gave herself up to police the next morning. Reports suggested she had been undergoing treatment for psychological problems. Other violent incidents resulted in 23 arrests for theft and criminal damage, and seven for throwing missiles at CRS policemen. A doctor was arrested for firing pistol shots in the air, apparently in exasperation at the noise of supporters near his apartment.[24]

The Aftermath of Victory

On Monday 13 July the nation greeted the French team on Champs-Elysées. After a morning downpour the sun came out on a Champs-Elysées red-white-and-blue with people and flags as the open-topped bus bearing the French team and officials, and the trophy (or rather a copy of it – the Cup itself was too valuable to be a allowed out),[25] tried to make its way from the Rond Point des Champs-Elysées to the Arc de Triomphe.

The Champs-Elysées again

Again people of all ages, from babes in arms to the retired, of both sexes and from all ethnic origins shouted and sang their euphoria among the packed crowd of half a million. A 78-year-old thought there had been more to celebrate the Liberation in 1944, but not since.[26] Workers threw confetti out of the shops and offices overlooking the route. Twenty-franc flags were snapped up. The most beautiful avenue in the world was awash with red white and blue. The chants were of 'Et un, et deux, et trois zéro'. Five hundred officers of the special security service, the RAID, tried to force a way through the crowd for the bus, but having managed 500 metres in nearly two hours, the bus then turned off before reaching the Arc de Triomphe.[27] The throng was unprecedented since the Libération, although there were those who found the comparison odious, preferring the memory of the 'dignified' march in support of de Gaulle during the Events of May–June 1968, and who had not been reconciled to football, its sights and sounds, and values. As the crowds prevented the bus from moving forward, it eventually took a side road. Some of the players, such as Stéphane Guivarc'h, Franck Leboeuf and Manu Petit, had enough energy left to spend the night, along with Aimé Jacquet, at the Lido nightclub.

The Republic honours Jacquet and French football

Tuesday 14 July saw the French Army in a show of strength in central Paris. In 1998 President Chirac's decision to phase out compulsory military service over the next five years and therefore modernise and professionalise the army has not been without its critics. Conscription has been seen as the key link between the citizens and the nation. In the 1998 Bastille Day parade on the Champs-Elysées, perhaps as a tribute to the recent calls on internal security forces during the World Cup, there were more police representatives than before, 374, headed by Lieutenant Sylvie Sanchis. They stole some of the thunder of the gendarmerie, their traditional rival in

14. Victory parade, Champs-Elysées, 13 July 1998.

matters of security and maintenance of order. Cadets from the Saint-Cyr military academy and from Polytechnique paraded in their nineteenth-century-style parade uniforms. As a tribute to the French footballers, the Garde Républicaine band played Gloria Gaynor's hit 'I will survive', that the team had adopted as their theme tune.[28] In the afternoon the President received the French team at the traditional Elysée Palace Garden Party and made Aimé Jacquet *Chevalier de la Légion d'honneur*. Michel Platini was promoted to the rank of *Officier de la Légion d'honneur* in the 14 July honours list. A week or so later, the Council of Ministers made all 22 players of the French World Cup squad *Chevaliers de la Légion d'honneur*, as well as the Chairman of the National Football League (LNF), Noël Le Graët. The President of the French Football Federation (FFF) Claude Simonet, was promoted to *Officier* rank in the Legion of Honour.[29]

Stade de France as multi-use arena

On Saturday 25 July the Stade de France proved that nostalgia is not what it used to be, as Mick Jagger celebrated his 55th birthday by performing with the Rolling Stones in the first ever pop concert held in the new national stadium, more or less full.[30] Nods and winks at the place of the Stade in the French World Cup epic were difficult to avoid. The opening act, Jean-Louis

Aubert, former singer with the first credible French rock group Téléphone, emerged with a tricolour flag he claimed someone had left in the dressing rooms. Chants of 'Et un, et deux, et trois zéro' greeted the Stones, and football fan Jagger (whose presence had been noted at some of the England matches) milked the easy applause with a statement of his pride at playing in the world champions' stadium. The audience, 99.99 per cent white, was not disappointed at what *Le Monde* called one of their best concerts.[31]

Changes of management for the French team

Aimé Jacquet remained unmoved at calls for him to go back on his long-standing wish to step down as national team manager and was moved upstairs on Friday 17 July with his appointment as *Directeur technique national du football français*, replacing Gérard Houllier (named as co-manager of Liverpool in the wake of the rising stock of French football in general). Houllier, aged 50, had formerly coached Lens and won the Championship with PSG, after making his name as manager of Noeux-les-Mines, taking them from the lower leagues to the second division. He had been selector and manager of the National Team from July 1992 to November 1993, when France failed to qualify for Atlanta 94, the point at which Jacquet had taken over.[32]

The announcement of Jacquet's replacement as national selector-manager was put off for ten days or so, after some problems of finding the right person who was free of other contracts. A poll of first division managers in France (and their English counterparts might have agreed) wanted Arsène Wenger in the job. The Federation wanted the ex-international of the 1980s, Jean Tigana, coach of Monaco. Tigana might well have accepted immediately despite a fall in salary since there were reports that he was on bad terms with his club chairman, but he was under contract. Monaco might let him go but only if they could have their former player Glen Hoddle as replacement. Meanwhile *L'Equipe* suggested that Auxerre's long-serving Guy Roux had put himself forward as a stop-gap. However, on Monday 27 July, Jacquet's former assistant took over the reins, chosen by the Federation for the sake of continuity. Roger Lemerre, aged 57, had been Jacquet's deputy since January 1998. This method of internal promotion after co-option into the coaching team has been the method used since Platini was succeeded by his assistant, Houllier.

Little known to the general public, Lemerre was a respectable professional footballer (six international caps between 1968 and 1971). He spent much of his managerial career in charge of the French army team (from 1986) that became world champions under his managership in 1995. Apart from running some training sessions, his role in the 1998 World Cup campaign was to be the interface between Jacquet and the players, who loved in particular his repertoire of dirty jokes which according to *Le Monde*, they insisted he trot out for the head of state's visit to Clairefontaine. He may not have the tactical awareness of Tigana, or the experience of Roux (but who has?) since he has not managed a big professional club. However, one of the reasons he was chosen was because he had the support of the players.[33]

Gendarme emerges from coma ...

On Tuesday 4 August Daniel Nivel, the gendarme left for dead by German thugs in Lens, emerged from his coma after six weeks in a Lille hospital, and was able to breathe without a respirator. Initially reported to have suffered irreversible brain damage, he still had great difficulty in speaking and understanding. Four suspects were charged with attempted murder. The savagery of the assault provoked much soul-searching in Germany. The German Football Federation collected about £200,000 from German clubs and police and set up a charitable foundation, while newspapers raised £100,000 for the victim's family. A benefit match between former French and German internationals was arranged for 20 September near the symbolic French–German border outside Strasbourg.

Football reasserts itself

Roger Lemerre's first test with *les Bleus* was a friendly match against Austria in Vienna on 19 August. Players wondered whether they should continue to use the familiar 'tu' to address their new coach. He had been their mate under Jacquet's reign, and on first-name terms. Thierry Henry was taking no chances; he was going to use 'vous', and call Lemerre 'coach'. The French press were not convinced by the performance as a style of play 'as modern as Lemerre's seventies' flares' produced a 2–2 draw, with France's goals again coming from defenders. *Plus ça change ... ?* The team is only as good as its last result in the eyes of the press, and although France may be qualified as-of-right for the next World Cup, they still have to qualify for the Euro 2000 Championship in Holland and Belgium.

NOTES

1 'Le chiffre du jour', *Le Monde supplément*, 28–29 June 1998, 14; *France Football*, 30 June 1998, 5.

2. S. Hoggart, 'Diary', *Guardian*, 30 June 1998, 12; J. Henley, 'Paris braced for fête du foot', *Guardian*, 9 June 1998, 8; F. Amalou, 'Deux mois de répétition sur les pistes d'un aéroport', *Le Monde supplément*, 10 June 1998, viii; A. Rémond, 'La marche du siècle', *Télérama*, 17 June 1998, 92.

3. E. Barth, 'Les Bleus encore décalés face à l'arbitrage new-look', *Le Monde*, 16 June 1998, iii.

4 J.-L. Pierrat, 'Platini: 'Il ne pouvait rien nous arriver', *Le Parisien*, 14 June 1998, 11.
5. 'Sepp Blatter et Michel Platini critiquent l'arbitrage', *Le Monde supplément*, 18 June 1998, IV; D. Lacey, 'Hoddle voices his fears as referees start to see red', *Guardian Sport*, 20 June 1998, p.3; 'Le patron des arbitres convoqué par le président de la FIFA', *Le Monde*, 25 June 1998, 32; F. Potet, 'Les arbitres, toujours les arbitres...', *Le Monde supplément*, 26 June 1998, vii.
6. F. Chambon, 'L'homme en noir roi de l'arène', *Le Monde supplément*, 20 June 1998, iii.
7. J. Henley, 'Police officer beaten at World Cup out of coma', *Guardian*, 5 July 1998, 2.
8. B. Pivot, 'Esfandlar Baharmast, arbitre trop vite vilipendié par le monde entier', *Journal du Dimanche*, 5 July 1998, H.
9. B. Hopquin, 'L'équipe de France version Mondial 98 ignore tout de la peur', *Le Monde supplément*, 9 July 1998, v.
10. P.V., 'France-Croatie: la victoire est dans la rue', *Lyon-Matin*, 9 July 1998, 6.
11. G. Desporetes, 'L'exploit des Bleus convertit la France au culte du ballon. Hommes, femmes, blancs, blacks, beurs...', *Libération*, 10 July 1998, 2; J. Buob, 'La France voit la vie en bleu', *Le Monde supplément*, 11 July 1998, i.
12. G. Dutheil, 'Après avoir critiqué Aimé Jacquet, L'Equipe se refuse au mea culpa', *Le Monde supplément*, 11 July 1998, iii.
13. F. Chambon, 'Les Bleus jouent pour ceux qui n'ont pas de billets', *Le Monde supplément*, 11 July 1998, VIII; J.LT, '"Notre vrai public, il est dans les rues" Les Bleus fulminent contre l'ambiance apathique du Stade de France, garni de VIP', *Libération*, 10 July 1998, 26.
14. G. Desporetes, 'L'exploit des Bleus convertit la France au culte du ballon', 2; J. Buob, 'La France voit la vie en bleu', *Le Monde supplément*, 11 July 1998, I; O. Bertrand *et al.*, 'Drapeau tricolore, foule multicolore', *Libération*, 10 July 1998, 2–5.
15. M. Dokan, 'Trois voix championnes du monde', *Journal du Dimanche Supplément féminin*, 5 July 1998, 4–7; R. Eggar, 'Fever pitch', *Air France In-flight magazine*, June 1998, 18–24.
16 A. Debièvre, 'Un feu d'artifice de polémique', *Journal du Dimanche*, 12 July 1998, 11; A. Techer and M. Laubeuf, 'Une deuxième voiture folle sur les Champs-Elysées', *Le Parisien*, 16 July 1998, 12.
17. After the World Cup there was a report that the Argentine international Juan Veron had been controlled positive for cocaine and ecstasy on 1 June, before the start of the tournament. Veron denied the report. See *Le Monde*, 24 July 1998, 17.
18. G. Roger, 'Le Tour sous le choc', *L'Equipe*, 12 July 1998, 20; J.-M. Rouet, 'Un mal pour un bien', *L'Equipe*, 12 July 1998, 20; P. Le Gars, 'Virenque: «Je suis effondré»', *L'Equipe*, 12 July 1998, 20; F. Chaptal, 'Dopage: la rumeur sprinte sur le Tour', *Le Journal du Dimanche supplément Sport*, 12 July 1998, J; P. Rochette and C. Losson, 'Une ouverture à l'ombre du dopage', *Libération*, 13 July 1998, 25–6; 'Neuf jours en enfer', *Le Figaro*, 17 July 1998, 10; Y. Bordenave, '«Si tu ne prends rien, tu ne peux rivaliser avec les meilleurs»', *Le Monde*, 18 July 1998, 16; 'Dopage: briser la loi du silence', *Le Monde* (editorial), 17 July 1998, 12
19. A Canal Plus advert in *Le Journal du Dimanche supplément Sport*, 12 July 1998, C.
20. P Georges, 'Pays plus équipé, cela fait un joli coup double', *Le Monde supplément*, 14 July 1998, I.
21. F. Galalmetz, 'Zizou entre Enzo et Eros', *L'Equipe*, 14 July 1998, 7.
22. F. Tonneau and P. Larue, 'Partout, une nuit de folie', *Le Parisien*, 14 July 1998, 6–7.
23. P. Broussard, 'Plus d'un million de personnes ont fêté la victoire sur les Champs-Elysées', *Le Monde supplément*, 14 July 1998, iii.
24. A. Techer and M. Laubeuf, 'Une deuxième voiture folle sur les Champs-Elysées', *Le Parisien*, 16 July 1998, 12.
25. D. Roamin, 'Ce n'était pas la vraie Coupe du monde', *Le Parisien*, 14 July 1998, 2.
26. P. Boutroux, '24 heures sur le toit du monde', *L'Equipe*, 14 July 1998, 4.
27. F. Michel and D. Roamin, 'Une marée humaine pour acclamer les Bleus', *Le Parisien*, 14 July 1998, 2–3.
28. P.-H. Desaubliaux, 'Un défilé, des évolutions', *Le Figaro*, 13 July 1998, 6; J. Isnard, 'Le 14 juillet, des policiers défileront sur les Champs-Elysées', *Le Monde*, 14 July 1998, 24.
29. *Le Monde*, 23 July 1998, 17.
30. Headline on front page of *Marianne*, 20–26 July 1998.

31. C. Tossan and A. Campion, 'Mick Jagger, 55 ans au Stade de France', *Journal du Dimanche*, 26 July 1998, 1; S. Siclier, 'Toujours flamboyants', *Le Monde*, 28 July 1998, 19.
32. I. Hawkey, 'France try on another Jacquet', *Sunday Times Supplement 2*, 19 July 1998, 9.
33. 'Houllier à Liverpool', *Le Figaro*, 17 July 1998, 11; and France-Info radio; F. Potet, 'Roger Lemerre sort du rang et succède à Aimé Jacquet', *Le Monde*, 28 July 1998, 16.

Conclusion: The Impact of France 98

HUGH DAUNCEY and GEOFF HARE

A Successful World Cup?

The world's media, notoriously difficult to please, seemed to agree that France 98 had been successfully organised, and that France's image had improved as a result. Telecommunications was a key issue in the media success of the tournament, and whereas IBM's image had not emerged unscathed from the Atlanta Olympics, France Telecom's technical expertise serving French and foreign media proved up to the task. The predicted indifference of the French to football proved mistaken. The same media's pre-tournament fears of chaos resulting from any combination of transport strikes, terrorism and hooligans did not materialise. A *Financial Times* reporter thought the World Cup transport system would probably never be bettered, and was particularly pleased at the absence of police in stadiums. The two problems recognised as such by organisers and foreign press were the violence in the towns of Marseille and Lens and the bad feeling over ticket allocation, but were partly forgotten by the end of the Finals. The departure of England no doubt helped the security issue. Some of the criticism of the allocation of tickets was arguably aimed at the wrong target and was an occasion for demagogic francophobia. There were certainly never going to be enough tickets to satisfy foreign fans, but the damage to 'real fans' was not due to the few dozen tickets in the hands of touts at several matches, or even the way the last-minute ticket 'hotline' raised vain hopes, but resulted from the hundreds of thousands of tickets that went to sponsors and companies buying corporate hospitality facilities.

A Success for the CFO

From the viewpoint of the CFO, there was general satisfaction at a job well done. Jacques Lambert, chief executive of the CFO, considered that the organisation of the CFO had been professional, detailed and worthy of the image of France. The CFO tended to play down the security aspects of the competition, although the events of Marseille and Lens, especially the attack on the gendarme, were described as a stain on the World Cup. Regarding in-stadium security, the CFO was pleased with the successful innovation of unpaid stewards. It considered ticketing to have been a success since all the stadiums had been full, including lesser attractions like the Romania–Tunisia game at the Stade de France when there was nothing at stake (since the one team was already qualified for the second round and the other could not qualify even by winning). His judgement reflected the priorities in the CFO's thinking from the start – the need to fill the stadiums and break even. Lambert argued that there were no perfect solutions for distributing two and a half million seats, and that in view of the difference between demand and supply, there was no miracle answer to the appearance of a black market. Despite criticisms that too many tickets had gone to VIPs, the CFO maintained that sufficient numbers of different national supporters had brought ambience to matches, and pointed out that for matches involving France, there was no real French national football fans' association that could have organised more atmosphere in grounds – his comment reflects the pattern of support for club matches in France.

Looking ahead, Lambert concluded that the successful organisation of the World Cup had showed how France could organise an Olympic Games, logistically and commercially. Thanks to France 98 France now has an Olympic Stadium (the new Stade de France), although it would still need other infrastructures.[1]

France 98: A Triple Success for the Government

In a provisional evaluation given the day of the Final, the Youth and Sports Ministry saw the World Cup as a triple success in terms of sport, spectating and popular impact.[2] Firstly, France 98 had been a sporting success because not only had the French team performed well, and indeed surpassed expectations, but all the matches had generally been played in a good spirit. Secondly, the competition had been a success as far as spectators were concerned because the stadiums had been practically filled to capacity, and the ticketing policy had offered inexpensive tickets to many fans. Thirdly, the World Cup had been a popular success within France itself as the event had been appropriated by the people outside the stadiums, helped by free transmissions on big screens.

The Ministry was satisfied that predicted catastrophes in terms of public transport strikes and exploitative rises in prices had not happened, and that pre-tournament concerns over policing and security before the tournament had not been justified since the problems of violence had been restricted to only two matches, thanks to work by the CFO inside the stadiums, the police outside the stadiums and international co-operation. They blamed what violence had occurred on 'openly xenophobic people motivated by an ideology of exclusion'. These motivations, the Ministry argued, contrasted with those of France, which had managed to organise the World Cup without renouncing its values. France 98 had not been dominated by money, but had been a *fête*, despite the ticketing problems which had come from an excess of demand inherent in the event itself. France had responded to the best of its abilities to this demand from home and abroad. These latter claims are debatable, and linked. The CFO, admittedly under pressure from FIFA rules and the need to make ends meet, exacerbated the problem of the huge numbers of tickets going to French and multinational companies for business hospitality purposes. They were unable to reverse the way the World Cup had sold out traditional stakeholders to big business. What the Ministry can and should be congratulated on is the way it encouraged local authorities to set up (and in many cases, subsidise) the many big screens that allowed the event to be a shared and expanded experience for the hundreds of thousands who viewed the games in this way, and were all the better able to participate collectively. As one might expect of the French Left, the government used the opportunity to point to the way the French victory had caused millions of French people to give collective expression to a sense of belonging to the national community, not through nationalism and exclusiveness, but rather through solidarity, diversity and positive, progressive, human values – in the image of the French team.

To build on what it hopes is a defining moment for French racial and social relations, and to prolong this positive dynamic in the nation in favour of sport and integration, the Ministry proposed a number of measures for the future. Firstly, funds will be set aside in the 1999 budget to support local sporting events and projects in the difficult estates and urban districts, in order to help build up social links and combat exclusion. Secondly, since the enthusiasm for the World Cup will create a desire to play football, among young girls as well as boys, in September 1998 the Ministry launched a *coupon sport*, to pay the registration fee for children of poorer families to join a sports club. Thirdly, in order to keep people going to sports stadiums, especially those who discovered that they could watch matches as families without fearing hooligan behaviour in the stadiums, the Ministry will work with the FFF and the League to bring football ticket prices in line with cinema prices, and indeed to provide some free places. These unapologetically interventionist policies confirm the continuing nature of the French State's public service mission to ensure that certain values prevail in French sport.

Footballing Success

France 98 was important in terms of football in a number of ways. In terms of the tournament it was the first time that the number of participating nations had been expanded to 32, including more teams from developing football countries, and involving the increase to 64 of the fixtures in the Finals phase. Equally, in terms of the world game, France 98 introduced new rulings on tackling from behind and other measures intended to protect the entertainment value of the sport. Regarding its relevance to France, the victory of *les Bleus* finally concluded the host country's search for footballing recognition, and in the process of winning, the French team under the guidance of Aimé Jacquet rewrote some of the rules about French footballing style and national sporting stereotypes.

Les Bleus *and Why They Won*

One reason behind France's success was arguably its coaching system. Platini drew attention to the fact that a generation of ex-players had invested a lot in football, and underlined that the French Federation had a good coaching policy. Whereas, as players, Platini's generation had been completely left to their own devices by their predecessors, the current national squad was coached by players such as Fernandez, Giresse and Tigana, from the Platini generation, and of course by Jacquet. Another reason was the continuity (which must have helped teamwork) which characterised Jacquet's teams. The typical French team for Euro 96 differed little in personnel from his *équipe type* in 1998.

Experience abroad was also a factor contributing to success: The notable difference in France 98 was that while in 1995/96 eight out of eleven first teamers played in French club football in the season preceding Euro 96, all except Guérin (who was under suspicion of doping at Paris Saint-Germain and did not make the 1998 squad) went on to gain experience with big foreign clubs before the World Cup. Lama (Paris Saint-Germain to West Ham), Thuram (Monaco to Parma), Blanc (Auxerre to Barcelona and back to Marseille), Desailly (AC Milan), Lizarazu (Bordeaux to Athletic Bilbao and Bayern Munich) Karembeu (Sampdoria to Real Madrid), Deschamps (Juventus), Zidane (Bordeaux to Juventus), Djorkaeff (Paris Saint-Germain to Inter Milan), Dugarry (Bordeaux to Barcelona and back to Marseille). Key newcomer Petit had of course won the League and Cup double with Arsenal, and goalkeeper Barthez had won the European Cup with Marseille in 1993 and had also gained European Cup experience with Monaco.

Team spirit, 'le collectif', strengthened the squad's self-belief as pre-tournament sessions at Tignes and travel to Morocco and Finland helped players to bond. It was noted that even the individualist Djorkaeff started to defend, and as the tournament progressed the team felt physically stronger than other teams, said captain Deschamps. Jacquet believed that his players were becoming a team. 'My aim has always been to bring together a side for the World Cup in 1998, and I am more confident that will happen,' he said. 'We have performed as a unit, and we are comfortable together now.'

The French team also learned self-belief and learned to 'play in the big league'. The Euro 96 experience – going out in the semi-final on a penalty shoot-out against the Czech Republic – was assessed at the time by Deschamps as a failure of character of the young France team: 'French sportsmen have never really learnt to cope with the pressures and expectation at the very top,' he said. 'We always seem to collapse on D-Day. In the next two years we must discover if the team can overcome this problem.'[3]

The National Team and French Style

As Marks points out above, one of the myths commonly mediated through football relates to national styles of play. Beaud and Noiriel see judgements on national style as a construction, a discourse that maintains chauvinism and xenophobia.[4] Wahl unearthed evidence of the search for a French sporting identity as early as the 1920s, a quest for a national style to replace the tough muscular play of the English.[5] Platini's teams were described as playing 'champagne football' characterised by improvisation and vivacity, making for a sparkling passing game, but one that was vulnerable and fragile.[6] One of the more detailed histories of French football picks out the lasting impact on French style of play made by the visiting Uruguayans in the 1924 Olympic Games held in Paris.[7] Until then influences had come mainly from across the Channel, but the Uruguayans were the revelation of the tournament, bringing a new type of football to France. Beating France 5–1 in the quarter-finals in front of 45,000 home spectators, they inspired admiration for their South American artistry, giving the French a football lesson, almost literally. Their style was described as combining artistry, a sense of entertainment, virtuosity, and the effectiveness and realism of professionals. Their influence in establishing a French style of play (or perhaps in establishing a conceptual framework through which to talk about football and style) was maintained by their continued international success: Olympic Champions again in 1928 and first World Cup winners in 1930.

The Uruguayan dialectic emerged in descriptions of French national styles in the mouths of national team managers over the years, as the mood swung between power and solidity on the one hand and finesse, flexibility and vivacity on the other. Albert Batteux, coach of the successful Reims teams, and successful national manager in 1958, and Michel Hidalgo, manager of the Platini teams of the 1980s, promoted an open, attacking style giving full scope to the individual brilliance of Kopa and Fontaine or Platini and Tigana. On the other hand, Georges Boulogne, national team manager in the 1970s, was a partisan of 'football labeur' ('football as hard work'). Both approaches appear to have at their base the same conception of French national character as undisciplined and individualistic, the one seeing it positively, the other negatively. Boulogne's response was to exercise total authority over the players, to instil a sense of solidarity and teamwork in players whom he saw as naturally individualistic because of competition for places in the team.[8] Partisans of football as hard labour drove out Just Fontaine as national team coach (1966–67).

As the Federation's Coaching Director in the late 1960s, Boulogne developed ideas on what he called 'modern football'. In order for French football to adapt to modern economic conditions and to international competition, he claimed football had to stop being an enjoyable game ('une activité ludique'). He used vocabulary based on economic thinking of the time: organisation, effort, productivity. His new direction meant giving up improvisation based on the individualism recommended by Batteux. Boulogne took over the national team in 1969 with the idea of instilling an ethic of discipline and effort, a more rigorous type of game based more on defence, therefore less entertaining and less spectacular. Players had to accept more discipline on the pitch. But France did not qualify for the 1970 and 1974 World Cups.

Michel Hidalgo, an ex-player, who took over as national team manager in 1976, was a firm partisan of Batteux's attacking style, of 'le plaisir de jouer', rejecting military vocabulary, telling his players 'to go out and enjoy themselves'. Win at all costs was not the main object, and style became just as important as effectiveness, or rather, style being the one of the key objectives, success was to be achieved by playing with style. The French public seemed to agree.

Equally the authoritarianism of Boulogne may be seen as reflecting the dominant Gaullist ideology of an earlier time, and while possibly in tune with the way industrial society was developing, was arguably becoming out of tune with a post-May '68 society. The basis of the Gaullist presidential regime of the Fifth Republic was to give the State and its (democratically elected) leaders the authority to take decisions in the national interest cutting across the myriad of individual interests represented in parliament with its multiparty system. Post-Gaullist France has been attempting little by little to dismantle some of the authoritarian institutional and mental structures of an earlier age. Hidalgo was more in tune with Mitterrand's France of the 1980s which culminated in both Mitterrand's presidential re-election campaign of 1988 and the Bicentenary celebrations of 1989 led by the fashion designer Jean-Paul Goude, both being the triumph of style over substance. As co-director of the Organising Committee, Platini's desire to turn the 1998 World Cup into 33 days of *fête* is in direct line of descent from Batteux, Hidalgo and May '68. However, that was not what could be said of the 1998 French team manager.

Was *L'Equipe* living in a romantic past in its constant criticism of Aimé Jacquet for his apparent attachment to the Boulogne type of workmanlike style, and his use of his famous tactical notebook, from which he passed on detailed instructions on how to cope with opponents and how to eradicate errors, and which of course allegedly stifled spontaneity? Jacquet's style, which, after his success, the press associated with his humble (in both senses, humility and lower social class) origins, and his ethic of hard work, honesty, no frills and provincial rural characteristics ('la France profonde'), were suddenly seen as in tune with the reality of late-twentieth-century French values that could unite the nation. The stereotypically undisciplined individualists Ginola and Cantona (geniuses maybe, and representing an out-of-date British idea of French football), were never mentioned in the French press as *les Bleus* progressed to the Final. Not even *L'Equipe*, it should be said, had pressed for their inclusion in the squad. Some might argue that Jacquet made a virtue out of necessity in his reliance on team work, and solid defence, having fewer creative players and strikers to field than Batteux or even Hidalgo, but it remains that his style seems in tune with the time, even if in France 98, for as jaundiced a judge as Johan Cruyff, overall standards of play had gone down 'in terms of our ideas and the lack of real genius'.[9] Perhaps Jacquet's genius was to bring out the best in players few of whom were in the genius category.

Economics, Politics, and the Feel-good Factor

Politically, hosting the World Cup has revealed a number of things about French society. Firstly, there was a certain amount of anti-World Cup feeling protesting against various aspects of the event. These protests were gradually drowned by rising enthusiasm for the success of the French team. Secondly, the same enthusiasm for the competition and for a successful France led to a growing feel-good factor, which affected the President's and the Prime Minister's standing slightly differently. Its causes were not wholly to do with football. The prime ministerial honeymoon period – the new government dated from May 1997 – had been prolonged by good economic results. World Cup success begged the question of whether the competition and victory would have further economic effects.

The Economic Impact of France 98

Two separate studies (from the Caisse des Dépôts and consultants Paine Webber) have concluded the economic effects of past World Cups had been small and difficult to quantify. In France 98 some SMEs will have done well, and there was increase in economic activity in the middle of the year, but one tentative study thought the fall-out from the tournament would be an increase of only 0.1 per cent of GDP, a little less than the overall cost of the operation. The most tangible results, according to the French Economic Statistical Agency (Institut national de la statistique et des études économiques – INSEE), were increases in television and video-recorder sales, an increase in consumption of certain services like hotels (but this was uneven across regions and quality of hotel), and an earlier rise in tourist hotel and restaurant prices than in other years. The impact on jobs was 'derisory', since many World Cup activities were undertaken by unpaid volunteers, and most other jobs were temporary. Commerce and the construction industry benefited. Building the Stade de France created between 1,400 and 3,000 jobs. One estimate put the organisation of the Cup as creating 15,450 jobs at its most intense point of activity. In the longer term, however, a World Cup effect is expected in tourism and more importantly on inward economic investment, but this will not become evident for a year or two.[10]

Regarding tourism, there was a drop in numbers of visitors coming to France in the period covering the tournament, Whereas the Musée d'Orsay in Paris was 15 per cent down and the Château de Versailles was 10 per cent down during the World Cup, hotels in Saint-Etienne (not a tourist haven) were nearly full in the second half of June. Equally, business in hotels, campsites and bars in and around Lens was up. The 'Lens effect' stretched as far as bars in Lille, but not as far as Calais (30 per cent of whose activity comes from tourism), where ferry traffic saw no increase. This confirms that for every football fan who crossed the channel other British tourists stayed away. The success of French railways and especially the TGV certainly did not help keep spectators in some provincial host towns. In Bordeaux, however, the local airport saw 50,000 extra travellers in June. Here too some hotels had a higher occupancy rate and bars did better business compared to the previous year. While overall numbers of visitors were down, consumption was up. Was this why the Chamber of Commerce took out advertisements in Scottish papers to thank Scottish supporters for their visit (and good behaviour)? In the Paris region, while five star hotels did well, the 1–3 star category had mediocre results. The Paris Tourist Office concluded early on that one million non-sport tourists had failed to arrive, whereas football had brought in half-a-million fans who would not otherwise have been there. However, preliminary evidence in August indicated that the month and a half following allowed a catching up, and a total of 60 million tourists finally visited France in summer 1998, thus retaining France's first place as a tourist destination.

Another important long-term factor was that French confidence was boosted by the World Cup victory in other ways. Jean-François Kahn identified a new and surprised realisation by the French or at least by public opinion (but this is confirmed by talking to ordinary people) that France could be proud of its achievements in general and that the rest of the world did have things to admire about France rather than just seeing the country as a nation of *râleurs* ('whingers').[11] Discussing 'the French success stories that the world envies us for', Kahn's *Marianne* vaunted the news that the French TGV had been sold to Taiwan as the latest in a series of deals underlining the success of this flagship example of French high technology. 'Playing in the major league' in this way in technology and industry is something France wants to be recognised for.

A World Cup Tournament is a Long Time in Politics

The anti-World Cup movements of Left and Right were swamped by football mania as *les Bleus* progressed. The neo-Trotskyist *Lutte ouvrière* (LO) castigated government and CFO for the capitalist exploitation of sport, and was similarly critical of how government and businesses had exploited the period of World Cup festivities to announce unpopular measures such as pay cuts and redundancies, hoping that protests would be stifled by fear of 'spoiling the party'. In a trenchant editorial in the party newspaper after France's first match, LO leader Arlette Laguiller emphasised that the World Cup was being used as a bread-and-circuses mollification of a divided French society, and sardonically demonstrated how after a single victory the nation's media were already creating the theme of 'Lionel Jospin – Aimé Jacquet: Same Struggle for a Winning Team France'. Laguiller concluded by warning that even a win in the Final might not be enough to buy Jospin more popularity.[12]

For the extreme-right weekly *Rivarol*, the World Cup offered the usual predictable examples of racial conflict, government incompetence and corruption, and media toadying to the 'Establishment line' on France's problems. Early in the competition, the newspaper commented on various claimed examples of disturbances between English and Scottish supporters and so-called bands of local youths of 'ethnic origin', who, according to *Rivarol* had manifestly failed to internalise the government's belief in the 'pacifying and integrating enthusiasm of the World Cup'. Pointing to the participation of Moroccan, Tunisian and Cameroon teams in the competition, *Rivarol* sneered at the divided loyalties it expected in what it called the 'néo-Français' of France's second-generation immigrant communities.[13]

The Comité pour l'organisation du boycott de la Coupe du monde de football en France (COBOF) had the highest profile and was the most political of various movements set up to contest the hosting of the Finals. Basing its rejection of France 98 on an analysis of football and the World Cup which interpreted them as the tools of Fascism or liberal capitalism and on the view that French society was in economic and social crisis, COBOF criticised French State funding of the World Cup, the intrusion of police video-surveillance, and rejected the duplicity of France's welcome to teams from countries with questionable attitudes towards human rights. COBOF argued that, in France's divided society, World Cup funding by the French State was irrational and would serve only the interests of the commercial partners of the CFO.[14] These anti-World Cup voices were, however, progressively drowned by the tide of euphoria swelling round by round.

World Cup wins (and losses) have had significant effects on the popularity of governments, as Harold Wilson saw in 1966 and 1970. Both the right-wing President Chirac and the left-wing Prime-Minister Jospin benefited from the euphoria of the World Cup win in the popularity polls of July 1998. The highly regarded IFOP-*Journal du Dimanche* opinion poll satisfaction barometer reported that President Chirac had gone up 11 points in a month to 59 per cent, catching up Prime Minister Jospin who had gone up 7 points.[15] Public opinion also not surprisingly felt good about the system of cohabitation (68 per cent of favourable opinions, up 9 points for *Paris Match*), where power is shared between President and Prime Minister. Because the terms of office of President and Parliament are different (seven and five years respectively, and indeed the President can dissolve parliament early, as Chirac did in 1997), a parliamentary election can give a different result to that of a previous presidential election. The left-wing coalition's parliamentary majority of 1997 forced Chirac to appoint a left-wing Prime Minister and government therefore, which takes over all the initiative for legislation. Foreign policy on the other hand tends to be shared in a 'two-heads-one-voice' situation. For the first time since 1990 there were roughly as many French people happy with the way they were being governed as those who were dissatisfied.[16] President Chirac had lost much political credibility after his misjudged dissolution of parliament, but cohabitationary periods have in the past benefited the popularity of the President. French public opinion seems to enjoy consensus politics.

Has Chirac's enthusiastic presence at the French matches, brandishing his number 23 shirt after the Final win and handing the Cup to the French captain, benefited him more politically than his left-wing rival? They both seem to have gained by being seen to be equally unconditional supporters. There were those who thought Jospin might have responded to Deschamps' post-semi-final criticism of the dark suits by wearing a blue strip to the Final, but he chose not to up-stage the head of state.[17] Jospin has benefited most from the improved economic situation, the drop in unemployment especially among young people, and the hope invested in the Euro single currency.[18]

Has Chirac's unconditional support of the team made the French public forgive or even forget his dissolution gaffe? As President, having lost influence over the right-wing parties, especially over his own neo-Gaullist party, le Rassemblement pour la République (RPR), he has derived far more political benefit from the World Cup than the right-wing politicians squabbling over the supposed succession following the 1997 defeat. As a lame-duck President, Chirac's political career seemed to be over, but a World Cup tournament is a long time in politics. He now seems still to be the only recourse for the Right in any forthcoming presidential election.

Chirac's Popularity and Problems of the Right in France

The strength of the vote (around 15 per cent) for the Front National (FN) and the fact that it splits the right-wing vote at most elections, have posed a political problem to the orthodox Right in France. Some politicians such as Charles Millon have eventually come out in favour of an alliance with the FN (in the Lyon region) after split regional assemblies forced the right-wing leaders to choose between accepting FN support or handing power to the Left. Alain Madelin, ambitious leader of the economic liberals, Démocratie libérale, seemed tempted to back Millon, but drew back. Former PM Balladur seems to have timed his call badly, just before the World Cup, for discussion of 'préférence nationale' ideas associated with the FN. Other right-wing leaders have preferred to maintain support for a Republican front against non-democratic parties such as the FN, meaning abstaining or even voting for a Socialist candidate rather than for the extreme Right. After the multiracial nationalistic fervour of victory, Charles Pasqua, with a reputation as former hard-line Gaullist Minister of the Interior, surprised everyone on Left and Right, in the wake of the multicultural nationalism of World Cup celebrations, by calling for the regularisation of all those illegal immigrants who had applied for the amnesty when the left-wing government came to office, saying they could not all, realistically, be deported. 'When France is strong, she can be generous.'[19] He may be using football as a basis for recapturing the Right for an anti-European, but equally *anti-Le Pen* nationalism.

For its part, the FN was unusually quiet during the World Cup. Le Pen has his own internal opposition in the form of Bruno Mégret, leader of the FN would-be respectable wing. However, Le Pen had deeper problems with the way events were turning out. In 1996 he had judged it artificial to bring players from abroad and baptise them 'équipe de France'. He did not believe they represented France. This time his comments were rather different. ('The FN has always recognised that French citizens can be of different races and religions provided they have in common the love of the *patrie* and the will to serve it.') He none the less called the victory 'a detail in the history of the war that peoples wage on sports fields', in an attempt to undermine praise for the multiracial team. (He had once called the Holocaust 'a detail of history'.) He criticised Chirac and Pasqua for having succumbed to the 'World Cup effect'.[20]

Problems experienced by the extreme Right were neatly summarised in a political cartoon by Plantu that appeared in the weekly news-magazine *L'Express* following the world Cup victory and showed the supposed disarray of Le Pen: as the black-white-and-Arab French team sing the Marseillaise and the French nation hail Thuram, Zidane and Karembeu, an aide consoles Le Pen by saying: 'Don't cry Jean-Marie, next time the Final might be between Nigeria and Cameroon', at which point Le Pen falls off his chair in anguish.

Football, Culture and Society

The passionate World Cup celebrations on the Champs-Elysées after the Final victory, when over a million people came together to express their elation – scenes repeated in French towns and cities across the country – showed a sense of fraternity after a history of 'guerre franco-française'. Many expressed their joy by waving the national flag. Over the course of the Finals, France saw a rise in the level of drama (close victory over Paraguay by Golden Goal, victory on penalties over Italy, late victory against Croatia, and then the Final), a rise in interest among old and new fans (especially new female fans), a rise in the feeling of solidarity among French people from all cultural and ethnic backgrounds. Debate in the French press following the victory endlessly rehearsed the basic issue: *une France fracturée* needed a *prétexte fédérateur*, and the football celebrations were celebrations of national unity. In the right-wing daily *Le Figaro*, the writer and ex-Gaullist minister Alain Peyrefitte declared that France was a multiracial country and would remain so. Only a few voices, on the extreme Right, begged to differ and even Le Pen appeared somewhat wrong-footed. A second cultural and psychological effect of the victory seems to be that the French have discovered that the world loves them and that they are not eternal losers. France has discovered the reality of 'Une France qui gagne', as well as the reality of 'Une France multiraciale'. The press elected Aimé Jacquet as symbol of these 'new' old values.

'Une France tricolore et multicolore': Multiracial National Team – Multicultural Society?

Since the oil crisis of the 1970s and more particularly since the economic difficulties of the early Mitterrand years in the mid-1980s, racism has increased in France, along with the alienation and exclusion of children of first generation immigrant families, the *Beurs*. Social problems in housing and schooling, rising inequalities, petty crime and anti-social behaviour, feelings of insecurity and disillusionment with the orthodox political parties' failure to solve the problems have been seized upon by the extreme

Right. The Front National, as it has grown in influence, has gradually given a kind of respectability to racist attitudes and has set a political agenda where the nationality laws have been tightened to make it more difficult, for the first time since the signing of the Declaration of the Rights of Man two centuries ago, for young people born in France of foreign parentage to become French citizens. Right and Left have opposing views on reforming the nationality laws in the direction of *le droit du sang* (the idea of nationality based on blood rights or parental lineage favoured by the Front National and others on the right) and *le droit du sol* (the French Republican ideal of nationality coming from the land in which one is born). In the pre-World Cup climate orthodox right-wing parties and an ex-Prime Minister (Balladur) felt able to call for a serious national debate on policies of racial discrimination (*préférence nationale*) in housing and social security and so on. The traditional French Republican approach to integration of foreigners into a single model of citizenship, as opposed to the creation of a multicultural society, was being called into question. The 'immigration issue' was defining a key ideological and political divide.

France has been undergoing a crisis of identity to do with the racial and cultural mix of its poor city suburbs that have become ghettos. It has been complicated by growing globalisation of the economy (for which, in France, read Americanisation), the inability to come to terms in the collective memory with Vichy and France's role in the Holocaust, or with resentments left over from the Algerian War. Has the World Cup victory been a defining moment in France's realisation that it is unalterably, and for better or worse (and probably for the better in the image of their football team) a mixed-race society? Has the victory crystallised a feeling that France is also undeniably in the big league and accepted as such by the rest of the world? There may be a feeling that the World Cup is lifting a long depression, and showing the way forward in terms of national identity.

Zizoumania: Politicisation or Depoliticisation of French Society?

A symbol of the new multiracial France is a slightly balding Kabyle named Zinedine Zidane. Since the two goals he scored in the World Cup Final on 12 July 1998, he is arguably the best-known Frenchman in the world. As Mignon and Marks have suggested above, support for the national football team in France's multicultural and often racist society is a matter of complex dynamics, and the opportunity to support a sporting success offered by the World Cup victory encouraged much ink to be spent on expressions of racial harmony. The French press, which before the Finals thought so much depended on Zidane's performance as France's playmaker, was, after the Final, relieved to see him confirm his status. Platini felt 'Zizou' had been the player to make the difference between the two sides.

France's most famous number 10 had always said Zidane was the only current player he would buy a ticket to see play.[21] Zizou's father arrived from Kabylie, the Berber region of Algeria, in the Paris red industrial belt in the 1960s, and moved to La Castellane in 1970, working as a warehouseman. It was on this poor Marseille estate that his son was brought up and learned to play football – with such success that the 26-year-old has become a local hero, the poor local boy made good, a source of pride who can serve as a model of social integration and 'getting on' for children from an area where unemployment is 40 per cent.[22]

From La Castellane to the Champs-Elysées, second generation North African immigrants (*les Beurs*) chanted his name. One anecdotal illustration of Zidane's symbolic value in race relations and national identity was that a *Beur* acting as self-appointed cheer-leader by the Saint-Denis big screen was determined to have the mainly white crowd chant 'Zizou', and thus recognise Zidane's contribution to the nation and the *Beurs'* place within it. On the Champs-Elysées other *Beurs* waved Algerian flags alongside the French tricolour, thus showing their dual cultural identity. As Benjamin Stora remarked: 'This closes a chapter of French history because it shows one can remain faithful to an Algerian nationalist father and yet be for France, that one can be a Moslem and be fully French.'[23] 'Father Christmas is Kabyle', read a home-made poster on the Champs-Elysées.[24]

The view that France was changing was expressed by demographer and immigration specialist Michèle Tribalat. She saw in the gusto with which the multicoloured team sang the Marseillaise (except Karembeu in the Final) and in the joyful nationalism of supporters from all backgrounds a moment of grace and identification with the nation, a magical day incarnating the ideal of the French melting pot. She compared the French system of republican integration of ethnic minorities with the German one that had produced a German team of all white faces and blond hair and no players of Turkish origin. In this way, she concluded, the French system visibly opts for 'universalism' with a very open nationality law whereas Germany's ethnic concept of the nation means Turkish children remain Turkish. For Tribalat, France 98 had showed that nationalism can be positive and elevated.[25]

The celebrations were widely portrayed as a festival of political theatre. One contributor to *Libération* saw the events as the first step backwards taken by the extreme Right.[26] Something was changing in people's heads. The fact that so many women joined in (after their notorious lack of interest in team sports) proved for some that 12 July was to do with more than just football. And other newspapers took a similar line. *Le Journal du Dimanche* drew the conclusion that, despite their social, political, cultural and urban divisions, French people could come together around the tricolour and the

Marseillaise, the traditional attributes of the nation and of patriotism that the extreme Right had stolen. For years the worry had been how to recapture the heritage monopolised by Le Pen, but the increasing movement of support for the multiracial national team demonstrated that 'Win or lose France has won a victory over itself.'[27]

There are those, however, who see the political and ideological interpretations of the fervour of 12 July as an out-of-date view of French culture in the widest sense, the implication being that football fervour is football fervour and should not be given a wider significance. Michel Vovelle saw popular rejoicing over the result of a football match as a sign of the depoliticisation of French society. The only comparable manifestations of the last 60 or so years have been the Liberation in 1944, certain marches at the time of the Popular Front in 1936, or in the events of May 1968. Since then there have been few comparable spontaneous collective mobilisations of people in the streets. In an entirely different register, he compared the spontaneous out-pouring of emotion to the reaction in Britain to the death of Diana, Princess of Wales. In both cases he saw a manifestation of the need to join in with other people across generations and social class barriers.[28] It was to do with a need for interpersonal relations rather than a political statement, and as such a depoliticisation of French culture.

Aimé Jacquet, or the Parable of a New France: Une France qui gagne?

After being the butt of Canal Plus's satirical *Les Guignols* and *L'Equipe*'s whipping boy for *les Bleus*'s inability to play attacking champagne football, the national team manager Aimé Jacquet suddenly found himself transformed in the press into an icon of the new France, a blend of new and old values. Having been mocked for his provincial accent and his inarticulacy, his refusal to play the communication game, and for generally being unfashionable, he now stood for the virtues of hard work, modesty, humility, respect, honesty, simplicity, authenticity, competence, professionalism. His approach to football had worked: methodical, protecting his players, building teamwork, generosity, valuing character, willingness to work meaning more than natural talent, getting a result rather than being flashy. He came to represent all those unpaid volunteers who coach young children in park football, but the term that fits him is not coach, or trainer, or manager, but the very French *éducateur*. Indeed the role of such people was compared to that of the 'hussars of the republic' in the late nineteenth and early twentieth century, the lay primary school teachers of the first universal free and secular State school system: transmitting Republican values to the youth of France, promoting a meritocracy, and creating the national unity that in the last decades had been eroded. The former skilled factory worker and then professional footballer had become a manager winning three championships and two French cups with Bordeaux before being sacked by President Bez for being 'too straight'. As national manager, for some he symbolises a new era of French football, the opposite of the Tapie years, the money years when lucre and appearances were everything. Furthermore, his 57-year-old shoulders have to bear a heavier burden of symbolism: the team he created becomes an analogy for the country, supposedly tired, suffering from an inferiority complex, judging itself to be a mere middle-ranking country, fearful of the challenges of modernisation, and of social integration. For having inspired a multiracial team, in France's image, to all pull together successfully in the same direction, Jacquet was presented as incarnating the three integrative forces of old: not only the primary school teacher (method and hard work), but also the provincial priest (community) and finally the Saint-Etienne factory worker (solidarity, *cohésion*). If the Republic is once again threatened in its cohesion, in its fraternity, in its *banlieues* and elsewhere, much of the French press saw Jacquet's traditional values and self-belief as the answer.[29]

As Robert Graham said, in a perceptive British view of events in the *Financial Times*, the reactions of all from the President downwards underlined France's hunger for good news. 'The weight of recent history hangs heavily on the national psyche – whether it be collaboration under Nazi occupation during the Second World War, De Gaulle's complex about playing second fiddle to the Americans and British, colonial defeat in Indo-China or colonial retreat from Algeria. This has been exacerbated latterly by a feeling of the odds stacked against France, with high unemployment, nagging strikes, a losing economic model and the absence of cultural icons.'[30] This sense of depression, as has been shown, has deflected attention from many areas where France has been a winner. One of the most important areas for further study emerging from France 98, precisely because it is so important for the future, is to observe how permanent is this change of national mood and purpose.

NOTES

1. Interview with Jacques Lambert on 98 Radio France, 11 July 1998.
2. A Ministry spokesman at a reception at La Plaine-Saint-Denis Forum on 12 July 1998.
3. D. Maddock, 'France preoccupied with World Cup', *Times*, 28 June 1996.
4. S. Beaud and G. Noiriel, 'L'immigration dans le football', *Vingtième siècle* (April–June 1990), 83–96.
5. A. Wahl, *Les Archives du football* (Paris, Gallimard, 1989), p.205.
6. P. Nussle, 'Jouons "à la française"', in J. Bureau (ed.), 'L'amour foot. Une passion planétaire', *Autrement*, 80 (May 1986), 24–5.

7. J. Thibert and J.-P. Rethacher, *La Fabuleuse Histoire du football* (Paris, Editions de la Martinière, 1996).

8. See Wahl, *Les Archives du football*, pp.297–9.

9. *Observer*, 19 July 1998.

10. *Wall Street Journal Europe*, 13 July 1998, 6; Y. Joly, 'Une première évaluation de l'effet "Coupe du Monde"', *Le Monde*, 1 July 1998, 5; 'Les bonnes affaires du Mondial', *Le Monde* supplément, 14 July 1998, XIV; C. Fouquet, 'Le Mondial n'a pas de fort impact sur l'économie française', *Les Echos*, 2 July 1998.

11. J.-F. Kahn, 'Les réussites françaises que le monde nous envie', *Marianne*, 20–26 July 1998, 24–32.

12. A. Laguiller, 'Du cirque et du pain', *Lutte ouvrière* No.1562, 19 June 1998, 3.

13. C. Lorne, 'M comme Mondial, métissage, meutes ethniques et magouilles', *Rivarol*, No. 2391, 19 June 1998, 12,

14. See http://perso.wanadoo.fr/cobof/Default.htm COBOF was supported by the famous satirical magazine *Charlie Hebdo*, which published a special issue in which sports sociologists and teachers presented subversive interpretations of the World Cup and French society's obsession with spectacularised sport; *Charlie Hebdo*, 308, 'L'horreur footballistique'.

15. J.-L. Parodi, 'Impressionnant record de Jacques Chirac', *Journal du Dimanche*, 26 July 1998, 1, 4.

16. 'Les Français plébiscitent la cohabitation selon un sondage', *Le Monde*, 23 July 1998, 6 (report on *Paris-Match* issue dated 23 July 1998).

17. C. Pasternak, 'Le hold-up sentimental', *Journal du Dimanche*, 26 July 1998, 4.

18. G. Courtois, 'Le Mondial a aidé Jacques Chirac à retrouver sa popularité', *Le Monde*, 28 July 1998, 5.

19. 'M. Pasqua: il faut régulariser tous les sans-papiers', *Le Monde*, 17 July 1998, 1.

20. 'Condamnation unanime des propos de M. Le Pen sur les footballeurs français', *Le Monde*, 26 June 1996, 8; R. Dely, 'Le Pen: "la Coupe du Monde est un détail de l'histoire"', *Libération*, 13 July 1998; B. Jeudy, 'Le Pen minimise "l'effet Mondial"', *Le Parisien*, 18–19 July 1998, 10.

21. J.-L. Pierrat, 'Platini: "Il ne pouvait rien nous arriver"', *Le Parisien*, 14 July 1998, 11.

22. K.N., 'La "Zizoumania" sur tous les fronts', *Le Parisien*, 14 July 1998, 10.

23. R. Graham, 'Tonique for the nation', *Financial Times*, 18 July 1998.

24. K. N., 'Zidane prend place sur le Toit du monde', *Le Parisien*, 14 July 1998, 10.

25. D. Simonnot, 'Ce jour est magique, il incarne l'idéal du creuset français', *Libération*, 5 July 1998, 5.

26. R. Castro, 'Allez la France Mondiale', *Libération*, 10 July 1998, 7.

27. A. Genestar, 'Autant en apporte la fête', *Le Journal du Dimanche*, 12 July 1998, 1.

28 J. Schlumberger, 'Le symbole du drapeau' (interview with Michel Vovelle), *Journal du Dimanche*, 19 July 1998, 20.

29. H. Haget, 'Vas-y Mémé', *L'Express Le Magazine*, 4 June 1998, 8–11; M. Chemin *et al.*, 'La saga Jacquet', *Libération*, 11–12 July 1998, 6–8; G.-M. Benamou, 'Le hussard de la France qui bouge', *Evénement du jeudi*, 16–22 July 1998, 3; J.-J. Bozonnet, 'Aimé Jacquet, le plus glorieux des humbles serviteurs du football', *Le Monde*, 12–13 July 1998, 16;. J.-M. Colombani, 'La parabole Jacquet', *Le Monde*, 14 July 1998, 1.

30. R. Graham, 'Tonique for the nation', *Financial Times*, 18 July 1998.

Notes on Contributors

Pierre Bourdieu holds the Chair of Sociology at the Collège de France, and is a Director of Research at the Ecole des Hautes Etudes en Sciences Sociales, Paris. Founder-director of the review *Actes de la Recherche en Sciences sociales*, he is also the author of, among other books, *La Distinction, Homo academicus, La Noblesse d'Etat, Les Règles de l'Art, Sur la Télévision*, and *La Domination masculine* (1998).

Hugh Dauncey is Lecturer in French Studies at the University of Newcastle. He has taught at university level in Bordeaux, Bath and Paris. His main research interests are in the study of French public policy, especially in high technology, new trends in French television programming and the political aspects of French football.

James Eastham is a fourth year Modern Languages student at the University of Durham. He is writer and editor of *Aux Armes!*, an English language fanzine about French football. He has also written about French football for *The Independent* and *The Guardian* and has worked with the sports department of the French regional daily newspaper *Midi Libre* in Montpellier.

Geoff Hare is Senior Lecturer in French at the University of Newcastle. He has worked at university level in Paris, Bradford, Leeds and Aberdeen. His main research interests are in the study of French broadcasting, especially radio and new broadcasting technologies, and in the interaction between television and French football.

Gérard Houllier is manager of Liverpool FC, having formerly coached Lens and won the French Championship with Paris Saint-Germain. He was French national team manager from July 1992 to November 1993, and then National Technical Director of French football, until joining Liverpool in summer 1998. He is co-author of *Entraîneur: compétence et passion, les détails qui font gagner* (Canal Plus/Albin Michel, 1993).

Claude Journès is Professor of Political Science at the University of Lyon 2. He has also lectured in Britain, Algeria and Cambodia. His main research interests have been policing in western democracies, especially in Britain and France. He has also published previously on political institutions and the history of ideas.

Lucy McKeever is Deputy Site Librarian at Sunderland University. She has previously worked at University College London and Bradford University. Her research interests include libraries in France, human aspects of digital libraries and the Internet, and French football and the media.

John Marks is a Reader in French Studies at Nottingham Trent University, having also taught at University level in Leeds and Loughborough. His main research interests have been in the area of contemporary French thought, particularly the work of Michel Foucault and Gilles Deleuze, and more recently the general area of cultural debates in France.

Patrick Mignon holds a research post in the Sociology Department of the Institut national du sport et de l'éducation physique, Paris, and teaches at the University of Paris-IV. A member of the editorial board of the review *Esprit*, he has authored numerous articles on the sociology of football fans in England and France, and the book *La Passion du football* (Odile Jacob, 1998).

Ian Pickup is Senior Lecturer in French Studies and Senior Tutor to Joint Honours students at the University of Birmingham. He has written on nineteenth-century French novelists, on the French educational system, on French song and on the language of sport in the French press. He is the author of the first English–French/French–English sports dictionary.

Index

The 1998 soccer World Cup was perhaps the greatest international event in recent French history. This collection examines the effects on the host nation of the major economic, political, cultural and sporting dimensions of this global sports event. It discusses issues such as the impact on traditional French approaches to sport of the commercialisation of football, the improvement of sporting infrastructures, the marketing of the competition, the role of commercial sponsors, media coverage of the matches, policing and security during the month-long competition, and the French nation's identification with the multiracial national team.

The analysis of France 98 is set within the recent history and organisation of French football (the links between football, money and politics; and the characteristics of the French football public), and more broadly within the French tradition of using major cultural and sporting events to focus world attention on France as a leader in the international community. The book concludes with an evocation of the day-to-day impact of four weeks of sporting festivities in France and an analysis of the lessons to be drawn about French national identity in the current climate of economic, political, cultural and sporting globalisation.

Geoff Hare is Senior Lecturer in French Studies at the University of Newcastle upon Tyne and has taught in higher education in Aberdeen, Leeds, Bradford and Paris. His main research interests have been in contemporary French society, particularly broadcasting and other aspects of popular culture. His life-long fascination with France has also involved him locally and nationally in the Alliance Française – leading to the award of a French government decoration, the Palmes Académiques. Playing football at the lowest possible level and life-long support of Lincoln City have brought fewer rewards.

Hugh Dauncey is a Lecturer in French Studies at the University of Newcastle upon Tyne, specialising in the teaching of French history, politics and society. He has also taught at University level in Bordeaux and Paris and at the University of Bath. His principal research interests have been the politics and economics of French space policy and high technology, and the cultural and political implications of programming trends in French radio and television. His interest in sport in France derives from the conviction that study and research in French Studies Departments should not ignore important dimensions of everyday experience. He won a runners-up medal in the Bath University Intra-Mural Football Cup in 1987.

Cover photographs (clockwise from left): Ronaldo, Zinedine Zidane, and the Stade de France (courtesy of Colin Dixon).

Books of Related Interest

Footbinding, Feminism and Freedom
The Liberation of Women's Bodies in Modern China
Fan Hong, *De Montfort University*

'...valuable for its survey of modern Chinese sports history and Chinese debates about women and physical activity – no English-language book has covered the subject so comprehensively...well written and enriched with thoughtfully chosen images from the historical periods discussed.'   **Choice**

1997 352 pages
0 7146 4633 4 cloth
0 7146 4334 3 paper
Sport in the Global Society No. 1

The Games Ethic and Imperialism
Aspects of the Diffusion of an Ideal
J A Mangan, *University of Strathclyde*
New Preface and Foreword

This book is more than a description of the imperial spread of public school games: it is a consideration of hegemony and patronage, ideals and idealism, educational values and aspirations, cultural assimilation and adaptation, and perhaps most fascinating of all, the dissemination throughout the empire of the hugely influential moralistic ideology of athleticism.

1985; new impression, 2nd edition 1998; 240 pages
0 7146 4399 8 paper
Sport in the Global Society No. 2

The Race Game
Sport and Politics in South Africa
Douglas Booth, *University of Otago*

In this book Douglas Booth takes a fresh look at the role of sport in the fostering of a new national identity in South Africa. Through careful analysis he argues that sport will never unite South Africans except in the most fleeting and superficial manner.

1998 280 pages illus
0 7146 4799 3 cloth   £37.50/$52.50
0 7146 4354 8 paper £17.50/$22.50
Sport in the Global Society No. 4

FRANK CASS PUBLISHERS
Newbury House, 900 Eastern Avenue, Newbury Park, Ilford, Essex IG2 7HH
Tel: +44 (0)181 599 8866 Fax: +44 (0)181 599 0984 E-mail: info@frankcass.com
NORTH AMERICA
c/o ISBS, 5804 NE Hassalo Street, Portland, OR 97213 3644, USA
Tel: 800 944 6190 Fax: 503 280 8832 E-mail: cass@isbs.com
Website: www.frankcass.com

Books of Related Interest

The First Black Footballer
Arthur Wharton 1865–1930: An Absence of Memory
Phil Vasili

With a Foreword by **Irvine Welsh** *and an Introduction by* **Tony Whelan,** *Manchester United FC*

'Arthur Wharton is hardly a household name, but perhaps he should be ... his sporting achievements elevate him way beyond many far better known and celebrated figures. He was a remarkable athlete who led a remarkable life through one of the most turbulent periods in British history.'

Irvine Welsh, author of *Trainspotting*

Arthur Wharton was the world's first Black professional footballer and 100 yards world record holder, and was probably the first African to play professional cricket in the Yorkshire and Lancashire leagues.

The late-Victorian context of Wharton's career, in a Britain at the height of its economic and political power, shaped the way he was forgotten: it just was not politically expedient to proclaim about the glories of an African sportsman, when the dominant ideas of the age labelled all Blacks as inferior. Arthur died a penniless coal miner. His absence from the histories of football, and to a lesser extent athletics, is now being revised.

1998 272 pages 25 photographs
0 7146 4903 1 cloth
0 7146 4459 5 paper
Sport in the Global Society No. 11

Cricket and England
A Cultural and Social History of Cricket in England between the Wars
Jack Williams, *John Moores University, Liverpool*

In this book Jack Williams takes a fresh look at cricket as a symbol of England in the 1920s and 1930s. Cricket had a vital role in how the English imagined themselves and their social world.

1999 224 pages illus
0 7146 4861 2 cloth
0 7146 4418 8 paper
Sport in the Global Society No. 8

FRANK CASS PUBLISHERS
Newbury House, 900 Eastern Avenue, Newbury Park, Ilford, Essex IG2 7HH
Tel: +44 (0)181 599 8866 Fax: +44 (0)181 599 0984 E-mail: info@frankcass.com
NORTH AMERICA
c/o ISBS, 5804 NE Hassalo Street, Portland, OR 97213 3644, USA
Tel: 800 944 6190 Fax: 503 280 8832 E-mail: cass@isbs.com
Website: www.frankcass.com

Books of Related Interest

Rugby's Great Split
Class, Culture and the Origins of Rugby League Football
Tony Collins

'.' ... *brilliantly records the early years when rugby and football emerged from the public schools and seduced the working classes ... a fine read which intelligently probes the connections between social class and sport whichs till holds sway today.'*
The Independent on Sunday

.. *Collins' book sets out to explain the fundamental question : why are there two forms of rugby? It describes the battle for Rugby's soul in a scholarly, yet readable way.'*   **Open Rugby**

1998 314 pages
0 7146 4867 1 cloth
0 7146 4424 2 paper
Sport in the Global Society No. 5

Scoring for Britain
International Football and International Politics, 1900–1939
Peter J Beck, *Kingston University*

This book considers the nature and development of linkages between international football and politics in Britain between 1900 and 1939 and also provides a history of international football in Britain.

1999 240 pages illus
0 7146 4899 X cloth
0 7146 4454 4 paper
Sport in the Global Society No. 9

FRANK CASS PUBLISHERS
Newbury House, 900 Eastern Avenue, Newbury Park, Ilford, Essex IG2 7HH
Tel: +44 (0)181 599 8866 Fax: +44 (0)181 599 0984 E-mail: info@frankcass.com
NORTH AMERICA
c/o ISBS, 5804 NE Hassalo Street, Portland, OR 97213 3644, USA
Tel: 800 944 6190 Fax: 503 280 8832 E-mail: cass@isbs.com
Website: www.frankcass.com